Breaking Free

Breaking Free

THE STORY OF A
Feminist Baptist Minister

Jann Aldredge-Clanton

EAKIN PRESS ◆ Austin, Texas

This book is dedicated

to my husband,

David,

and my sons,

Chad and Brett,

with deep love and gratitude.

FIRST EDITION
Copyright © 2002
By Jann Aldredge-Clanton
Published in the United States of America
By Eakin Press
A Division of Sunbelt Media, Inc.
P.O. Drawer 90159 ⌨ Austin, Texas 78709-0159
email: sales@eakinpress.com
💻 website: www.eakinpress.com 💻
ALL RIGHTS RESERVED.
1   2   3   4   5   6   7   8   9
1-57168-724-6

Library of Congress Cataloging-in-Publication Data
Aldredge-Clanton, Jann
    Breaking free: the story of a feminist Baptist minister / Jann
Aldredge-Clanton.– 1st ed.
       p.   cm.
    ISBN 1-57168-724-6
    1. Aldredge-Clanton, Jann, 1946–. 2. Baptist Church–Clergy–
Biography. 3. Feminist theology. I. Title.
BX6495.A37 A3   2002
286'.1'092–dc21   2002012517

Contents

Foreword
by Liz Carpenter

Jann Aldredge-Clanton can write. And she can remember minute details. Indeed, she writes the details so well, you are carried along from sentence to sentence (uncomplicated sentences are her specialty) and suddenly you are caught up in more about the Baptist church than you thought you wanted to know. But it is fascinating because she tells of her very personal story of victory over the barriers which the Southern Baptist church has used to thwart its female members from being ordained as ministers. Since there are fifteen million Southern Baptists, that's a lot of thwarting.

But she made it along with a small but growing number of women ministers who refused to take "no" to their ambitions. At the moment, the conservative (often right-wing) Southern Baptists remain unchanged, but other Baptists are out front, leading for a more liberal attitude. Now there are about 1,700 women who are ordained Baptist ministers.

Jann has sometimes described herself as a Methobaptist, because she was an ordained Baptist minister serving as associate pastor in a Methodist church for a while. Jann knows Protestant hymns and weaves them into the text at charming places. If you are a hymn-singer, as I am, you hum along the text with the familiar tunes—"He Leadeth Me," converted to "SHE Leadeth Me." She wrote all new words to "Mine Eyes Have Seen the Glory," calling her version "We Sound a Call to Freedom." (Having grown up in the Methodist church, hymns from the old Cokesbury hymnal come to me quickly. I can do all the stanzas of "Love Lifted Me," which we youngsters wickedly labeled "The Nightgown Song.")

What shaped a Christian feminist like Jann? A father who was a minister, more liberal than his church on civil rights, and who was cheering her on—"You beat a boy!" he said, when she was chosen the high school class valedictorian. A mother who's a gifted preacher, even though her Baptist church hasn't ordained her or any other women. A brilliant sister who's been ahead of her time on everything, including feminism. And her husband, David, and two sons, who have encouraged her not only to be a minister but to write about her journey to become one. Plus the networking of feminists has given her support.

She now passes that along: "I see myself as freeing others with my own liberation." With the words of Martin Luther King, Jr., Jann can join in, "Free! Free at last! Thank God, I'm free at last!" Her readers will be shouting that too.

Acknowledgments

My deepest gratitude goes to my family, who contributed a wealth of material and inspiration for this book. My son Chad used his considerable persuasive gifts to convince me to write my memoir, gave insightful editorial comments, and cheered me all the way through until I found the right publisher. My son Brett encouraged my writing, inspired me with his own writing, and introduced me to his favorite University of Texas writing teacher, John Trimble, who critiqued several chapters of this book. David, my husband, took the photographs for the cover and gave me valuable suggestions and support throughout the process. Through some of the most difficult times, my sister, Anne, and my mother, Eva, energized me with their constant belief in my work and their enthusiastic evaluations of it. And the influence of my father, Truman, is vital to my story.

My special appreciation goes to JoAnne Prichard, a friend and editor who played a crucial part in the development of this book. JoAnne's incisive editorial recommendations greatly improved the book, and her affirmation increased my confidence. I am also grateful to my sister Anne, John Trimble and Brian Burton, who read sections of this work and gave me perceptive, affirming feedback. My hearty thanks to my friends Kay and Walter Shurden and Mary Carol Kendzia for reading the manuscript and offering affirming comments, and to agent and friend Susan Sanders for all her encouragement and support. I owe an enormous debt also to New Wineskins feminist ritual community. Thank you, gracious sisters and brothers, for your strong support of this book, for providing a chapter of the material, and for your partnership in feminist ministry.

My deep gratitude also goes to my publishing partners and friends at Eakin Press. President Virginia Messer gave her enthusiastic support, creativity, and excitement from the beginning of the project. Melissa Roberts contributed her outstanding editorial skills, creative energy, encouragement, and patient attention to details.

Introduction

On a bullet train from Paris to Lyon I finally got the message. David and I had saved up for this trip to France in celebration of our thirtieth wedding anniversary. We'd finished putting our two sons through college, so now was our chance. I wanted to slow down and savor the wine vineyards laid out in symmetrical rows on hillsides below picture-book chateaus. I kept pointing for David to take pictures. But the scenes flashed by so fast that he couldn't catch them with his camera.

The bullet train seemed a metaphor for my life. I couldn't believe that thirty years of marriage had rushed by and that I'd already passed my fiftieth birthday. I couldn't slow down my life any more than I could the train. But maybe I could capture the scenes with words. Now I knew for sure that I had to get on with telling my story.

For several years my oldest son, Chad, had been trying to convince me. He'd say, "Mom, you simply must write your memoir. What you've done is really unusual. A Baptist woman minister, born and raised in the South, who's written books on feminism. There're not many in your tribe."

But I worried I might hurt someone if I told the truth of my experience. And it felt too egotistical to write an autobiography.

"A memoir would be too presumptuous," I told Chad. "Memoirs are for famous people to write."

When Chad gets an idea in his head, he rarely lets go. This determination helped him as a boy to win tennis matches against stronger opponents. And now in his twenties he was already making his mark on Capitol Hill in Washington, as well as on national and international political campaigns. So Chad prodded me gently, but persistently. He suggested that I drive over to my hometown, Minden, Louisiana, to recapture memories of growing up. He brought me James McBride's *The Color of Water* and Willie Morris's *North Toward Home* as powerful examples of how memoirs can touch people. When I told Chad that Willie's dog Skip reminded me of my Flossie, he said, "So, you can write about Flossie in your book."

About this same time my son Brett had inspired me to take up my journal again. He had been recording some of his experiences in his first year of teaching English at an "underresourced" high school in the Mississippi delta. Natalie Goldberg's *Wild Mind* had stimulated him to write every day in his journal and to begin a moonlighting job with the local newspaper. I'd worked through *Wild Mind,* but had slipped away from daily writing. My job as chaplain sapped so much of my energy that I didn't think I had any left for writing during the week. Hearing Brett's enthusiasm for writing reminded me that writing feeds instead of drains me. Brett also introduced me to his favorite University of Texas writing teacher, John Trimble, who gave me an encouraging critique of some autobiographical work I'd sent him.

All the while, words from Jeanne Achterberg's *Woman as Healer* echoed in my mind:

> It is especially important that women make a written record of our ideas, our accomplishments, and the way the world appears to us. From the very earliest roots of Western medicine, in ancient Sumer, the scribes structured reality. By selectively omitting women from their writings, they left us with an obtuse lineage . . . Women's names and their ideas have been quickly buried under the avalanche of words that have flowed from the pens of men.

I had heard Achterberg say at a conference, "Things will

change as women tell our stories, as we give voice to ourselves—our struggles and our visions."

On a much slower train in southern France, David and I sipped red wine and munched baguettes. I took out my journal and jotted down my impressions of the Louvre and of the ancient labyrinth at Chartres Cathedral. I wanted to make sure I remembered to tell my friend Raynal what I'd seen because she used to love taking student groups to France. My mind flashed back to images of Raynal and me: sitting together in a graduate Renaissance Drama course at Texas Christian University, and standing against the president of Dallas Baptist College when he tried to make all the faculty sign a fundamentalist creed. My imagination fast-forwarded to a meeting of the Baptist Studies Advisory Board at Brite Divinity School, where I introduced myself as a "Baptist feminist" and explained why I thought any true Baptist should also be a feminist.

In the background I kept hearing Alice Walker say that each of us has a small part of the whole story. I looked out the window at the Mediterranean Sea as we rolled along the coast toward Nice. I'd never seen a clearer, deeper blue. The name "Azure Coast" was indeed appropriate. Above, a flock of seagulls danced in the late afternoon sunlight. One by one the seagulls broke away to soar and flounce and flip, then return to form with the others a perfect "V." Maybe I did have a part of the whole story.

For many years I'd felt my call as a minister to include social justice work. My feminism had come with a spiritual awakening to inequities in church and society. China Galland's merging of the spiritual and the political in her book *The Bond Between Women* struck a deep chord within me. I had written books, such as *In Search of the Christ-Sophia,* to persuade churches to include feminine divine images for the sake of justice. But I'd written little about my personal experiences of injustice. At the beginning of her book Galland writes that when she went to Argentina, she "was able to see and hear firsthand how corrosive silence is, how it engenders complicity." So she decided to include more of her own experience in the book. She had come to agree with Brazilian Catholic liberation theologian Ivone Gebara: "Women have to resist silence. . . women have to speak up, to cry out."

My mind wandered back to a scene in First Baptist Church of Minden, where my daddy pastored for sixteen years. It was a Girls' Auxiliary coronation. Girls in this mission organization marched down the aisles of the sanctuary to receive awards for memorizing Bible verses, names of Southern Baptist missionaries around the world, and directors of mission boards. I had gone through all the steps to become maiden, then lady in waiting, then princess. And now several other girls and I paraded to the altar in long white taffeta evening gowns to be crowned queen. Little boys in white suits marched before us bearing our crowns on white satin pillows.

Baptist churches honored girls as queens, but kept adult women from any positions of leadership. At twelve, I stood proud and unaware of the incongruity and unfairness.

At the conclusion of the coronation, I sang loudly along with the congregation the Girls' Auxiliary hymn, never dreaming the new meaning these words would one day have for me:

> We've a story to tell to the nations,
> That shall turn their hearts to the right,
> A story of truth and mercy,
> A story of peace and light.

I knew I had a story to tell. The more I got into my story, the more certainty I had about telling it. Some days as I walked about Baylor Medical Center on my chaplain rounds, I could hear a voice inside growing louder and louder, "You must write. You must write. Make time to write."

What follows is the part of the whole story that is mine to tell. It is my experience of becoming an ordained Baptist woman and feminist theologian. I guess Chad's right. There aren't too many in my tribe.

Chapter One

Breaking Through Walls

On Sunday evening, September 18, 1977, my friend Raynal Barber and I rushed to Cliff Temple Baptist Church. I'd asked her to go with me to a worship service. We'd miss the evening service at our own Calvary Baptist, a few blocks away. But I told Raynal that this service at Cliff Temple would surely be a historical event. I wanted to go partly out of curiosity and partly because of my growing uneasiness with the exclusion of women from church leadership.

As we approached the church that covers several blocks in the Oak Cliff area of Dallas, we saw crowds of people scurrying up the massive steps into the sanctuary and reporters lugging TV cameras. Raynal and I were early enough to get a good seat in the center of the sanctuary. We overheard several people behind us talking about a group from Criswell Bible College who had come to protest. "That must be the group," I whispered to Raynal as I looked over at the young men in dark suits and crew cuts who filled the first three rows of the left section.

Martha Gilmore was about to become the first woman in the

South to be ordained by a Baptist church. It was no surprise that students from Criswell College would oppose the ordination. W.A. Criswell, founder of the college and leader of Baptist fundamentalists, had been one of Martha's most vociferous opponents. The *Dallas Morning News* had quoted his pronouncements against the ordination of women. *The Baptist Standard,* the news journal of Texas Baptists, had published a debate between Martha Gilmore and Criswell. My husband David had photographed Martha for the *Standard*. In fact, it was from David that I first heard about Martha's ordination. He came home from the photo shoot and said to me, "You ought to get to know her. She's an impressive woman." As I read the debate in the *Standard,* I thought Criswell's quoting of a Bible verse that tells women to keep silent in church was silenced by Martha's powerful reminder of Acts 2:17, "your sons and your daughters shall prophesy," and Galatians 3:28, "there is no longer Jew or Greek, there is no longer slave or free, there is no longer male and female; for all of you are one in Christ Jesus."

Baptists and Ordination

Unlike some denominations, Baptists don't consider ordination a sacrament of the church. Baptists historically have protested a class of priests. One of the most sacred tenets among Baptists is priesthood of all believers. Baptists value democratic church polity. But as in Orwell's *Animal Farm,* where "all are equal, but some are more equal than others," the practice of Baptist churches reveals that some are more priests than others. Ordination conveys leadership power upon pastors and deacons.

A few Baptist leaders have opposed ordaining anyone. Ethicist T.B. Maston, who taught for many years at Southwestern Baptist Theological Seminary, refused ordination because he believed it unbiblical. But Baptists have mainly opposed the ordination of women. Southern Baptists have been especially reluctant to give this power to women. My friend

Glenda Fontenot struggled with the decision about her ordination—not because she didn't believe women should be ordained, but because she didn't believe in the hierarchy usually resulting from the distinction between clergy and laity. She finally decided to be ordained by a Baptist church, saying, "We have to have power in order to give it away."

In 1984 the Southern Baptist Convention passed a resolution against the ordination of women, citing a biblical passage prohibiting women from having "authority over a man" and conveniently overlooking in the same passage the injunction against wearing gold, pearls, or expensive clothes. Then as late as June of 2000, the Southern Baptist Convention adopted into a more permanent document of beliefs, *The Baptist Faith and Message,* a statement limiting the office of pastor to men. Again, the men who wrote this statement claimed to be following the Bible.

Southern Baptists are the largest religious group in the South, with over eight million members. Baptists' attitudes toward women reflect and shape Southern culture. The ideal of a Southern lady persists: lovely, demure, and deferring to male leaders. Southerners put women on pedestals more often than behind pulpits. Formidable cultural as well as theological walls stand against giving women equal rights.

In a TV interview, Martha Gilmore responded to an accusation that she sought ordination just for the power. "Yes," she said, unapologetically, "I want power. Power to use the gifts God has given me. Power to take part in decisions that affect the course of the church. Power to break through walls of prejudice that make women second-class citizens in church and society." Growing up in the South, I'd absorbed the belief that it was wrong for women to seek power. Now I heard Martha saying that power was a good thing.

Martha's opponent questioned, "Why can't you serve God without ordination? Plenty of people do wonderful ministry without ordination."

"That's true," Martha replied. "But it's also true that Baptist churches require ordination for the offices of pastor and deacon. Refusing to ordain women puts a male-only label on these ministry opportunities. Baptists could do away with ordination altogether. But as long as we ordain men, then it's only fair that we ordain women as well. Only then will we live up to our belief in freedom for everyone to follow God's call."

Local churches can choose whether or not to follow the Southern Baptist Convention resolution against women's ordination and the statement against women pastors. According to Baptist polity, each church is autonomous. Individual churches, not a group of bishops or a denominational board, decide whom to ordain. The ordination service takes place in a local church, not at a convention. But denominational resolutions and statements of faith definitely influence churches. Most Southern Baptist churches still refuse to ordain women. But since the 1970s some churches have ordained women, and no resolution or decree can annul this ordination.

Martha's Ordination

Martha's ordination service began with prayers and hymns, like worship services I'd attended all my life. But from the beginning, I saw a difference. Women took part in worship leadership. And I heard a new interpretation of a passage in Ephesians on breaking down walls of prejudice that divide people. Doug Waterson, pastor of Cliff Temple Baptist Church, applied the Apostle Paul's words to breaking down centuries-old barriers that have kept women out of ministerial leadership.

Then, for the first time in my life, I saw a woman kneeling before the church as a long line of people—women as well as men—passed by to lay hands of blessing upon her. My childhood memory of ordination was of a man kneeling at the altar while other men filed by like soldiers to place their hands on his head and whisper in his ears. Only the ordained—all men—could participate in this sacred ritual. Only men could ordain only men. The message I internalized was that this was a male ritual, from which women were forever excluded.

Now something new was happening. A woman was receiving the sacred blessing. From somewhere deep within my soul I felt the rightness of it. Tears streamed down my face as I made a solemn vow to do all in my power to spread this truth I was discovering. I would write articles, teach, and persuade. I would give chapter and verse to support the ordination of women.

The service ended, and people started leaving the sanctuary to go to the reception in the church parlor. I sat transfixed, with no strength or will to leave this holy place.

Raynal turned to me and said, "Jann, one day we'll be going to your ordination!"

I gave her a look of shock, stammering something like, "No way can I do this! I'll support others, but I don't want all the struggle and criticism. Besides, you know I'm finishing my Ph.D. in English. I didn't spend all that time and energy for nothing!" Raynal had completed her Ph.D several years before. We had become friends in a graduate course at Texas Christian University, and we now taught together at Dallas Baptist College.

She continued, "Well, I just see you—see the way you relate to the students. You give them so much time and counseling. I can see you as a minister."

"I'm determined to do all I can to support the ordination of women, but not me."

The prophetic word could not be unspoken. In fact, it came again a year later through another friend and colleague, Jill Pickett. Jill taught English part-time at DBC, and was a member of Cliff Temple Baptist Church, where David and I moved our membership shortly after Martha's ordination. At a Cliff Temple Sunday school party, Jill and I were talking about how much we appreciated the sermons of our new pastor, Dan Griffin. We especially relished his literary allusions and illustrations. Jill expressed her opinion that his sermons were so eloquent because he'd been an English major. Then she said to me, "Maybe your next calling is the ministry."

My Ordination

Eight years later, Raynal stood at my ordination service to read the words of the prophet Habakkuk: "Write the vision; make it plain on tablets, so that a runner may read it. For there is still a vision for the appointed time; it speaks of the end, and does not lie. If it seems to tarry, wait for it; it will surely come, it will not delay." Raynal's voice broke as she read, and I had to strain to hear her. But it seemed as though a runner leaped out of the pages of Scripture and across the centuries to deliver those words of Habakkuk directly to me as I sat trembling on the front pew in the sanctuary of Seventh and James Baptist Church on November 24, 1985. I remembered saying about a year before Martha's ordination, "One day Baptist churches will see the light and ordain women. It's the right thing to do. But I probably won't live to see it." Now I marveled, "I've not only seen a woman ordained, but I'm about to be ordained myself."

Martha Gilmore preached my ordination sermon, proclaiming that I was "the vision made flesh, the vision that God indeed calls women to ordination." Martha declared that in addition to being a symbol, I had also become "a statement, a promise for many men and women and a hope for many women who may be frightened to hear God's call and to become bearers of the Word of God." It helped to hear her bless me as a "statement," because that word had been used pejoratively in reference to me and other women who had chosen nontraditional paths. People had tried to dismiss me by saying, "Oh, you're just trying to make a statement." I realized that we were in a time in history when statements about the worth of women needed to be made. And now I could accept making this statement as part of my divine call. Martha assured me that most important of all, the Spirit would give me power for my ministry. "I need that power right now," I thought, knowing I had to go up to the pulpit next to give the "Response of the Candidate."

Knees quivering and heat rising up from my stomach to my

face, I stood before the large congregation to proclaim my call to ministry. I confessed that when I was growing up, I was so fearful of public speaking that I refused several times to go to church camp to avoid giving the inevitable report to the church when I came back. And here I was standing before them, behind an imposing pulpit in a large sanctuary, there by some power beyond my own, proclaiming a call different from anything I had ever imagined. I quoted Shakespeare's Hamlet speaking to the rational Horatio, "There are more things in heaven and earth than are dreamed of in your philosophy."

Then I invited all who wished to come forward to lay on hands of blessing. Even though Baptists traditionally invite only ordained pastors and deacons, usually all men, to lay on hands, I wanted this ritual to symbolize the inclusiveness that I believed formed the foundation of the Baptist belief in priesthood of all believers. And I couldn't bear to exclude my mother, my sister Anne, and many friends, just because they weren't ordained.

As I knelt at the front of the sanctuary, women and men, unordained and ordained, Baptist and Methodist and Episcopalian and Catholic and Presbyterian, children and adults—hundreds of grace-filled people came by with words and hands of blessing. Powerful feelings washed over my spirit like waves washing over rocks along the seashore. Hard places softened with tears of joy, and determination strengthened with tears of sadness over the hundreds of years women had been denied this sacred blessing. I wept for my mother, faithful daughter of the church. I wept for my grandmother, Greek scholar. They were never given official sanction or blessing by the church. I wept for my sisters in all faiths who were still denied this blessing. At the same time waves of hope washed my soul, filling me with fresh faith to live the vision. In that mystical moment, I felt the reality of Martha's proclamation: I had become "the vision made flesh."

During the laying on of hands, the organ played "Lead, Kindly Light." I'd requested this hymn because the words described my experience of the last few years: "Lead kindly Light amid the encircling gloom; lead Thou me on; the night is dark, and I am far from home; lead Thou me on. Keep Thou my feet; I do not ask to see the distant scene; one step enough for me." I closed my eyes and saw myself in my red Toyota Corolla driving back and forth on the endless dark road between Waco and Dallas and Fort Worth as I completed my theological education. On those predawn and night trips several times a week for two years, my eyes strained to stay awake as I wondered if I would ever reach home and if I would ever find a welcoming place for my ministry.

Now I was being ordained by a Baptist church. My ordination service intensified my belief in the power of imagination. For several months I had been envisioning this service and all the people I wanted to participate. Every person I invited was able to come, many from out-of-town. Women and men shared worship leadership. All the language in hymns, litanies, prayers, scripture readings, and homilies was inclusive of male and female, just as I had envisioned and planned. The first hymn we sang was "In Unity We Lift Our Song," written by Ken Medema to the tune of "A Mighty Fortress":

In unity we lift our song of grateful adoration,
For brothers brave and sisters strong,
What cause for celebration.
For those whose faithfulness has kept us through distress,
Who've shared with us our plight, who've held us in the night,
The blessed congregation.

For God our way, our bread, our rest,
Of all these gifts the giver.
Our strength, our guide, our nurturing breast,
Whose hand will yet deliver.
Who keeps us till the day when night shall pass away,
When hate and fear are gone, and all our work is done,
And we shall sing forever.

I remembered the electricity that surged through me several years before at a Baptist Women in Ministry meeting when I first sang this hymn, more timidly when I came to the phrase "our nurturing breast." Now as I sang "our nurturing breast" at my ordination, I thrilled to the power of Feminine Divine imagery. The theme of the service, from the Habakkuk passage, was "Make the Vision Plain." The service, more than I had imagined, made plain the vision of shared spiritual power. I saw a glimpse of what could be when women and men receive equal value as proclaimers of sacred truth.

After the ordination service, a vision came to me: I saw everyone in that congregation kneeling to receive the divine blessing. From that moment on, my vision included breaking down walls between ordained and unordained, extending ordination to all women and men because all have a sacred calling. I longed for my mother, who for many years had been advocating for the ordination of women in First Baptist Church, San Angelo, Texas, to receive this blessing upon her faithful service. I longed for my sister to receive blessing upon the spiritual path she had chosen, a path away from traditional religion. With tears in her eyes she told me after the service, "This was so powerful, different from anything I've ever experienced. I need more ritual in my life." Although at this time I didn't know where she might find this kind of inclusive ritual either outside or within the institutional church, a desire stirred in me to continue trying to create this new experience.

The day after my ordination, Mother wrote a letter, beginning with this blessing: "Yesterday was a giant hour! I do bless you with all spiritual blessings and commit myself to pray that you have your father's gifts of ministry as well as developing your own unique gifts." I treasured her words, but grieved that she could not affirm her own gifts of ministry because they had never been given official blessing. She had the gift of the Word, but not the "Y" chromosome that many people thought necessary to preach it.

Chapter Two

Beginnings

Both my parents were preachers, but only one was ordained. I grew up in a small town in Louisiana in the 1950s and '60s.

Anyone who listened to the cadences of his resonant baritone voice and watched his long arms waving emphatically would think my daddy, Henry Truman Aldredge, was a typical Southern Baptist preacher. But those who could hear beneath the volume and see past the index finger that looked like it pointed right at them learned otherwise. Most people in First Baptist Church, Minden, Louisiana, called him "Brother Aldredge," and many said that he preached over their heads. He believed it was his calling to make people think as well as repent. Growing up during the depression, Daddy was the only one of six children with more than a high school education. He worked his way through both college and seminary, so he placed a high value on education. In his sermons he quoted Shakespeare and Kierkegaard and William James and Emily Dickinson, right along with the Bible. His use of the Revised Standard instead of the King James Version gave some people cause to question his orthodoxy.

But what really made them sit up in their pews was his

stand on integration. It was the early 1960s, when the civil rights movement was gaining momentum. The deacons of the church fumed that Martin Luther King, Jr. was nothing but a "communist agitator." They believed that King was stirring up trouble everywhere, including the churches. Some members of the church even supported their racist attitudes by claiming that the biblical "curse on Ham" rendered people of color inferior and subservient. One of the deacons made a motion to "refuse to seat any Negroes who come to First Baptist Church." He bellowed, "They'd just be coming to cause trouble! Not for the right reasons." Daddy rose to his full height of five feet, ten inches and boomed with his large voice: "When have we ever questioned the motives of people coming here to worship? If African Americans come to this church, they will be welcome! As long as I'm pastor here, everyone is welcome." Daddy knew that he might not be welcome there much longer.

My belief in miracles might be traced to this time when, in spite of his prophetic preaching and actions, Daddy didn't get voted out of First Baptist Church, the largest church in town and the one most invested in the status quo. He did, however, get voted off the board of trustees of Midwestern Baptist Theological Seminary because of another stand for conscience' sake. A controversy had arisen in the Southern Baptist Convention over a Genesis commentary written by a Midwestern professor. Because of his symbolic rather than literalistic approach to the creation narratives, Professor Ralph Elliot came under attack as a "liberal," a label that carried the same connotations for Southern Baptists as "anathema" did for traditional Catholics. Swayed by the outcry, leaders in the Convention wanted to fire Professor Elliot and called for a vote from the board. Daddy voted to keep Elliot at the seminary because he so strongly believed in the principle of academic freedom, and because he agreed with Elliot's interpretation of Genesis. The trustees voted by secret ballot, or so they thought. Somehow the vote leaked out. The next year the Convention voted off the board those trustees who had supported Elliot.

My mother, Eva Louise Hickerson Aldredge, worked hard to fit the mold of a Baptist preacher's wife. She entertained visiting preachers and evangelists in the best tradition of Southern hospitality, cooking and serving elegant meals on our long dining room table adorned with fresh flowers, starched linen tablecloth, china, crystal, and silver. She poured her creative energy into parties for the deacons and the young people of the church. For these occasions, Mother not only prepared the food but planned games and made elaborate decorations. Also for the church, Mother held offices in the Woman's Missionary Union, visited prospective church members, and directed a youth Sunday School department.

No matter how good she was as preacher's wife, Mother's exuberant spirit couldn't be confined to this narrow role. The minute we got out of Minden on family vacations, she broke loose. She seemed transformed by the temporary freedom. One time at a gas station, she tied a scarf around her nose and mouth, got a carrot out of our food bag, went up behind the man filling up our car, and poked the carrot in his back, saying, "Stick 'em up!" My sister Anne and I laughed hysterically, while Daddy tried to pretend he didn't know her. When we visited our grandparents Aldredge in Abilene, Texas, Mother led Anne, Cousin Kathy, and me in late-night expeditions to "roll" yards with toilet paper.

Mother's time and place and religion were filled with contradictions concerning women. There was no way for her to escape them. A woman could go to college, but the main purpose was to be an educated wife and to have something to fall back on if her husband died. So bright that she skipped one grade in high school, Mother earned her bachelor's degree by the time she was twenty and began teaching high school English and home economics in the small town of Van, Texas. The next year she married Daddy and moved with him to Fort Worth, Texas, where he would attend Southwestern Baptist Theological Seminary. She also went to seminary and got a master of religious education degree to learn how to support Daddy's ministry, not to pursue professional ministry herself.

Women could vote, but they usually asked their husbands how to vote, and they never ran for office. Churches praised the contributions of women but gave them no decision-making power. Mother grew up singing the gospel hymn "Wherever He Leads, I'll Go," but her culture clearly defined where she could and could not go. She could be a preacher's wife, but not a preacher. Her younger brother, Julius Raught Hickerson, could receive a divine call directly to missionary service. Mother could be called, but only indirectly through her husband. Daddy never felt called to foreign missions, so at that time Mother assumed she wasn't either. She had gotten the message from her own mother that the "He" in "Wherever He Leads, I'll Go" meant husband more than God.

Grandmother Hickerson taught classical Greek at Sioux Falls College in South Dakota until at age twenty-six she married a tobacco farmer. She left academia to follow her husband to his farm in Tennessee, where she became a full-time cook and dishwasher for forty field hands. Later, when Grandpa Hickerson became a Baptist preacher, she followed him to Texas. The role of preacher's wife in Southern churches brought respect and dignity, but no salary. Churches revered their "first ladies," placing them on a spiritual pedestal. No one seemed to question the ethics of churches who got two qualified workers for the price of one. One of my most distinct memories of Grandmother Hickerson is of her hands and feet constantly moving. When she drove her white Chevrolet, she pumped the accelerator, giving my stomach the sensation of riding the bumper cars at the fair. Her hands danced all over the steering wheel, or even more precariously left the wheel to accentuate her animated voice. All the energy of her stifled intellect and creativity seemed to find some release through her restless movement. Grandmother Hickerson never seemed to question the injustice of her circumstances. Neither did Mother.

Although Mother always served as a minister, she was never ordained or paid. At that time it never entered her mind that things could or should be otherwise. Her gregarious personality, dynamic speaking voice, and exceptional leadership skills made her every bit as qualified as Daddy to pastor a church. But she praised Daddy and downplayed her own strengths. She was always taking care of the underdog, never realizing that she was one. Every Sunday morning she drove miles outside Minden to pick up a Native American boy named Herman and take him to church. Mother believed in getting people "saved" and into the church, but that was not her only concern. She gave Herman and his family clothes and food and anything else they needed.

Mother took some risks in her social ministry. She often invited an alcoholic woman named Marie into our home for counseling and for dinner. I was embarrassed when this woman showed up at our front door, looking like a prostitute with scarlet lipstick smeared around her mouth and breasts bulging out of an orange sequined sweater. Some of the ladies in our church criticized Mother for taking in this woman. But she was a person in need, and Mother didn't care what any of us thought. She was going to help her.

A Budding Preacher

My vocation as a preacher began perhaps when I was three years old at Mrs. Bowers's house in Breckenridge, Texas. At that time Daddy pastored First Baptist Church of Breckenridge, a small West Texas town advertised as the "Home of the Breckenridge Buckaroos." The town focused more on football and rodeos than health care. Mother and Daddy had to drive sixty miles to the hospital in Abilene when I was born.

One of First Baptist Breckenridge's most faithful members was Mrs. Bowers, short and stout with dishwater blond hair piled haphazardly on her head. She looked like Aunt Bea on "The Andy Griffith Show." Anne and I loved to stay with Mrs. Bowers when our parents went out of town because she let us do anything we wanted. Mrs. Bowers won prizes for her cooking at the

Stephens County Fair, and she often invited our family for Sunday lunch.

One Sunday at the conclusion of a seven-day-long revival meeting, Mrs. Bowers invited the visiting evangelist and his family, the revival singer and his family, and our family over for lunch. Twelve people gathered around her dining room table loaded with country fried chicken, honey-baked ham, roast beef, mashed potatoes, cream gravy, brown gravy, candied yams, corn on the cob, baked beans, green beans swimming in bacon grease, black-eyed peas, fried okra, green Jell-o salad with fruit cocktail, cornbread, and hot yeast rolls. It was before the days of low-fat and low-carbohydrate diets. "And biscuits are in the oven," Mrs. Bowers said. "They'll be coming out tender and butter-melting hot right after the blessing."

At that moment I raised my hand and asked to say the blessing. Anne, three and a half years older, usually got most of the air time allowed children. In fact, Mother swears that she began making complete sentences before she turned a year old and never quit talking. But I was learning one sure way to get the floor. Of course, no one at the table could deny a little girl's request to pray, especially a blond, rosy-cheeked girl who looked like Little Miss Sunbeam on the bread wrapper. One year Mother even entered me in a contest sponsored by Sunbeam bread. She felt sure the judges would pick me as the Little Miss Sunbeam look-a-like. She always fixed my golden blond hair in a curly top-knot with three ringlets down my neck, like Miss Sunbeam's. And for the contest she made me a blue and white plaid dress, exactly like that of Miss Sunbeam. When a girl with dark brown hair won, Mother railed against the contest as rigged.

But at lunch that Sunday I did win the heart of Mrs. Bowers. She said, "How sweet! Of course, you can say the blessing." I began praying. I blessed the fried chicken, the mashed potatoes, the sweet potatoes, the gravy, each food item on the table individually, then the plates, forks, knives, spoons, glasses. Open-eyed, looking around for more material, I went on to bless the table, chairs, every piece of furniture in the room, the lights overhead, every person at the table individually by name. I knew that no one could interrupt me, because I was praying. I held all those people in my power. When I finally said, "Amen," Mrs. Bowers rushed to the oven. A wail came from the kitchen, "Oh, my biscuits, my biscuits . . . they're ruined. My biscuits burned. Jann made me burn my biscuits." Everyone laughed and talked about my long-winded prayer in ways that made me feel important.

Mother and Daddy told this story over and over, each time praising my spunk and my smart method of gaining attention. At only three years old I had learned the power of my own voice and ways to use it to my advantage.

Somewhere along the way toward adolescence, I lost my voice to stronger voices telling me how to look and act "like a lady." In *Reviving Ophelia: Saving the Selves of Adolescent Girls,* Mary Pipher illustrates the struggle adolescent girls still have to maintain a sense of themselves in a "girl-poisoning" society. Pipher says that in their struggle to stay within a narrow definition of female, many girls lose spark and even IQ points. I almost lost my life. The strong, self-assured voice of the little girl giving the blessing at Sunday lunch would not emerge until years later.

Minden's Kissing Expert and Colored Water

In 1950, when I was almost four years old, we moved to Minden, a small town in north Louisiana. Minden lay between Arcadia, where notorious killers Bonnie and Clyde finally met their deaths, and Shreveport, home of the "Louisiana Hayride" made famous by Governor Jimmy Davis's singing of "You Are My Sunshine." About ten miles west of Minden stands a striking symbol of this juxtaposition of violence and warm hospitality: a sign that reads "Goodwill Road—Ammunition Plant." Minden is closer to the East Texas culture of towns like Tyler than to the Cajun culture of New Orleans. As I recently drove on Interstate 20 toward Minden, I heard a Tyler radio station broadcasting a program called "Gun Talk." The host kept encouraging listeners to "defend your gun rights" and to visit a website regarding the Second Amendment. He ended the program by saying, "Go out and do some shootin'." I was stunned. I couldn't believe that this town, famous for growing some of the loveliest roses in the world, could also produce a radio show promoting "shootin'." I struggled to understand the contradictions of my land.

Church was serious business in our family. First Baptist Church of Minden not only provided our livelihood but also gave us our identity. Daddy was the preacher, Mother was the preacher's wife, and Anne and I were PKs (preacher's kids). Church demanded much of our time. Sunday mornings we went to Sunday School and worship service, Sunday nights to Training Union and worship service, Wednesday nights to prayer meeting, and Tuesday afternoons to Girls' Auxiliary. On top of that were social events on many Friday or Saturday nights and weeklong revivals twice a year.

Anne and I bonded in rebellion against so much church. I followed her in terrorizing various Sunday School teachers. When Mother thought I was old enough, she let me leave her side and sit with Anne on the second row of the large sanctuary. Several rows back, Mother thought she could still keep a watchful eye on us. But we found ways to break the monotony of services and entertain each other. We wrote notes to each other, making jokes with the words in the hymnal: "I was sinking deep in sin—whoopee!" We almost gave away our clandestine activities when one Sunday we came to "my spirit pants for thee" in the hymn "Break Thou the Bread of Life." Anne and I doubled over to keep from laughing out loud. When we got home, we sang "my spirit pants for thee" over and over again, laughing so hard that tears ran down our cheeks. Mother's explanation of the meaning of "pants" in this hymn made no difference. We were singing about our underpants.

Minden gave me mixed messages about growing up female. It was important for girls to do well in school, but not to have much career ambition. Being a "good girl," defined as not having sex before marriage, stood at the apex of values. But looking good and pleasing men came close behind. I could see strong women all around me, especially Mother, but not in leadership positions at church or in the community. The *Minden Herald* of the 1950s carried a one-page section with the heading "News of Interest to Women," consisting mainly of wedding announcements and club meetings. Only beauty queens made any other page of the paper. One notable exception was Ruby Graham, the "Kissing Expert." On the front page of the February 20, 1953, issue I found a picture of Ruby and her wide, smiling lips. She was holding up a matching pair of lips which she'd smacked on a piece of paper. The caption read, "Kissing Expert—Ruby Graham, a clerk-typist in the office of the Webster Parish Clerk of Court, displays the 'kissprint' with which she won a new bedroom suite in a contest conducted by a Shreveport furniture store. Ruby is married and has a two-and-a-half-year-old son."

I grew up in a time in the South when water fountains were "colored" and "white," and gays and lesbians existed only in jokes or sermons. When I was around five years old, I asked Mother if I could drink some of that pretty "colored" water in West Bros. Department Store, and got a hushed "no." When I was in high school, I asked Mother why my friends had laughed at me when we were on a band trip to march in a Christmas parade in Natchitoches, Louisiana, and I had remarked that another band's uniforms looked "queer." Mother answered, "I don't know. It's a perfectly good word to me." Naiveté, Mother's and mine, thus deferred my struggle with the homophobia in our culture.

When I was growing up in Minden, black was black and white was white, and they didn't cross the tracks to meet. But I was largely unaware of the racism in our community. I heard whispers of a favorite activity of some of the teenage boys— sneaking out after dark to Caney Lake to spy on meetings of the Ku Klux Klan. And there were rumors of crosses burning on the lawn in front of the Catholic church, the one church in town where a few blacks mixed with whites. Growing up in segregated schools and church, I had little contact with African Americans except Lucille and Icey May, who worked from time to time as maids in our home. Both were kind and hard-working and deferential, even to Anne and me. Icey May stayed with us many nights when Mother and Daddy were out on church business. One night especially stands out in my memory. I was around five and terribly afraid of kidnappers. Icey May was busy ironing after she'd tucked Anne and me in bed in the next room. Suddenly, I heard what I thought was the sound of a door slowly opening and then *"creak, creak, creak"*—footsteps on the hardwood floor. I cowered down in bed and cried out to Icey May, who immediately came to me with all the comfort of her large body and soul. She hugged me and said, "Honey, you can be sure God will protect you, and I'll protect you. If anybody tries to get you, I'll get 'em with my iron." I trusted Icey May's protection more than God's. So I went with her back to the utility room and sat on the floor, watching her strong arm wield the hot iron, and believing she could indeed get anybody who tried to get me.

Recent conversations with two African-American colleagues at Baylor University Medical Center further impressed upon me the extent of the racism in the Louisiana of my growing-up years. I learned that Ella Steverson, the nursing supervisor on one of the units I serve as chaplain, is from Doyline, a small town about ten miles south of Minden. Ella and I reminisced about places and foods we had in common as children. But it became quickly obvious that our experiences, though parallel in time and place, were far apart. Racial prejudice and division had created two different worlds. Ella told about how her mother had protected her and her siblings from the discrimination in Minden. Instead of taking them to "town," where they would face the harsh realities that they couldn't eat in most restaurants or even try on clothes at department stores, her mother kept them close to home. She would trace their feet on cardboard and take the cardboard impressions to a store in Minden to make sure she bought shoes that fit them.

Ella told me that Cynthia Robinson, a marrow transplant insurance coordinator at Baylor, had grown up in Minden. When I graduated from Minden High School in 1964, it was still an all-white school, and Webster High School was the all-black school. Cynthia, almost ten years younger than I, could have gone to Minden High; busing had begun in 1969. But she chose to stay at Webster High because of tales she'd heard about the struggles of the few black teenagers who went to Minden High at that time. Cynthia had been drum major in the Webster High band, and I had been a majorette in the Minden High band. Her parents were leaders in the largest black Baptist church in town, and mine were leaders in the largest white church. But what struck me most as I talked with Cynthia was that she knew more white people in Minden than I knew black people. Her dad had worked in the construction business for white supervisors. I realized that the main reason for her superior knowledge of the other race relates to the history of survival of subordinate groups. Just as women have had to understand more about men than men have had to know about women, blacks have had to know whites as a factor in survival.

Flossie, the Church Dog

Several years ago my son Chad gave me Willie Morris's *My Dog Skip,* with these words inscribed by the author: "In memory of your noble Flossie." Chad had told Willie about the dog I grew up with. Flossie was every bit as remarkable as Skip, even though no movie has been made about her yet.

Soon after we brought Flossie home, it became clear that she was my dog. That suited me and the rest of the family just fine. I was nine years old and the one most interested in playing with Flossie, stroking her sleek black coat and caring for her. Flossie was a straight-haired cocker spaniel. To me, this difference between Flossie and other cocker spaniels made her special. I thought that her straight hair was a sign of her superior intelligence. Another sign was that she foiled all our efforts to keep her in our back yard.

We could not stop Flossie from going to church. Flossie had a soul. I was convinced of that, not only by her determination to attend church services, but also by her large, compassionate brown eyes. As much as Flossie loved to come in the house for me to rub her bald stomach and to eat bites of meat I gave her from my plate, she knew there was more to life than stomach rubs and roast beef scraps. She ventured out of our back yard on her quest. Her search almost always led her to First Baptist Church. We built a fence around our back yard, but Flossie escaped through the holes she dug under it. Over my objections, Mother tied her on a long leash to the clothesline. But it didn't take her long to manage somehow to get her head out of the collar that held her to the leash. Off she ran again to church.

Flossie was not just a Sunday church-goer. On weekdays, Daddy would find her walking around the sanctuary and would lock her in one of the church restrooms until he got ready to go home. Being confined all day long didn't deter Flossie from her spiritual pilgrimage. She went back, day after day, hoping for some beatific vision, even in a church restroom. But she especially loved to go to worship services. One Sunday evening, Daddy looked up and saw Flossie resting her paws on the balcony railing and leaning her head over, listening attentively to his message. Seated on the second row downstairs, I didn't see Flossie. I was shocked when Daddy stopped preaching and rudely said, "Jann, go up to the balcony and get Flossie and take her home." I could tell Flossie's feelings were hurt too.

What I most regret doing to Flossie was dragging her down the streets of Minden dressed as a Mouseketeer in the Pet Parade of 1958. Mother made her a costume just like the one worn by Annette Funnicello, my favorite Mouseketeer on the television show "The Mickey Mouse Club." Even though Flossie tried to resist, I pulled her front legs through the arms of the white sweater with a big letter "M" stitched on it and slipped the little red skirt over her back legs. Then I took the

Mickey Mouse ears I'd bought on our summer vacation to Disney Land, punched holes in the sides of the hat, pulled black ribbon through the holes, put the ears over Flossie's ears, and secured them on her head by tying the ribbon under her chin. We lined up on Main Street with hundreds of other gussied-up dogs, cats, rabbits, chickens, various other animals, and their owners. I was twelve, and Flossie was three. Mother sent Anne, fifteen, to watch out for us. Not wanting to be seen by her teenage friends in such an assemblage, Anne slinked along the outskirts of the parade. The Mouseketeer ears must have been humiliating to Flossie, because she kept tossing her head to shake them off. She succeeded only in moving them under her chin. Over and over, I'd bend down to set them straight on her head, but they kept falling down. For most of the two-mile parade, Flossie shuffled along to my gentle tugs on her leash, her head hung low, her own small black ears pressed close against the top of her head and two large black plastic ears dangling below her chin. Her dignity was not restored when she won the prize for the "dog with the most creative costume."

Flossie remained loyal to me and our whole family, in spite of being excluded from church services and paraded around ignominiously. Years later, when Daddy died, First Baptist Church overflowed with people and flowers for his memorial service. After the final prayer, the funeral directors escorted us out to the limousine that would take us to the graveside. We walked down the hall past Daddy's study. There stood Flossie, still and mournful. I bent down and hugged her neck, and we grieved together.

Starving to Fit the Feminine Ideal

When I was eleven, I developed an illness that wasn't even named at that time. Perhaps this marks the beginning of being ahead of my time, although I'm not proud of this part of my story. As a pre-adolescent, my body began a normal rounding process. I felt hurt and embarrassed when several people called me "chubby," and I determined to do something about my body. I started a diet that became an obsession. Even when I had lost over twenty pounds and people started saying how skinny I looked, all I could see when I looked in the mirror was a fat girl. This was in 1957, before eating disorders had been identified. My family referred to "Jann's diet" in hushed tones. Mother and Daddy got scared when I lost down to around sixty pounds. They took me to our local physician, who prescribed a rich diet that included milk with thick cream. I refused to comply. They took me to a psychiatrist in Shreveport, who threatened me with hospitalization. I pretended to eat a little more and flushed food down the toilet when I thought Mother and Daddy weren't looking. They took me to a hypnotherapist in Monroe, but my strong determination kept me from going under his spell.

Finally, over a year later, I looked in the mirror and snapped back into reality. I saw a gaunt face, accentuated by hair pulled back in a pony tail, and a baggy dress hanging on a skeletal body. I looked like one of the child survivors of Auschwitz I had seen in pictures. Some of my friends were attracting attention from boys, and I wanted boys to notice me too. It helped that Daddy looked past my emaciated appearance and simply remarked, "Jann, boys are beginning to notice how pretty you are." With as much resolution as I had begun the diet, I ended it. Now I cringe to admit that a desire to please boys, not love of my own life, motivated my recovery.

Years later I learned the name of my illness: anorexia nervosa. When I heard that popular singer Karen Carpenter had died from anorexia, I suddenly realized that I could have died also. I'm amazed that I recovered from anorexia without adequate professional interventions. When I studied the psychology of this illness, I knew that I fit the profile, except that I was a precocious anorectic. Most anorectics are women in their teens or early twenties, but I was only eleven. Like the profile, I had perfectionistic drive, strong control needs, a distorted self-image, and a strict home environment. Often anorectics seek control over their weight because they feel that they have little control over anything else.

Cultural forces, I believe, contributed even more to my anorexia than psychological factors. The overwhelming majority of young people with anorexia nervosa are female. Many young women starve themselves to fit the thin Barbie Doll image held up by our society as the feminine ideal. I grew up believing that thinness was vital to female attractiveness. If I had grown up with images of powerful, beautiful women of various sizes and shapes, including Divine Feminine images, I could have valued my changing body and saved myself and my family all the suffering we went through with my anorexia.

"Whose Opinion Do You Want?"

In the Baptist church, when I was growing up, there was an eleventh commandment: "Thou shalt not dance." Because Daddy focused his sermons on what he considered more important issues, some members of First Baptist wrote letters telling him that he should preach against dancing. He didn't bow to this pressure. But he and Mother thought it wise not to allow Anne to dance. Instead of school proms, Anne had to go to the parties in First Baptist Church's big recreation center. Anne protested loudly against this injustice but couldn't sway Mother and Daddy. Not until Mother went to a conference on parenting at Glorieta Baptist Assembly did they change. It was too late for Anne; she was already a freshman in college. But I was in my high school prime, my sophomore year. Mother returned from Glorieta, where she'd learned the value of giving teenagers choices on such "moral" issues as dancing. "If they don't have opportunities to choose, then they'll not develop their moral decision-making capacity," so the teaching went. "Give them the choice. Hope and pray that they make the right choice." In spite of all Mother's prayers, I chose to dance.

As the older child, Anne had a harder time as a PK than I

did. And her rebellion was more sincere and highly developed. Our grandmother Aldredge from the beginning labeled me "sweet innocent Jann." Mimi Aldredge married when she was sixteen, had six children, suffered through the Great Depression and her own depression, and believed that God didn't intend women to vote or work outside the home. She never knew how to take Anne's independent, questioning nature and didn't live to see mine.

Mother and Daddy, mellowed by Anne, better tolerated criticism of my behavior. When I was a sophomore in high school, they allowed me to be a majorette in the band, even though Daddy got letters demanding, "Why do you allow your daughter to prance down the streets of Minden in shorts? The Bible says a preacher must be able to control his own children!" One time I went into a local drugstore in shorts, and Daddy got another anonymous letter about his "unruly" daughter. But Daddy never said a word to me about these letters. Mother told me about them, but she didn't ask me to stop wearing shorts.

Anne, now a child psychologist, tells me that research shows that a father's affirmation of his daughter greatly influences her achievement and success. Mother and Daddy both cheered my achievements in school and in extracurricular activities. "I'm busting my buttons" was always Daddy's enthusiastic response.

His pronouncements helped me to develop internal standards of success. When I was in eighth grade, I played an oboe solo in an annual band festival in Monroe, Louisiana. Our band director, Mr. Grambling, always encouraged his students to compete in this contest. The year before, I had played a clarinet solo and received a number one, a "Superior" rating, so I didn't hesitate to compete again, even though I had been playing the oboe less than a year. I loved the haunting sound of the oboe, like what I imagined from the Bible verse about the Spirit's sighs too deep for words. And I relished the challenge of a new instrument. The oboe proved to be more difficult than I realized, with its temperamental intonation and delicate reeds that had to be just the right shape and thickness to produce the sonorous tones.

As I was practicing several hours before my performance at the contest, I chipped my best reed on my front teeth. Fighting back panic and tears, I got a spare reed out of my case. The solo I had worked on so hard to master now came out of my oboe with a tinny sound, punctuated by squeaks. There was no time to get the reed in shape or to buy another one. So I stood before the panel of five judges, determined to do my best anyway. I played my solo from memory perfectly. All the right notes were there. But I realized halfway through the solo that I was off-key, even though I had carefully tuned my horn with the piano before beginning. There was nothing I could do about the intonation nor about the thin tone with intermittent squeaks. The judges' rating reflected the weaknesses, not the strengths, of my performance.

Walking in the door that evening, I sobbed out my distress: "My best reed chipped, and I had to use this awful one that kept squeaking and going out of tune. I had worked so hard, and I got a three, a 'Very Good.' Everybody knows that means 'it stinks.' What am I going to tell everyone at church and school when they ask how I did?"

Mother hugged me, and Daddy declared, "You can say, 'Whose opinion do you want, mine or the judges?'"

The next year, when I was in ninth grade, I also played the xylophone. The xylophone extended from my pelvic bone up to the top of my head. Balancing this instrument while playing the music from memory while marching eight large steps to ten long yards, left right, left right, in tempo with the music and in step with the band while keeping in line as we spelled out "Minden High" and made other impressive formations with our bodies would have been a feat even for someone well-coordinated. I was not. I can still hear Mr. Grambling's voice booming out during practice: "Jann, you're out of line! Jann, keep in step!"

One evening during the Minden High School Band's half-time performance, I got caught up in the notes I was ringing out on my bells. I didn't notice that the band had turned one direction, and I had turned another. Suddenly, I was marching alone down the football field.

After the game that night, I hurried home, chagrined and humiliated. Before I could say anything or even begin to cry out my feelings, Daddy said, "Jann, I noticed that the other band members turned the wrong way on the field tonight. You were the only one going the right way."

In a recent poem I expressed the confidence Daddy's words gave me to choose different paths.

> The band marches down the field mindlessly
> like ants moving straight and relentlessly,
> in line and on task continually.
> One member of the band alone,
> half-covered with her xylophone,
> steps out of line.
> Heads turn,
> but she continues making music.
> Then the band turns right,
> and she turns left and marches solo down the field,
> ringing out her crystal notes.
> Marching out of line, away from the band,
> she creates her own music.

On the whole, however, I walked in step with the Southern culture in which I was growing up. In the minutes of the Minden High School Student Council meeting, October 16, 1963, I wrote: "Stan Belton moved that the boys on the Council put up a new flagpole and that the girls on the Council serve refreshments to them." In the last extant minutes of that school year, May 6, 1964, I recorded: "The Council decided that the boys would trim yards the following Saturday. The Council voted to have the end-of-the year party Wednesday, May 13. The girls on the Council were appointed to bring the food." I was totally oblivious to the sexism in these arrangements. And I never questioned why Harmon Drew was president and I was secretary of the Student Council. Just as flutes and clarinets were for girls and trombones and drums were for boys, so secretaries were girls and presidents were boys. That's just the way things were. Sitting there taking minutes in my white sweater and red felt circular skirt, hair teased regally, I felt pleased with myself and my world. Mother and Daddy, having converted the upstairs of our house to my campaign headquarters, were also proud of my extracurricular success. Even Flossie had contributed to my election as secretary of the Student Council. She had stood patiently for hours tied to the flagpole in front of the high school, wearing around her middle a piece of a sheet with red letters that spelled "Doggone it, Vote Jann."

At a recent family gathering my nephew David read from my Student Council minutes, which Mother had unearthed and brought to me. As David dramatically read our ponderous deliberations concerning the victory bell, an issue that was discussed for over five months, Anne and I laughed in recognition. So this was what had prepared us as adults to sit for hours in meeting after meeting, discussing and debating and planning and appointing committees and recording and reporting, until we have little time left for the work we're plotting. The Minden High School Student Council from December 1963 through April 1964 planned the dedication of the victory bell, formed a committee to make rules concerning the victory bell, discussed possible locations for the victory bell, passed a motion that specified five occasions to ring the victory bell, and amended the motion so that the bell would be rung immediately after football victories as well as on the school day following victories.

A Girl's Worth

Just as football validated boys in Minden, beauty pageants proved a girl's worth. Every year each class selected ten girls to be in the Minden High School Darling Pageant. As I anxiously awaited the results of the voting, my grades no longer mattered.

The MHS Darling Pageant seemed the apex of success to me, and I desperately wanted in. When I heard my name read over the intercom, I could hardly contain myself. I ran home and burst open the door, shouting to Mother, "I got voted in! I'm in the pageant!" Mother and I went to Shreveport to pick out my evening gown, a powder blue taffeta with a tight bodice and a full skirt with layers of net on top and layers of petticoats underneath. Decked in this gown, hair teased and flipped, I paraded around the stage in the Minden High auditorium, feeling like a queen.

At football games I now marched as a majorette. Mr. Grambling had selected me for the front line of the band, I think, because he hoped I could stay in step better without the cumbersome xylophone. I proved only slightly more coordinated with a baton. At summer camp in Kilgore, Texas, I was the only one of the Minden High majorettes who didn't win some twirling award. At the recognition ceremony I heard my friends' names called—Waynette Farrington, Mary Margaret Evans, Eve Baskerville, and Betty Lou Cunningham. I kept hoping I'd at least win "most improved." I'd worked so hard in classes, taught by Gussie Nell Davis, director of the famous Kilgore Rangerettes. I did, however, learn some routines well enough to perform with the group without embarrassing anyone. I practiced our routine to "Baby Elephant Walk" so many times that when I hear that music even now, I remember the steps and twirls. My best moments in halftime performances were when we twirled fire batons. With the stadium lights out, no one could tell if my dance steps weren't synchronized or my twirling lacked precision. And it didn't matter that I singed most of the hair on my arms. I felt like Prometheus, dazzling the crowd with my gift of fire.

My senior year I entered the Miss Minden Pageant. In the MHS Darling Pageant I'd had to compete only in evening gown. The Miss Minden Pageant, a stepping stone to Miss Louisiana and then to Miss America, added swimsuit and talent competitions. I entered this contest with enthusiasm for the new challenge. I diligently practiced my piano solo,

Rachmaninoff's Prelude No. 2 in C# Minor, and planned how I would present my talent with the flair of Liberace, complete with candelabra on the piano. Selecting a swimsuit proved more difficult because I thought my breasts were too small and my hips too large. Finally, I found a black suit that made me look almost balanced.

In 1964, sleek, straight gowns were in fashion, especially since that's what the girl who won the Miss Minden crown the year before had worn. I had a seamstress make me a fitted rose-colored satin gown with a scooped neck bordered by tiny beads and pearls. I performed the Rachmaninoff piece with precision and flair. Recently I tried to play this dramatic piece and could barely stumble through the huge chords and daunting arpeggios, all in four sharps. I marvel that at age eighteen I had such confidence to play this piece before a panel of judges and a large hometown crowd. I didn't make as good a showing in the swimsuit competition, but I walked and posed and turned in my black suit and high-heeled shoes. My scores in the evening gown and talent competitions placed me in the top five. To decide among us, the judges presented us with a question: "What do you think is the greatest discovery of all time?" My quick answer was "the wheel." I went on to elaborate on the ways human history had been affected by the discovery of the wheel. Daddy became incensed when I wasn't chosen Miss Minden, because he thought my answer to the question was much better than that of the winner. He fumed, "This just proves what I've thought all along about these contests. They're just horse shows." Although later I came to agree with his assessment, at the time I felt pangs of jealousy and disappointment over not winning the Miss Minden crown. Being named first runner-up was some consolation.

Reading Jill Conner Browne's *The Sweet Potato Queens' Book of Love* reminded me of how I had longed to win a crown when I was a teenager. I never won a beauty contest, and I was never elected Homecoming Queen. I laughed in recognition as I read Browne's line, "There's just nothing better in life than to ride around on the back of a convertible with a crown on your head." I achieved only partial fulfillment in the Minden High School Homecoming Parade of 1963. How I loved sitting on a convertible in my royal blue wool suit and velvet hat, feeling proud and pretty. But I didn't get the crown. The student body hadn't elected me Homecoming Queen. I was only a lowly "maid." Each football player picked a "maid" for the Homecoming Court, and my boyfriend Bobby Hale chose me. My glory was derivative and uncrowned, but at least I got to ride on the back of a convertible.

The Minden Lions' Club

Several years ago my son Chad called to tell me that he was embarking on a ten-day tour of Louisiana with Senator Mary Landrieu. Chad held the position of deputy director of communications for Senator Landrieu, the youngest member of the U.S. Senate and the first woman senator from Louisiana. How proud I was of him for working with this trail-blazing woman.

Chad said, "We'll spend about five hours Wednesday afternoon in Minden. We're beginning with a luncheon meeting of the Lions' Club."

"That's great!" I responded. "You're going to Minden. I can't wait to tell your dad you're going to Minden, and not DeRidder."

"Yeah, that'll really get to him."

"Be sure to tell people in Minden that your name is Chad ALDREDGE Clanton. Your granddaddy Aldredge was a member of the Lions' Club."

I gave Chad names of people to look up as my memory took me back to Minden and the mystique surrounding the Lions' Club when I was growing up. There was no question then that it was a male-only club. Daddy, like other men in the club, guarded the secrets which I later discovered were not that profound. I remember as a young child asking Daddy what the Lions did, and he'd laughingly respond, "Oh, we growl and roar and then settle down when the lion tamer cracks his whip." My imagination conjured up pictures of grown men clad in lion suits, hollering and running wildly about the "Lions' den." Then the lion tamer, like Daniel in my Bible storybooks, would calm them down.

This terrifying picture faded after several years, but the mystery continued until I played an oboe solo at a Lions' Club meeting. This was the year after my ill-fated performance at the band festival. For several hours a day, every day of the past year, including summer vacation, I had diligently practiced my oboe. So determined was I to make a "Superior" rating at this year's festival that I'd convinced Mother and Daddy to take me to Shreveport every Saturday for lessons with Mickey Hooten, first chair oboist of the Shreveport Symphony. I even learned to make and restore my own reeds, so that I could salvage my performance if something happened to a trusted reed. That year my perseverance was rewarded by a number one and a comment from one of the judges that I "sounded like a professional." Even so, I approached the invitation to play for the Lions' Club with trepidation. These were important men, like my daddy, the leaders of the community.

The real "Lions' den" appeared larger and brighter than the one in my imagination. The May sunlight streamed through the windows surrounding the meeting room on the second floor of a downtown office building. The men greeted me with friendly informality and seated me, along with several other band members who were to play solos, at the head table. I thought I might enjoy this gathering if I could just get my solo over with. But lunch was first on the agenda. Throat dry and stomach queasy, I could eat very little. I looked out at the sea of men dressed in dark suits and narrow ties. My dad smiled and nodded at me, making me even more nervous. I wanted to make him proud of me. After lunch, I learned what the "lion tamer" really did—he cracked jokes, not a whip.

Finally, it came time for the program: first, the trumpet solo, then mine, then the flute solo. The trumpet solo seemed longer and louder than when I'd heard it before. When I rose to play my solo, my legs almost gave way. They continued to tremble until I played the first line of the solo, and then the music transported me to some place outside that room, to some faraway land first imagined by Handel when he composed this poignant Oboe Concerto in G Minor several centuries before. The music came from somewhere deep within my soul, filling my whole body, flowing out through my oboe. The music was all that existed. Then it was over, and the loud clapping brought me back to the Minden "Lions' den." After the meeting, Daddy hugged me and spoke those familiar words: "I was busting my buttons." Somehow, from the look in his eyes, I knew he'd gone with me on the wings of my music to a land beyond Minden.

Chad came back home to Dallas after his trip to Minden. With animation, he began telling me of his experience with the Minden Lions' Club, of people he met who talked to him about me and about Daddy. Then he jotted down these recollections for me.

It was another Wednesday Lions' Club lunch in Minden, Louisiana, with a room full of bankers, lawyers, preachers, and business people. But there was something unusual about this day. The first female U.S. Senator from Louisiana was the invited guest speaker, and the grandson of the most deeply revered Baptist minister this small town ever knew accompanied her as a press aide.

After loading up a plate with sweet potato pie, fresh collard greens and fried chicken and then grabbing a tall glass of sweet tea, I could have sat down almost anywhere. At least twenty seats were empty for the taking. So I slid into a seat in the back, next to an affable-looking gentleman wearing khaki pants and a red-striped necktie.

I extended the obligatory outstretched hand with a warm greeting, a drill familiar to anyone who works for a politician: "How you doin', I'm Chad Clanton with Senator Landrieu's office." The man shook with the same firm, self-assured grip that stings your hand a little, a macho handshake I had become familiar with during this trip through rural northwest Louisiana. Then he asked me where I came from.

"Well, I'm a native Texan. But my parents are both from Louisiana. In fact, my mother is from right here in Minden."

"You've got to be kidding. This is a small town where everyone knows everyone. What's her name?"

"You'd know her as Jann Aldredge."

When I informed him of this, he dropped a fork full of sweet potatoes, leaned across the table with eyes wider than Lake Ponchatrain, paused for a moment, and said, "Good heavens, I used to date your mother. She was an incredible kisser. You've got to remember to tell her you ate lunch with Paul Kitchens."

I learned that Paul attended First Baptist Church, where my granddad had pastored. And so did several others in the room, he said. "Come with me after the senator finishes speaking and I'll introduce you to them. Your granddad was a fine man. They will want to meet Truman Aldredge's grandson."

I was the last one in the room to stand up and clap as Senator Landrieu concluded her remarks and began making her way to the door. Kitchens led me over to the front table where his brother and several other comrades were sitting. He told them about my roots and relatives. "So very nice to meet you," they said one after another in almost rhythmic fashion.

But there was something deeper there. You could see it in their reverent faces and smiles. And after several volleys of platitudes, they began spouting an almost bottomless well of remembrances of my granddaddy Aldredge, ranging from his preaching style to his bowling game. Each one conveyed the kind of genuine respect and admiration that not even thirty years of time can wash away. Truman Aldredge was always an invisible man to me since he died before my birth. I lingered to learn more about him.

George Turner, now more than eighty years old and a senior deacon at First Baptist Church, shared the most vivid memories: "He was a compassionate man. Many times I went with him and fellow deacons on hospital visits. And Dr. Aldredge was not your ordinary preacher, no sir. Your granddaddy was different than the shallow preachers of today who skim the surface without getting to the heart of things. He was a true intellectual. He studied hard and drew from a wide variety of sources in his sermons. It was almost like a college classroom."

As I read Chad's account of his brief visit in Minden, I chuckled over Paul's remark to my son that I was "an incredible kisser." I'd probably aspired to follow in the footsteps of Ruby Graham, the 1953 "kissing expert." I was thrilled over Chad's opportunity to know Daddy better. I'd told both my sons stories about him and given them some of Daddy's sermons and articles to read. But it was clear that visiting Minden and talking to people with whom Daddy ministered for over sixteen years helped Daddy come alive for Chad. It also delighted me that George Turner commended Daddy for the depth of his preaching, because I knew that not everyone in First Baptist had appreciated his intellectualism.

That Mournful November Day

When President John F. Kennedy was shot in downtown Dallas, I was sitting in Mr. Prothro's civics class. Mr. Williams, principal of Minden High, made the announcement over the intercom. Mr. Prothro stared long and wild-eyed up at the little brown box near the ceiling, as though he were pleading for another message that would annul the horrible one it had just delivered. I sat frozen at my desk. The brown box kept speaking ominous words: "The reporter says the president has been rushed to Parkland Hospital. They're saying they think the president has fatal wounds." About thirty minutes later, this usually lively class still sat transfixed, waiting for more words from the brown box. Finally, a little after 1:OO P.M., we heard,

"I'm sorry to have to announce that President Kennedy is dead. It's been confirmed by Walter Cronkite. You're dismissed for the rest of the day." No one jumped up. Mr. Prothro still stared. My classmates started filing slowly out of the room. Suddenly, panic swept through me, even more than when a tornado warning had sent us ducking for cover under our desks several months earlier. I just wanted to get home to Mother and Daddy. As I hurried out, I noticed that the flag in front of the school was already at half mast. It was Friday afternoon, November 22, 1963.

The only time I left the TV the rest of that day and the next three days was to go to church, reluctantly. There was no school that Monday, the day of the funeral, and I thought we shouldn't have had church on Sunday. Images and sounds that played over and over on TV, often in slow motion, remain indelibly in my memory: President Kennedy waving as his motorcade approached Dealey Plaza, shots ringing out like firecrackers, Jackie in pink suit and trademark pillbox hat holding the president's head in her lap, the shaky voice of the Parkland Hospital surgeon announcing President Kennedy's death, Judge Sarah T. Hughes administering the presidential oath of office to Lyndon Johnson, with Lady Bird and Jackie standing on either side, President Johnson delivering to the nation a moving condolence speech, written by Texan Liz Carpenter, Jack Ruby gunning down Lee Harvey Oswald as he was being transferred from the city to the county jail, Kennedy's coffin lying in state in the Capitol rotunda as thousands of mourners passed by, the Navy hymn punctuated by the *clump, clump, clump* of the horse-drawn caisson carrying the coffin, John John saluting his daddy's casket, Jackie Kennedy in black suit and veil walking regally behind the caisson, national and international dignitaries among the crowds gathered inside and outside St. Matthew's Cathedral for the funeral mass, trumpets playing taps at the Arlington Cemetery burial, the eternal flame marking the grave.

My memories also include Daddy's fervent Sunday morning pastoral prayer for the Kennedy family and for the nation. Few members of First Baptist Church had voted for Kennedy, and neither had Daddy. But he hadn't spouted anti-Catholic rhetoric against Kennedy, like some Baptist preachers. If I'd been old enough, I knew I would have voted for Kennedy. I'd been enamored with the Camelot image of John and Jackie Kennedy. I thought Mother looked like Jackie—a classic beauty with high cheek bones, olive complexion, and thick dark hair. I told Mother that, and she seemed pleased.

Ambivalence Toward My Mind

"You beat a boy," Daddy cheered when I told him that I was valedictorian of my graduating class. All through high school David Hinton and I were neck-and-neck competitors for the top rank. He had always scored higher on IQ tests. But my Taurus tenacity and drive to achieve gave me the edge over my rival. A countercultural message from Mother and Daddy also helped. Southern culture gave girls the clear word, "Don't dare compete and beat the boys." But at home I heard, "God wants you to do your very best in everything."

There were plenty of people around me saying that if I wanted to be popular with the boys, I better play down my intelligence. One boy I dated told me, "No matter how smart a girl is, if she doesn't have looks, she's nothing." This message reverberated in my ears even as I sat atop the monkey bars with nine of my classmates posed beneath me for the picture of the Top 10 of our graduating class. As I sat up there, instead of thinking about my academic achievement and where it might lead me in the future, I worried about what the wind might be doing to my carefully flipped hair. It was not enough to be valedictorian; I had to look good too. Cultural voices told me that my greatest value lay in my looks.

I grew up with ambivalent feelings toward my mind. Feeling I had to compensate for my intelligence, I acted as though I had little common sense, especially in relationships with boys. But when I was alone with my books and tests, I went for the top.

Daddy helped me write my valedictory address, beginning with a quote from Tennyson, "Knowledge comes, but Wisdom lingers." I delivered the address perfectly from memory without realizing at that time the import of my words. I'm glad I worked hard to gain knowledge, but the wisdom to follow my own voice both in my vocation and in my relationships came much later. That warm May evening in 1964 as I gave my graduation speech to a crowd of over 500 people sitting in the bleachers of the Minden High football stadium, neither Daddy nor I could have known the part Wisdom would play in my life. I would later call her by her Greek name, *Sophia*.

The Life Service Band and Other "Really Juicy Stuff"

My explorations into ministry began when I was eleven years old. At Girls' Auxiliary mission camp, I sat spellbound by Wana Ann Fort's stories of her adventures as a missionary doctor in a faraway land called Africa. She showed slides of beautiful ebony children and exotic settings. The passion in her voice as she told of her divine mission warmed my heart with longing. I wanted to be like this woman missionary doctor and give my whole life to a mission that would change the world. She challenged us girls to develop our gifts and to follow God's call above all else. She put no limitations on what we could do in ministry. Mary Frank Kirkpatrick also inspired me to be a missionary. She left her position as our youth minister at First Baptist to follow her call to Nigeria. When she came home on furlough, Mary Frank spoke eloquently about the rewards of mission work and the need for more missionaries. Dark-haired and over six feet tall, Mary Frank stood as an imposing presence in the pulpit. She quoted Jesus' words: "The harvest is plentiful, but the laborers are few."

In the military parlance so prevalent in Baptist tradition, I "surrendered" to "special service." Anne later quipped, "If you're a preacher's kid and you're a boy, you're called to be a preacher. If you're a preacher's kid and a girl, you're called to be a missionary." She knew then what I'd later discover all too clearly about my religious tradition's gender labels and limitations. A woman could be a missionary but not a preacher. She could preach, baptize, and serve communion overseas but not at home. If a woman were a missionary, she could stand in any pulpit on Sunday morning. She could "speak" (not preach) and give a "testimony" (not a sermon).

The gender roles were already clearly defined in our high school "Life Service Band." This group of teenagers called to special service met in the church parlor, the place that rivals the sanctuary for sacredness in a Baptist church. The walls of the parlor were "church green," a leftover-English-pea color ubiquitous at that time in churches across the South. Over punch and cookies the Life Service Band elected officers, organized projects, and discussed our future vocations. We never questioned whether our pool of candidates for president should extend beyond the two or three upperclass males in the Life Service Band. We elected a boy named Sam, who combined the evangelistic piety of Billy Graham and the lackluster personality of Bob Dole.

Sam pursued my sister Anne with the zeal with which he followed his divine call. His unrelenting solicitation was probably one of the reasons Anne dropped out of the Life Service Band. The group elected me to fill the secretary's position Anne vacated. I helped organize our project of painting two large white wooden signs with bright red and blue letters, announcing the hours of worship and Bible study at First Baptist. We placed these signs at the northern and southern entrances into town, quite confident that we were "rescuing the perishing," just as one of our gospel hymns instructed us to do.

The Life Service Band's most ambitious project was conducting a worship service in the Webster Parish Jail one Sunday afternoon each month. Sam and other boys did the preaching while the girls helped with the music and with getting the inmates seated. The warden met us at the back of the jail and led us up one dark, narrow, creaky staircase after another. Keys jangling from his belt, he unlocked door after door for us to enter and then clanged the massive doors shut with us inside. Later I dreamed of being locked up in that jail, groping my way down the halls, banging on one door after another, yelling for help. I tried to cover my ears to the sound of the criminals laughing and shouting at me, "Come on back here, honey. We'll take care of you!"

The jail of my teenage memories had surely been there over a hundred years. But on a recent trip back to Minden I learned that the jail was the fourth floor of a courthouse completed in 1953, making it only about seven years old when I went there with the Life Service Band. In the May 4, 1951, issue of the *Minden Herald* I found an appeal for this new jail. The Police Grand Jury had condemned the old Webster Parish Jail, built in 1905, for the fifth time since 1946, stating, "We feel that the jail is inadequate and outmoded and should be replaced by a new and more modern structure. We further feel that the jail is unsanitary and an unfit place to keep prisoners." I couldn't believe that the jail described in this article was not the one I'd visited as a teenager. I kept checking and rechecking the dates. Either my fears upon first encountering a jail distorted my memories, or the condition of even a new jail in Louisiana in the 1950s was not too good.

The boys in the Life Service Band lugged a dilapidated pump organ and small wooden pulpit into the stark meeting room, while the girls went cell to cell with the warden. We stood as far away from the bars as possible while we invited the prisoners to the worship service. The dingy cells reeked of urine and contained only a cot, a toilet, and gaunt, staring men.

As the warden unlocked the cells, I welcomed the chance to get away into the meeting room to begin my other task, playing the pump organ. Though by this age I was proficient in playing all the hymns in *The Baptist Hymnal,* coordinating my feet with my hands was a struggle. I'd be playing along only to realize that no sound was coming from the organ because I had stopped pedaling or wasn't pedaling vigorously enough.

As in the Larry Gatlin song about people at the rescue mission "getting saved" many times a week, some of these men "got saved" every Sunday afternoon we came—perhaps for our approval or the approval of wardens or for some diversion from their bleak existence, or maybe from sincere repentance. Only God knows. What truly amazes me looking back on this experience is the graciousness of these men toward a bunch of teenagers trying out our call on them.

Recently one of my best high school friends, Waynette Farrington, answered my letter in which I'd asked about her recollections of the Webster Parish Jail and our Life Service Band. She wrote:

> When I think of Jann Aldredge and all of us growing up, my first memory is not of the Webster Parish Jail or any other Christian activities. We were as "wild" as we dared to be, although not as "wild" as some other girls our age. I have thoughts of rolling the old cemetery with toilet paper on Halloween night, about 1960. Then there was majorette camp at Kilgore one year and at Ole Miss, another. There was that infamous trip to New Orleans with the Teentone Choir—remember? Also the slumber parties at your house, where your mom placed pots and pans outside the front door—as sort of a noise-alarm, so that if we tried to escape, she'd hear us. Remember Anne Kathryn would hold a flashlight under her chin, and with no other lights in the room, she'd tell us ghost stories? And of course, the night we all— about 13 or 14 of us—crammed ourselves in Celia's Volkswagen and went cruising around Minden at 2:00 in the morning trying to find a gas station open. All we had on was baby doll pj's. So let Mary Margaret and I help you out with the memories. I would just hate to see your memoir published with nothing but tales of all your Christian activities as a child, when there was such REALLY wonderful juicy stuff that went on with us girls.

I do indeed remember with fondness this "juicy stuff," and cannot improve on Waynette's vivid account. My only post-script concerns the "infamous trip to New Orleans." The

Teentone Choir of First Baptist Church attended a youth music week at New Orleans Baptist Theological Seminary. Waynette, Mary Margaret, Mary Linda, Celia, and I smeared Vaseline on the toilets and short-sheeted the beds of the chaperones of a group of girls from DeRidder, Louisiana. Years later, in a receiving line at my wedding announcement party, I learned that one of the recipients of those pranks was standing there beside me—Evelyn Clanton, my future mother-in-law.

Chapter Three

Louisiana Tech Days

The descent from Minden High School valedictorian to Louisiana Tech freshman came all too soon. Always eager to move on with life and goals, I decided to begin my college education the summer after graduation. After surviving registration that took hours in those days before computers, I walked proudly into the Student Center, called the "Tonk." The bookstore swarmed with students carrying armloads of books and grabbing from the table stacked with discounted used books. I took my load back to Aswell Hall, where I roomed with Waynette. I couldn't believe the number and weight of books required for just two courses. Still filled with naive confidence, I strolled out past the Lady of the Mist fountain in the center of campus to Prescott Memorial Library. Walking around the three-story library, I was overcome by the sudden awareness that here were thousands and thousands of books I had never even seen before. I recalled the daunting feelings I had that day in the library when I later taught Alexander Pope's *Essay on Criticism* to college freshmen and came across these couplets:

A little learning is a dangerous thing;

Drink deep, or taste not the Pierian spring:
There shallow draughts intoxicate the brain,
And drinking largely sobers us again.

Mother and Daddy had let me choose the college I would attend. Their choice of Louisiana College for Anne had backfired. They had hoped this small Baptist college in the piney woods of central Louisiana would forever instill traditional Baptist values in my sister. Her sophomore year she eloped with Bill Herring, whom she had dated in high school and who attended Louisiana State University. Although Bill was a Baptist boy, marrying before completing college and without a church wedding was definitely not according to script.

Now it became even more important for me to graduate from college before marrying. At that time my focus was more on the marrying than the college. I did want to uphold my reputation as a good student, but finding the right guy took precedence over pursuing a career. I had heard the unspoken message to Southern girls that we needed a college degree mainly to make us more refined wives and to help us get good jobs if we "had" to work later on. My choice of a college reflects my reticence to venture out from the norm. I followed many of my Minden friends, including a boyfriend, thirty miles east to Louisiana Tech in Ruston. It never occurred to me to look any farther from home than Baylor in Waco, Texas. There were rumors that students lost their religion even as close to home as Tech or Baylor, a Baptist university called by its devotees "Jerusalem on the Brazos," so good Minden young people were not encouraged to venture north.

Preordained Paths

By this time my call and the Life Service Band had faded into the background. If I fell in love with a guy who felt called to missions, then I would bring my call back up. But in the meantime, I chose to major in elementary education, because that's what most girls did. When my children went to school and if I wanted to go to work then, a teaching schedule could best accommodate the family, so the message went. Girls could also be nurses or secretaries, but teaching appealed to me more. I soon discovered how little self-knowledge went into my choice of elementary education. I had scant experience with children and wasn't even sure if I enjoyed being around them.

My slow awakening began in an art course my first fall semester. Having little interest or talent in art, I enrolled in the course only because my advisor told me that it was required in my degree plan. When I walked into the classroom in the art building and looked around at all the baggy shirts hanging out over frayed and faded jeans and the long, straggly ponytails on boys as well as girls, I knew I was in a foreign land. It was 1964, and I had heard of hippies, but never seen any in person. Our first assignment further confirmed that I was in the wrong class, a beginning course for art majors, not the one for elementary education majors that I thought I had selected. It was hard to hide my first attempt at a still-life drawing because our desks were close together, and the instructor paced around the room peering over our shoulders. The girl next to me eagerly and skillfully sketched the bowl of apples, pears, and oranges sitting on a table at the front of the room, while I drew unrecognizable circles. She glanced over and haughtily asked, "Are we looking at the same thing?" The professor more politely gave me some tips, "Try shading to bring more dimension to the fruit." Slaving over the drawing that evening, trying to make it presentable, brought back memories of trying to stand on my head to get an A in my high school gym class. At home I would practice for hours—kick up, *plop,* kick up, *plop*—but no matter how many times and ways I tried, I couldn't get myself upside down. I guess I should have been pleased with the B I got on that drawing of fruit, but I wanted A's on all my work.

Although I hadn't succeeded in headstands, my perseverance brought an A on free throws when we had basketball in high school physical education. Daddy took me every night for several weeks to our church's recreation center to practice. He patiently coached, and I determinedly practiced until I could make ten out of ten. So I believed that if I just worked diligently enough in this art class, I could succeed in it as well. Assignments kept coming back with B's and C's, but I persisted. Then one day a tall, slender woman in black tights and tank top came and sat on the table at the front of our art classroom, where the fruit had been. Before the professor spoke the assignment, fear began churning in the pit of my stomach, burned up my lungs into my throat, and blushed through my face. Drawing that model felt just as impossible to me as making my oboe solo sound good with the bad reed at my eighth-grade band festival. Try as hard as I might, there was absolutely no way. Again, I felt the raw, nauseating pain of my limitations. I doodled a little while in my sketchbook and then drew something little better than a childish stick figure. After the interminable class, I quickly closed my sketchbook and rushed out, burning with the shame of failure.

The next day I went to the registrar's office and dropped the course. When I looked in the catalog and saw two more art courses required for elementary education, I decided to change my major to secondary education with a specialization in English. The cultural expectation that I had to be a teacher, nurse, or secretary still guided me. And perhaps I chose English because girls were supposed to excel more in verbal than in mathematical skills. The choices seemed simple then. All I had to do was walk down preordained paths. Later I realized that the humiliating experience in art class led me out of a haphazardly chosen field for which I was ill-suited. Perhaps Shakespeare was right, that "there's a divinity that shapes our ends, rough-hew them how we will."

The Other Side of Rush

In the summer of 1997 as we were returning from a visit with our son Brett, who was in graduate school at the

University of Mississippi, my husband and I stopped by Ruston to take a nostalgic walk back into our Tech days together. We parked near Prescott Memorial Library, now even larger than it was when I first entered as a gawking freshman. The Lady of the Mist still sat pensively in the center of campus, but the fountain was turned off that evening. Entering the "Tonk," we heard a cacophony of music and conversations, much like when we met there for dates. Many rooms had been added; we entered one where an old James Bond movie was showing for a group of about twelve students. Out in front of the "Tonk," instead of the white concrete sidewalks we had strolled along hand in hand, we found red bricks fanning out in all directions. The bricks were divided into sections according to years, and there was a brick for each student who graduated that year. Under 1966, we found "David McPhail Clanton," and under 1968, we found "Peggy Janine Aldredge." Seeing my name and standing in this place took me back to the time over thirty years before when I had stood there in my long pink taffeta skirt and white blouse with my Phi Mu Sorority sisters, performing for Sing Week.

Accepting without question the belief common among my peers that a sorority was the only road to success as a college girl, I went through rush my first fall at Tech. All the goodness and glamour surrounding rush kept me from seeing the class system of sororities. I heard whisperings that some sororities were topnotch; others, second-class; and still others, undesirable. I was naively going from party to party, enjoying the fun and attention. When I mentioned to a friend, who was a legacy of one of the topnotch sororities, that I liked a sorority outside this group, she frowned and said, "Surely, you wouldn't think of pledging that one! You can do better!"

The sororities within the top group carried labels: Alpha Chi's were the beauties, Sigma Kappa's were the most popular, and Phi Mu's were the brains. I'll admit that I wanted all these labels, but I found myself gravitating toward Phi Mu. It was definitely my first choice after an elegant dinner party in a two-story antebellum home. At the conclusion of the party

Martha Lou Worley descended a winding staircase, regally dressed in a white satin evening gown and singing in her rich contralto voice, "There's a place for you," adapting the words of "Somewhere" from *West Side Story*. Thirty or so freshmen girls stood weeping at the bottom of the staircase as Martha Lou sang invitingly of the place Phi Mu had for all of us.

Later that evening the members of Phi Mu met for hours to choose which girls would be offered bids. The others would find a place in one of the other "good" sororities, if they were lucky. I watched girls who didn't get the desired bids cry as though they'd just heard their mothers had died.

The next year, on the other side of rush, I saw a spirit incongruous with the values of sisterhood and service we sang. The first Phi Mu bid session I attended, I found myself constantly countering critical remarks about the girls going through rush.

"She's too fat. Did you see how thick her thighs are?"

"She seemed witty and sharp to me," I defended.

"Did you see what she had on? She must have gotten that outfit at K-Mart. She has no taste."

"She was in the top ten percent in her graduating class. I really liked talking with her," I continued.

"I heard she had a bad reputation in high school. But I'm surprised boys even wanted to go out with that cow." They all laughed, as I fought back tears. I didn't know this girl that well, so why did she matter to me? But I felt hurt for her. I also grieved the loss of my idealistic feelings about Phi Mu.

As my Phi Mu sisters continued to pick apart girl after girl, I sat there thinking, "This is so cruel and so petty." I made a few more unsuccessful attempts to speak up for girls they attacked. Finally I got up and left, crying, resolving never again to go to a bid session. I would have let anyone in who wanted to join our sorority. My conscience nagged me about being part of an "in" group and keeping others out.

Even though I had been president of my Phi Mu pledge class, after that bid session at the beginning of my sophomore year I became inactive. Baptist Student Union (BSU) began to fill the gap. My first year at Tech I enjoyed my freedom from parents and from being known as a PK. If I went to religious services, it was because I wanted to. I did join Temple Baptist Church, but I chose not to go as often as I chose to go, and that felt good. The BSU held chapel services daily, but I went only occasionally. Walking back from chapel one weekday, I thought, "I went because I wanted to, not because I had to."

"Ph.D. Material"

I had met David Clanton on a BSU retreat in August of 1964. He was beginning his junior year, and I was a freshman. David came from DeRidder, Louisiana, a close counterpart to Minden. He had grown up in First Baptist Church, standing tall downtown with white-columned facade and the largest membership of any church in town, just like First Baptist Minden. DeRidder and Minden had both won the "Cleanest City in Louisiana" awards, although I teased David that Minden was far lovelier. Except for the shrimp gumbo his dad often cooked, the culture David grew up in resembled more the north Louisiana culture of Minden than the Cajun culture of Lake Charles, only forty miles south of DeRidder.

As social chairman of the BSU, David had helped plan the entertainment for the retreat. David himself was the most entertaining. He performed a skit called "Herbert, the Lion." With tongue pressed between his lower lip and teeth, he told a silly, gory story about how Herbert devoured each member of his family and later burped them up. I still laugh when I remember how David looked and sounded with his tongue in his lip, moaning, "Hubbut had et his mudder," and then at the conclusion, exclaiming "Hubbut had bupped!" When I've tried to get David to tell the story of "Hubbut" to our sons, he denies ever knowing it.

David also denies dressing up as wizard, wearing a high pointed black hat and a sweeping black cloak, and sitting atop a ladder at a BSU Halloween party. It was parents' weekend, and Mother attended that party, so I have a witness. When David first asked me out, I thought, "He'll be good for a laugh," without considering that this might become a serious relationship.

David never believed the "dumb blond" act I played to get along with boys. I had practiced lack of common sense until it had become as much a part of me as my Southern drawl. David's brother Mark used to call me "spacy." One evening after a movie in the one theater in downtown Ruston, David and I were strolling back to Tech campus. I asked some silly question about one of the buildings we passed by, and David responded, "I know you're smart, so why don't you act like it?" Later, in my first year of teaching at Dallas Baptist College, the chair of the English department said to me, "You're smart, but you don't sound like it." David had no such prejudice against my Southern accent. His mother Evelyn, from Alabama, could out-drawl me any day. But he wearied of my "spacy" facade. Another night when we were walking around the Tech campus, we found the perfect place to "go parking" without a car. Climbing down into a concrete alcove outside the basement of the science building, David remarked, "Aldredge, you're Ph.D. material." This affirmation of my intelligence, probably as much as his expertise in necking, won my heart.

Praying for a Miracle

In March of 1966, Mother and Daddy came to hear me play oboe in the Ruston Civic Symphony. It was my sophomore year at Tech, but my first year in the symphony. I took a break from the oboe my freshman year. But I kept hearing Daddy's question, "What are you doing for your aesthetic development?" I knew he would be pleased when I joined the Ruston Symphony because orchestral music was his favorite. I remembered his taking me to Shreveport Symphony concerts from the time I was around ten. He sat enthralled by the symphony, motionless except for an occasional tear I would see running down his cheek. Nothing, not even steadily increasing back pain, could keep him from coming to that first concert of the spring season of the Ruston Symphony. Before the concert, he came back stage and gave me a big hug. I noticed that he was walking slowly, slightly hunched. Mother carried big pillows to cushion his back when he sat down. When I asked him about the pain, he said, "Oh, it's nothing. The doctor thinks I pulled a muscle in my back. I've been going to the chiropractor for adjustments." After the concert, he told me with more feeling than ever before, "I was busting my buttons! I'm so proud of you." Even though I'd had only a few solo lines, he praised, "The concert was marvelous, and your solo was the best part!"

Several weeks later I was in the Miss Louisiana Tech Pageant, but Mother and Daddy could not come because he had just been admitted to Schumpert Hospital in Shreveport for tests and possible surgery. The back pain had continued to increase, so he questioned the accuracy of the diagnosis of pulled muscles. I was worried about him, but Mother and Daddy encouraged me to go ahead and be in the pageant. Several days later Mother called me from a phone outside his hospital room.

"Can you come to the hospital?" Her voice trembled.

"Sure, Mother, what's wrong?"

"The surgery—well—they couldn't do that much. It . . . it doesn't look good." Her voice broke. "Come on, and I'll explain when you get here. Be careful. I love you."

I made the seventy-mile drive from Ruston to Shreveport in less than an hour. All the while I tried to hold back the tears and tell myself that the pain was caused by pulled muscles, as several doctors had diagnosed. Surely that's all it was, I tried to reassure myself.

One look at Mother's face told me otherwise.

"The myelogram showed blockage in his spine, but they couldn't tell what it was," she explained. "When they opened him up, it was all over his spinal column. They took out only enough for tests and just sewed him back up. Because of where it was and how extensive, they couldn't get it."

"What? Couldn't get *what?*"

Mother began to sob, and I knew before she said, "Cancer. One of the fastest moving, most aggressive cancers."

Tears flooded my eyes as questions exploded in my mind: How can this be? Can there be some mistake? What about pulled muscles or maybe a slipped disc? How can this be, when he's only fifty-four? Why would this happen to someone who's given his life to the ministry? Why would it happen when he's in the prime of his ministry? God, you won't let this happen, will you?

I washed my face and tried to compose myself before entering Daddy's room. He smiled up at me and asked, "What are you doing here, Jann? Aren't you supposed to be in class?"

"Don't worry. I'm only missing a few classes, and I have A averages in them."

"How was the Miss Tech Pageant? Did you win?"

"It went fine, but I didn't win."

"What was wrong with those judges?" he demanded.

Down in the cafeteria, Mother tried to give Anne and me a more detailed explanation of Daddy's diagnosis. Physicians at that time labeled it "lymphosarcoma" of the spine with probable metastasis to the liver and bone. Years later I learned that it was lymphoma. Today there are many more treatments for lymphoma, including marrow transplant, than there were in 1966. Mother explained to us what Dr. Holabeck, the internist, had told her concerning treatment options. At that time chemotherapy was in its infancy; mustard gas was all that was available. In addition, Daddy received cobalt treatments. But from the beginning Dr. Holabeck said that little could be done for Daddy and that only a miracle could save his life. Anne and I sat there in that phase of denial that kept us objectively discussing the disease as though it were happening to someone else's daddy, while Mother held on to the word "miracle" in Dr. Holabeck's prognosis.

For the next eight weeks Mother threw her whole being

into praying and working for that miracle. She called churches in Minden and others she knew around the country to pray for Daddy. The charismatic faith healers gave her the most hope, so she called them to pray over Daddy. Richard Knox, a soft-spoken Minden Presbyterian minister who had begun to explore charismatic traditions, was the first to come. Other than dabbing a little oil on Daddy's forehead, Reverend Knox didn't do anything outside my notions of ministers. Then came Reverend Hennigan, Minden's only woman minister, a Pentecostal with coils of red hair piled high on her head and not a trace of makeup on her face. She too dabbed oil on Daddy, and then she began to pray, loudly and demandingly. She called on Jesus to defeat the power of the devil and to heal Daddy. Somewhere in the midst of her lengthy prayer, I realized she had begun to utter sounds that made no sense to me. After she finished in the room, she led Mother, Anne, and me out to a nearby stairwell to pray some more. This time she began her prayer by speaking in tongues. This was my first experience of charismatic tongues and my first experience of a woman minister. I found them equally strange.

Mother went beyond Minden in her quest for miracle-workers. She called Oral Roberts, Katherine Kuhlman, Robert Schuller, and other nationally known faith healers. Mother was only forty-eight, and Daddy was only fifty-four. He'd been healthy and vibrant a little over a month before. Now physicians were saying that he was dying of cancer. She simply could not accept this prognosis and fought desperately against it. In addition to the faith healers, she called physicians and scientists around the country. She called her cousin Jim Coon, a physicist at Los Alamos, New Mexico, to help her research experimental treatments.

All the while, our family didn't talk about our worst fears. Mother wouldn't talk with Daddy about what the doctors told her concerning his prognosis. She tried to get the doctors not to say too much to Daddy, because she was afraid he would lose hope of getting well. Daddy was too smart not to know exactly what was going on, but out of love for Mother, he went along with her and the faith healers' theology that he would be healed if we just had enough faith. Anne and I didn't say a word to Daddy about our fears for him, and he tried to spare us his. He didn't know I was standing outside his hospital door one day and heard his agonized cry that he wished, like Job, that he had never been born.

The burden of faith felt heavy on me. Because of what the faith healers told us, I felt I had to pray with absolute belief in divine healing for Daddy. If I let a negative thought enter my mind, then he might not be healed. I drove back and forth from Shreveport to Ruston several times a week. Anne drove to the hospital from Baton Rouge. A letter I wrote Anne and her husband Bill during this time shows how hard I tried to believe Daddy would be cured:

> I know ya'll are continuing to surround Daddy with love and prayer. I know it's hard to believe that a miracle will happen and completely cure Daddy. But I know it will happen if we can have enough faith. "All things whatsoever ye shall ask in prayer, *believing* ye shall receive." (Matthew 21:22). I can't help but believe this. No matter how much evidence there is to the contrary, we must keep believing that God will heal him.

I was trying to finish the spring semester, and Daddy kept asking if I were missing classes. One night after driving back to Tech from the hospital, not wanting to leave because Daddy was getting worse, I got down on my knees in my dorm room and prayed with as much faith and fervor as I could muster. Finally, exhausted after fighting back thoughts of losing Daddy for what seemed hours, I heard a knock at my door. It was Mrs. Penney, my dorm mother. She put her large, kind arms around me while I sobbed out my fears and the guilt I felt about not having enough faith. She said, "Honey, it's not in your hands. Your daddy's in God's hands." And she prayed a soothing prayer of comfort and trust.

At Tech I also poured out my grief to David. Although he'd

never lost anyone in his family and sometimes seemed uncomfortable when I talked about the details of Daddy's illness, he listened caringly. He gave me nonjudgmental support as I raised questions about God. David drove me to Shreveport many times, and waited patiently as I visited Daddy. My love and respect for David grew stronger during this painful time.

On one of his better days in the hospital, Daddy smiled up at me and asked, "Jann, who are you dating now? What's going on with you and the boys?"

"Mainly David Clanton. I've just about narrowed it down to him."

"David's a fine young man, a very fine young man," Daddy replied.

As I watched Daddy suffer devastating losses and agonizing pain, I began to struggle with issues I later learned to call "theodicy." How can we affirm the goodness and justice of God in the face of suffering? If God is benevolent and omnipotent, then why is there so much pain in the world? My more immediate existential question was how a loving God could let my daddy, such a good man and faithful minister, suffer so horribly. The spread of the cancer in his spinal column and into his brain caused paralysis from his waist down and then blindness. Although he tried to be brave, I could tell that he found the loss of his eyesight almost unbearable. He had already lost so much control, and now he couldn't read or even feed himself. Mercifully and inexplicably, he regained his sight after a few weeks. Mother took the doctor's inability to explain the restored sight to be confirmation of a miracle, and she redoubled her efforts toward a miracle of complete healing. But Daddy's cancer kept spreading, now through his liver, increasing his pain and coloring his skin a ghastly yellow.

One day my uncle Leland, a jovial man who'd been sending Daddy humorous cards every day, arrived from Abilene to see Daddy in the hospital. When he saw how gaunt and jaundiced Daddy looked, he choked and staggered out of the room to throw up. Uncle Leland came back in and tried to joke with his only brother, but Daddy knew how shaken he was.

It also wrenched my heart to see the suffering of Mimi and Papa Aldredge. They stayed for several months at our home in Minden, and members of First Baptist drove them every day to the hospital in Shreveport. Papa tried to keep his usual cheerful demeanor, but I could see how deeply he hurt as he watched his son dying. Mimi Aldredge wept openly as she stood at Daddy's bedside, stroking his head and arms.

On May 3, 1966, we celebrated my twentieth birthday in Daddy's hospital room. I didn't feel like celebrating, but Mother insisted and Daddy seemed to enjoy some diversion. Mother had always looked for any reason to throw a party, and she turned every holiday, including the lesser ones like St. Patrick's Day and Labor Day, into what Daddy called an "auspicious occasion." In spite of her exhaustion from staying with Daddy constantly for the past five weeks, Mother managed to create a birthday party for me. She decorated the room with bright balloons and crepe paper. Mother, Anne, and Daddy sang "Happy Birthday" while I held a large cake with twenty flaming candles. As I blew them out, the only wish I could make was for the miracle we all still prayed for. They gave me presents, but I have no memory of what any of them were. All I wanted for my birthday was for Daddy to get well.

One of Daddy's most earnest prayers was answered: that he not lose any mental functioning. His mind and spirit seemed to grow fuller and his voice to grow richer, even as his body continued to deteriorate. His deep baritone singing of "There is a Balm in Gilead" filled the room and the entire hall with hope and beauty. But it was not until his last week that we all talked honestly about his illness. Mother said to him, "I know it's not your faith or our faith or lack of faith. It's all up to God." He responded, "Well, that's what I've believed all along." Although it was hard to talk about his dying, Anne and I felt relieved that we didn't have to try to keep working up "enough" faith.

A few days later, Daddy seemed to rally a little bit. He kept encouraging me to go back to Ruston to take my final exams. Because of his worsening condition in May, when my finals were scheduled, I had asked the professors of two of my courses to give me an "Incomplete" and let me take the finals later. That week in June Daddy seemed to be a little better, so I went to Ruston on Thursday and Friday to take my finals. I completed the last one on June 10 and drove back that Friday evening to Shreveport to tell Daddy of my accomplishment. When I walked in the room, I saw Mother's distress and looked over at Daddy, who was laboring to breathe in spite of the oxygen mask. Even so, he smiled and waved at me. I walked over and hugged him and then Anne and Mother. We stood around his bed as he gasped over and over, "I love you, Eva. I love you, Anne. I love you, Jann." Through our tears we tried to tell him how much we loved him. Daddy asked us to sing his favorite hymns. He died as we were singing "Amazing Grace."

First Baptist Church was packed, downstairs and balcony, for Daddy's memorial service. Mother, Anne, and I led the large group of family members to the first four pews of the middle section: Mimi and Papa Aldredge, Daddy's brother Leland and four sisters—Lavelle, Polly, Katie, and Betty—along with their children, some of Daddy's aunts and uncles, Grandmother Hickerson, Mother's sister-in-law Vivian, and her daughter Julie. The congregation sang "How Firm a Foundation," and the choir sang the "Hallelujah Chorus." Two ministers gave glowing eulogies. But seeing Daddy's coffin right below the pulpit from which he preached for sixteen years made me feel as though I were in a surreal dream.

In the following weeks, Mother's devastation jolted me back to reality. During this time our roles reversed, as I put my grief on hold to try to help Mother. She was only forty-eight and a "widow," a word she couldn't stand to hear or use in reference to herself. Even though people kept telling her it wasn't wise to make important decisions after such a loss, she had to decide where she would go and what she would do. The church poured out support and generosity, but we knew we would need to move out of the parsonage so that the next pastor could live there. Forever etched in my mind is Mother's lament: "I've not only lost my best friend, my lover, my husband, but I've also lost my job and my identity." Her identity was being a preacher's wife. Suddenly, the life-changing question came to me: "If your identity is the wife of somebody and your husband dies, then who are you?" I made a solemn vow not to attach my identity to a husband or anyone else.

That summer following Daddy's death I remember the depth of Mother's grief and her agonizing questions: "What do I do? Where will I go? Who am I?" Anne visited as much as she could, but at this time she was struggling with her own identity crisis. She had a two-year-old son and a one-year-old daughter, and had deferred her educational goals while her husband, Bill, finished college. Their marriage was becoming more and more difficult. Anne and I did most of the work clearing out Daddy's study at the church because Mother found it too painful to go there. Shared grief and memories strengthened our bond as sisters. We marveled at the variety of books Daddy had collected, as many in psychology and history as in theology. When Anne was much younger, she had developed a fascination with psychology as she read some of his books at home. Daddy and Mother had underestimated her precociousness and her insatiable curiosity.

Teaching in Head Start

Richard Knox, who had prayed so fervently for Daddy's healing, now stepped in to help Mother. Considered "liberal" for his social activism as well as his charismatic leanings, Knox supported the Head Start program, beginning that summer in Minden. He suggested to Mother that teaching in this program might help her work through her grief. She had earlier remarked, "I've lost the three men in my life—my brother, my father, and now my husband." Mother's younger brother Julius had died in 1952 in a plane crash as he was traveling to his missionary assignment in Columbia, and her father had died in 1956 of what was then diagnosed as "hardening of the arteries." Always taught to look to male authorities, especially clergy, she now followed Knox's advice. Although I'd discovered in my first year at Louisiana Tech that elementary education was not for me, I followed Mother into the Head Start program because I wanted to be close by if Mother needed me and because I also listened to the male authority. I could work as a teacher's assistant in the program, Knox told me, even though I had completed only two years of college.

First Baptist members wanted to support us in this time of grief, but some raised eyebrows about our working in Head Start that summer of 1966, three years before Minden schools began to integrate. Many white Mindenites looked with suspicion on the Head Start program, seeing it as a step toward integration in that it gave African-American children some of the educational advantages that white preschoolers had in their more affluent families. A few people resorted to phoning Mother anonymously and taunting, "Is this Eva, the maid?" It didn't help that President Lyndon Johnson had initiated Head Start. The majority of people in First Baptist Minden were Republicans who had little use for LBJ, even though his great-grandfather, George Washington Baines, had founded the church and served as the first pastor from 1845 to 1849.

The school where Mother and I taught was definitely "across the tracks." As I saw the poverty of the all-black community we drove through to get to Jerry A. Moore Elementary School, the lie of "separate but equal" sank into my awareness. This dilapidated, drab school with second-hand books and supplies was far from equal to the elementary school I'd attended. When Mrs. Avery, the veteran teacher with whom I worked, deferred to me, I felt for the first time the guilt of my undeserved privileged status. Mrs. Avery had been teaching at Moore Elementary School for over thirty years. She was a large, slightly slumped, imposing woman, who sounded like Maya Angelou when she read to the children or spoke to her African-American colleagues. Her voice became like a thin, raspy reed and her gaze lowered when she spoke to me and the few other white aids and teachers.

Mother taught in the room across the hall from Mrs. Avery

and me. Mother's grief hung as heavy as the thick, humid air in the unairconditioned, overcrowded school room. But her indomitable spirit kept her lovingly engaged with the thirty children who clung to her for attention. Many days I would go over to get her for lunch and find her with several children in her lap, consoling them after some hurt, while tears rolled down her own cheeks.

A little more than thirty years later, I sat in the gymnasium of Gentry High School, Indianola, Mississippi, proudly watching my son Brett as he presided over a program in remembrance of civil rights leader Medgar Evers, murdered in 1963 by Byron De La Beckwith. Willie Morris, author of *The Ghosts of Medgar Evers,* had been giving Brett encouragement on his teaching and writing. Willie offered to speak to Brett's English students and to even bring along his friends Charles Evers, brother of Medgar, and Bobby DeLaughter, the assistant district attorney who, finally, after thirty years, brought De La Beckwith to justice. Brett seized this unique opportunity for a civil rights lesson and planned an assembly program so that all the students at Gentry High could hear the stories of heroes of the movement. Hundreds of teenagers sat mesmerized as Charles Evers told of growing up in Mississippi in the 1930s in separate but certainly not equal schools—with books dog-eared and discarded by white children, chalk used down to a nub in white schools, no electric lights, crates for chairs, and homemade desks.

After the program I walked by the principal's office and stopped to look at a display case filled with articles from the Indianola newspaper. *The Enterprise-Tocsin* featured outstanding students from Gentry High and from the private Indianola Academy. I stood staring at the pictures above the articles—all the Gentry students were black, and all the Academy students, white. These schools, in 1999, were as segregated as Webster High and Minden High when I was a student in the early sixties. "Surely, more equal now," I thought. "At least black and white students are side by side in the paper, something that never happened when I was in school." But I still wondered how much difference Head Start and desegregation laws had made in the South.

Head Start did help point Mother back to her premarital identity as teacher. That fall after Daddy died, she began a teaching fellowship at Louisiana Tech, while working toward her M.A. in English. She and I moved into an apartment at Tech Town Village. I still marvel that in several weeks we moved from the two-story parsonage we'd lived in for sixteen years into a furnished apartment. Grandmother Hickerson stored some furniture in her home in Dallas, and we rented storage space for the rest. One of my jobs in the move was to tackle the attic that contained magazines, stacked floor to ceiling, and medicine cabinets filled with half-used, outdated prescriptions. My "gift of throwing away" quickly developed.

Louisiana Tech with Mother

That fall semester Mother and I took a Shakespeare course together, a course that counted for both graduate and undergraduate English majors. I was beginning my junior year. Mother, close to panic, lamented, "I haven't read anything but Sunday School and Woman's Missionary Union literature for over twenty years. Here I am back in school. What am I doing here?"

Our Shakespeare professor, Colonel Moss, smoked a cigar and paced as he lectured. He'd stop to ask a question or to call on students to read passages from the plays. Instead of verbally correcting a student, he would walk to the open window and shake the ashes from his cigar, a symbolic gesture that reminded me of Jesus' admonition to his disciples to shake the dust of a recalcitrant place from their feet.

Mother covered her anxiety with overeagerness. Colonel Moss arranged us in alphabetical order, so Mother and I sat together on the front row. Colonel Moss seemed to relish beginning roll call by bellowing out, "Mrs. Aldredge, Miss Aldredge." Mother would reply just as emphatically, "Present."

I gave a soft, embarrassed "Here," and kept trying all semester to convince Mother that this was the modern way of responding to roll call. The first play we read was *Julius Caesar*. Mother enthusiastically raised her hand when Colonel Moss asked the first question: "What was Brutus' fatal flaw?" She answered, "He was weak." Colonel Moss said nothing, but moved toward the window, where he slowly and deliberately shook the ashes from his cigar. Mother looked crestfallen.

When it came time for the first test, she moaned, "Oh, Jann, I just can't do it. I'm going to fail. You're young and smart, but I've been out of school so long."

"Mother, I know you'll do great! You're smart, and you can do it," I encouraged. We studied together.

She made 100 and I made 90 on that test. From that point on, she knew she could make it, and I knew I had an intrepid competitor.

Her teaching fellowship gave her two classes of freshmen English and little pay. But teaching provided another boost to her self-confidence and determination. The first semester she had a sixty-year-old student named Mr. Smelley. In his first assigned composition he wrote that his goal was to become a lawyer. He'd always had this goal but had not been able to afford a college education until now. Even though he was just starting out as a college freshman, he felt sure that he could accomplish his goal. Mother quipped as she read his composition to me, "I guess he can be a lawyer in heaven." But Smelley increased Mother's resolve to pursue her goals. "If he can start out in a new direction at sixty, surely I can at forty-eight," she said.

A chapter in our family history that has been almost as hushed-up as my preadolescent anorexia involved my parents' adoption of a baby girl two years before Daddy's death. Alisa lived with Mother and me in the small Tech Town apartment. Since I had already left home for college when Mother and Daddy adopted Alisa, I had little emotional bond with her. Getting her to day care, helping Mother with her in the evenings, waking up to her crying at night—all made her feel like a burden to me, although I felt guilty about this attitude. Mother suffered guilt about her as well, as the reality hit that now Alisa would have only one parent.

Alisa had helped fulfill Mother's need for vocation and identity. Her job was preacher's wife and mother. When I left for college and her nest was empty, her abundant drive and energy had insufficient outlet. She could have gone back to teaching. But several years before, when she was offered a teaching job, she learned that the women of the church were praying that she wouldn't take it. Mother was their "First Lady," and they didn't want her to have any other job. Mother didn't want to lose their approval, so she turned down the teaching offer and later filled the void by mothering a new baby.

As Mother and I struggled to study with two-year-old Alisa underfoot, I began to question whether or not I ever wanted children. At any rate, I strengthened my resolve that my identity would not be tied to the roles of wife or mother. Mother continued to excel as teacher and student at Tech, and her sense of vocational identity expanded. After one year with Alisa at Tech, Mother decided to seek other adoptive parents for her. Although this was a painful decision for Mother, she knew that it was best for Alisa and for her. I agreed, and tried to support Mother through the grief of losing Alisa, added to her grief over the loss of Daddy.

Mother's resilience won out, and she immersed herself in her books as she prepared to take her comprehensive exams for her master's degree. My drive to achieve kept me studying hard through my senior year when many of my friends were partying. When we were not sleeping or eating or going to class, we studied. My clearest memory of that year is sitting with Mother at our kitchen table with books and papers spread all over the table. Mother said that I was like a slave-driver, letting her up only for water and bathroom breaks, but I believe her own competitive spirit drove her on. To save money and time, we often picked up hamburgers at the McDonald's close to Tech Town. At that time McDonald's sold small hamburgers—nothing but meat, buns, a tiny pickle, and a dab of ketchup—for only fifteen cents. We'd get two hamburgers apiece and take them home and add lettuce and tomato.

Choosing Lingerie Over Graduate School

David, then a student at Southwestern Baptist Theological Seminary in Fort Worth, Texas, came to see me in Ruston almost every weekend for over a year, catching a ride with a friend who pastored a church near Ruston. As our relationship became more serious, David began to express fears. He thought we might be rushing things. He'd kidded that I had pursued him at Tech—throwing rocks up at his dorm window to get his attention. I laughed at his tale, but knew its partial truth. I had always been goal-oriented, and he was now my goal. I had decided I wanted to marry him, though not before I graduated from Tech. The clear message from my parents was the importance of finishing my college degree before I married. I don't think they ever said that I needed to marry right after graduation. But the cultural admonition, especially for girls, was to find a husband in college, or perhaps lose any chance of marriage. And that would be the greatest tragedy.

I breathed in these messages along with the sultry, pine-scented Louisiana air. I had decided David was the one even before Daddy blessed him, saying, "David's a fine young man." But David needed to make sure I was right for him. So he suggested that we date other people for a while.

For the next few months David didn't come to Ruston, and we both dated others. I think this would have been a more painful time for me had I not been so convinced that David and I would get back together. I'm not sure who proposed to whom. I'd like to think, with my current level of feminist consciousness, that it was a mutual proposal. I had gone to Fort Worth for a missions conference at the seminary, a good excuse to see David. We went out, and started talking about getting married.

Though I had poured so much energy into my academic achievement, as graduation drew near, my focus turned to marriage. Two of my English professors at Louisiana Tech urged me to apply for Woodrow Wilson and Fulbright fellowships. I half-heartedly filled out the application for the Woodrow Wilson Fellowship, but didn't even touch the Fulbright. Planning a big church wedding and gathering my trousseau appealed to me more than graduate studies.

Louisiana Tech changed from the semester to the quarter system in the fall of 1967, so I graduated in February 1968 instead of May, as originally planned. I graduated summa cum laude, and then worked the next three months in a clerical job I hated in order to buy lingerie in every color imaginable, as well as help with wedding expenses.

My job was typing income tax returns in an accountant's office. Every morning I walked up a narrow staircase to a small, stuffy office packed with papers. I sat at a cramped desk for over eight hours each day typing on an old manual typewriter, pounding out number after number into small squares on form after form. The only relief came when Mrs. Williard, who had continued her husband's accounting business after he died, called me to come "C" and "P" in her office. These initials stood for "check" and "prove," a meticulous process in the days before computer programs, a process which took two people. I remember how David teased me about "C and P'ing" with Mrs. Williard. If David had ever met her, he'd have known that she was not the sort of person to play around with. Probably in her early sixties, she looked over eighty. A female version of the High Lama in *Lost Horizon,* she had straggly gray hair pinned up in a bun, thin lips pursed tightly, and impassive eyes. She was always there at her desk before I arrived at 8:00 A.M. and after I left around 5:30 P.M. I don't recall her taking breaks or showing any emotion, even on the morning after Martin Luther King, Jr. was assassinated. I walked into her office to express my shock and sorrow, and she just stared at me without comment.

It didn't enter my mind at the time to question what I was

doing in that job or to look for anything more in keeping with my education and aptitude. All I cared about was making enough money so that I could buy matching underwear and negligees in turquoise, rose, white, pink, forest green, baby blue. I even bought a turquoise girdle, though I'd never worn a girdle before. I suffered from an overdose of romantic Sandra Dee and Rock Hudson movies. During the long, boring hours of typing numbers on income tax forms, my mind filled with fantasies of marriage. I labored under the Cinderella Complex before there was a book on it. David would rescue me from this drudgery, and we would live happily ever after. My call and my vocation receded in the picture. Although I had vowed not to attach my identity to a husband, I was getting some vicarious fulfillment from David's being in seminary preparing to be a minister.

"Come on Back and Be Free"

Mother's ambivalence about her identity as a woman paralleled mine. Messages of the importance of marriage sounded strongly in her ears. No matter how much she excelled at Tech, she felt incomplete without a husband. She lamented, "The world's designed for couples. I feel like a fifth wheel going out with other couples or by myself." For a Southern woman of Mother's generation, a man was necessary for success as well as for security. The summer before when Mother, Grandmother Hickerson, and I had gone to Glorieta Baptist Assembly, Mother began looking and praying for a man.

That fall Mother began corresponding with Taylor Henley, whose wife had recently died of cancer. Their relationship moved quickly from shared grief to marriage plans. Taylor, another Baptist minister who at that time was director of a Baptist geriatric center in San Angelo, Texas, spared no expense or time in courting Mother. Although she could see that she was about to recover her lost identity as preacher's wife, her drive for academic achievement never slacked. During that spring of 1968, she pored over her books in preparation for her comprehensive exams. Since at that time the master's degree was the terminal degree in English at Louisiana Tech, the comprehensive exams equaled those of doctoral programs in length and difficulty. Mother scored higher than any of the other students on these exams and received her M.A. degree in May. Mother's energy seemed limitless that spring as she dated Taylor, completed her master's degree, and planned two weddings.

No matter how pressed she was for time and no matter how little space there was in our apartment, Mother determined to host an announcement party for me. I encouraged her to have a small informal gathering, but she could not be so stifled. Always the consummate Southern hostess, she got out her finest linens, the large silver punch bowl given to her by First Baptist Minden, her china cups and saucers, and her best silverware. On the table she also placed the tiered cake she had ordered from the best bakery in town, iced cupcakes she had made, mixed nuts, and party mints. For the occasion Mother made "Baptist punch," a mixture of lime sherbet and ginger ale, which she had served for many church parties and receptions. Our small combined kitchen/dining room seemed transformed into an elegant Hilton reception room. Mother and Grandmother Hickerson and I, dressed in our Sunday best, stood at the door to greet the guests.

About midway through the party, a man arrived dressed in frayed jeans and a faded T-shirt on which was a large peace sign stenciled in black. He had long tangled black hair down to his shoulders and was carrying wildflowers. Immediately I recognized him as Bill Iles, an art professor at Tech. He was David's best friend from DeRidder and was now also a great friend to Mother and me. Although the long wig threw her off at first, Mother soon realized it was Bill. We began to laugh almost hysterically, while trying to tell Grandmother Hickerson who he was. Bill began to move through the circle of guests seated decorously around the room. He went from person to person, bowing graciously and giving each a flower as he spoke the word "peace." Some smiled and said "thank you." Others chuckled, while some stared incredulously at him.

Bill stood in the middle of the gathering at our Tech Town apartment and proclaimed, "Jann's a member of our commune. She's a beautiful, wonderful flower child. She shows the world the meaning of peace and harmony. I've come here today on a mission to take her back to the commune." Bill then turned to me and began to plead, "Jann, come back. Don't get married and become part of the establishment. Come on back and be free." I laughed and complimented Bill on his creative joke, but the word "free" struck a chord. Even though this was many years before my "consciousness" was raised, I knew at some level that I was giving up more freedom than David was.

"Love, Honor, and Obey?"

My mind and conscience must have been buried beneath layers of convention when I took the vow to "love, honor, and obey." David teases me about the "obey," and I've tried to deny that I ever spoke the word. But a copy of the wedding ceremony proves that I allowed that horrid vow in my service. I moved unquestioningly through other patriarchal traditions, including being "given" away by one man to another and changing my name. When I was growing up in school, we girls used to try out our first names with the last names of our boyfriends. We believed it would be a great accomplishment to change our names and a disgrace to get stuck with a maiden name, the symbol of the "Old Maid." I remembered playing a card game called "Old Maid" with Anne, cousin Kathy, and grandfather Aldredge. The one who drew the scraggly-haired, pimple-faced Old Maid card lost the game. I blithely complied with the prejudices of my time and place, unaware of how oppressive they were. Kate Millett, in *Sexual Politics,* describes the state of naiveté in which I lived: "Many women do not recognize themselves as discriminated against; no better proof could be found of the totality of their conditioning."

Over a thousand people filled First Baptist Church in Minden for our wedding at 8:00 P.M. on May 18, 1968. As I walked down the long aisle on my grandfather Aldredge's arm, feeling like a queen from my veiled head down to the white satin train flowing behind my feet, with all eyes beaming approvingly on me, I wondered if anyone would notice how shriveled up my fingers still were from my three-hour bath. Some bride's magazine had given me the notion that I was supposed to spend my entire wedding day, if not many days before, soaking in perfumed bath oils and preening my body to its highest perfection. The night before the wedding I had spent several hours talking on the phone to Mike Burge, a good friend I'd once dated, commiserating with him that our relationship could never be the same after the next day. Feeling guilty that I was behind on my physical regimen, I got up the next morning about 8:00, ate a quick breakfast, and got into a bubbled, oily bath. Sometime between the second and third hour in the bathtub, long after the bubbles had melted, I jumped out, yelling, "That's enough! This is ridiculous! Why should I be doing all this when David's out having fun with his friends?" My consciousness was rising, slowly.

From as early as I can remember, I dreamed of a fairy-tale wedding, believing it would be the summum bonum of my life. In my dreams my husband was always a shadowy figure. I was the main character, the loveliest of brides. There was one other prominent character in this scene: my daddy. He played a versatile role, moving from "giving me away" to singing a solo to performing the ceremony. That dream could never come true. I was glad Papa Aldredge could "give me away," but my wedding was another poignant awakening to the reality of Daddy's death.

It was painful to see Walter Shurden standing where Daddy should have stood, performing the marriage ceremony. Later I wondered whether or not Daddy would have used that archaic vow—"love, honor, and obey."

Shurden, more progressive than most Baptist ministers, should have been aware of the oppressive language and symbolism of the traditional wedding. In his premarital counseling, he'd had an egalitarian perspective. I remember being embarrassed when he talked about how David and I could achieve equal sexual satisfaction in the marriage. Dr. Shurden had been generous in his pastoral care of Mother and me when we were together at First Baptist in Ruston after Daddy died. And Shurden's wife, Kay, broke out of the traditional preacher's wife mold to pursue a master's degree in English at Louisiana Tech. She and Mother supported each other through this degree program. Later Shurden became an avid supporter of ordained Baptist women and of my ministry, inviting me to contribute a sermon to a series he edited on the priesthood of all believers. Back in 1968 he probably pulled the "love, honor, and obey" vow out of some marriage book without even thinking about it. After all, he couldn't help being influenced by androcentric culture and religion. And neither could Daddy. Recently I listened to tapes of some of Daddy's sermons, and realized that he didn't escape the sexism of his time and place and religion.

Not quite two months after my wedding, Mother married Taylor Henley. The wedding took place in Grandmother Hickerson's church, Wilshire Baptist in Dallas. A month before, Grandmother and I had watched Mother walk across the stage of Howard Auditorium at Louisiana Tech to receive her master's hood and diploma. Although Grandmother expressed pride in Mother's academic accomplishment, she seemed to take even greater pleasure in Mother's marriage to Taylor. She kept making remarks to me like, "I'm so glad Eva has someone to take care of her now." Such comments seemed strange coming from Grandmother, who had gotten along quite well on her own since my grandfather's death over ten years earlier. In fact, she seemed to thrive on her independence, driving around the country and wearing red lipstick, as she'd never done before. I even heard her say, "I'd never marry again because I don't want some old man to take care of."

Standing beside Mother as she married, I felt more than a little ambivalent. It was a small wedding with Anne and me as matrons of honor and Taylor's son, John, as best man. Only a few other family members and several friends attended the ceremony. Anne and I wore matching dresses of aqua polished cotton, and Mother looked radiant in a street-length turquoise silk dress. Although the preacher who performed the ceremony didn't use that onerous vow of "love, honor, and obey," I couldn't help remembering Mother's lament about her lost identity after Daddy died. Here she was, becoming a preacher's wife again and planning to move with Taylor to San Angelo. What about the master's degree she had worked so hard to earn?

That question awakened Mother after a year of marriage. Though wifely functions, such as entertaining the board of directors of Baptist Memorials Geriatric Center and traveling around Texas with Taylor on his fund-raising duties, brought her some satisfaction, they were not enough. Through her graduate studies and teaching, she had discovered a self beyond the one dependent upon a husband. That self nudged her to begin teaching English at Central High School in San Angelo, where she enjoyed her own success and creative development. I was also an English teacher and planned to continue teaching until I had children, if things went according to script.

Chapter Four

Superwoman Years

My first teaching assignment soon went awry of my careful plans. I had held the illusion that if I worked hard enough to make my lessons stimulating and to communicate my great love for literature to my students, then they would work assiduously and joyously. It was the fall of 1969, and I was teaching three classes of sophomore English and two classes of speech at Paschal High School in Fort Worth, Texas. David was studying at Southwestern Baptist Theological Seminary, where he also worked as a photographer. My growing social conscience celebrated the fact that I was teaching in a recently integrated school. There were, however, only a small number of African Americans in the high school and only eight among my 150 students. Though racial conflict did cause some unrest in the school that year, it had nothing to do with the problems I encountered.

The bane of my tenure at Paschal was a fifteen-year-old named Fred, a brilliant Anglo boy who came from an upper-middle-class, well-educated family. Fred managed almost single-handedly to make a Tower of Babel of my third-period English class and my fifth-period speech class. In my calmer moments, I realized that Fred tried to compensate for his small size and physical unattractiveness with his bravado behavior. The cultural stereotypes for boys could be as insidious as those for girls. Boys gained popularity more through brawn than through brains. If they excelled too much intellectually, they risked being labeled a "nerd" or a "geek." Too small for football, Fred attempted to prove his masculinity through his rowdy, defiant behavior in class. What Fred lacked in size he made up for with the ingenuity of his methods of disrupting classes. Sometimes he blatantly challenged my authority, but more often he was like a ventriloquist, throwing a variety of aggravating sounds around the room or stealthily prodding other students into outbursts of anger or laughter. Though I might suspect that Fred instigated most of the pranks, he usually made it difficult for me to prove his guilt.

Still idealistic, I believed I could control Fred. I tried everything from reasoning with him to cajoling him to threatening him. Believing I could bolster his self-esteem by giving him a special assignment, I asked him to serve as teacher's assistant. Nothing worked. Fred achieved his goal of gaining the attention of his classmates, and some followed in his footsteps. Though none equaled Fred as a troublemaker, several others contributed to making that year of teaching a nightmare.

Many days I'd come home crying. I had recurrent dreams of my students screaming and running wildly around the classroom as I stood in the doorway, trying in vain to keep them from taking their havoc out into the hallways. My anxiety and flagging self-confidence brought on a relapse of anorexia. Many days I'd eat nothing but grapes for lunch, sitting in my car alone, glad to be away from students and other teachers. If I had no control over my students, I at least had control over what I ate.

This time my anorexia was not as severe nor as long-lasting as my preadolescent bout with the illness. And I didn't have Daddy's strong voice of affirmation to help me toward health. I was beginning to hear another voice, small but persistent—my own. Almost simultaneously, I left behind the anorexia and high school teaching. Slowly I was gaining some internal clarity about my gifts and my vocation. It was obvious that I was not a disciplinarian; I had little skill in confrontation and even less desire to be authoritarian. My love of literature and cultural forces that limited vocational choices for women had led me into high school English teaching. I had come to realize, however, that in high school teaching I had to expend so much energy trying to police classes that I had little left for the subject matter I so loved. Just as the ill-fated art class had helped widen my options beyond elementary education, my miserable experience with Fred and his followers led me to begin looking outside the narrow lines that had confined my perceptions of women's vocations.

The Mysteries of Providence

In the spring of 1969 I began applying to graduate programs of several universities in the Dallas-Fort Worth area. David had one more year at Southwestern Baptist Theological Seminary in Fort Worth, so I believed my choices to be limited by geography as well as finances. At that time it would have been inconceivable to me to look at studying in a city away from David or of asking him to move with me. But, contrary to prevailing messages of women's roles, I believed I had to bear my weight financially. Watching Mother struggle to make a living after Daddy died indelibly impressed upon me the importance of being able to support myself. So my choice of schools also depended upon the results of my applications for a teaching assistantship. Late that spring I received a letter of acceptance into the master's degree program in English at Texas Christian University, along with a teaching assistantship that would pay my tuition and a small salary.

"Ms. Clanton. Ms. Clanton? Jann Clanton?"

"Yes," I responded to roll call the first day of my first class at TCU.

"Oh, you're Fred's English teacher! He came home almost every day last year singing your praises," said my Renaissance

Drama professor—the father of my most obstreperous student at Paschal High. Stunned, I stared at him. Also, I felt relieved, given the context in which I now found myself, that Fred's comments about me to his father had been so positive.

"You're Fred's father. Well, of course . . . he . . ."

"Fred loved you so much," he interrupted, giving me time to think of something good to say about Fred.

"Fred is a very smart boy," I managed, truthfully.

"Yes, but I know he can be quite a handful. He's our only child. His mother and I have had trouble controlling him, and we're so grateful to you for all you did for him."

I just smiled and nodded, awed by the mysterious ways of Providence. My professor would never know that Fred was one of the main reasons that I was now sitting in his class at TCU instead of standing before a class at Paschal High School.

His remarks about Fred and my teaching him didn't stop after that first day in his class. I began to wonder if perhaps his father's doting had contributed to Fred's rebelliousness. Worried that others in the class would think he gave me preferential treatment, I worked hard to make nearly perfect scores on tests and papers so that there would be no question that I earned my grades. But I became embarrassed by his constant references and felt my classmates' annoyance.

"You really made an impression on Fred—and on our professor!" Raynal Barber teased.

Superwoman and Other Models

Raynal and I sat next to each other in the Renaissance Drama course and quickly discovered all we had in common. Growing up in Southern Baptist families, we both remained active in Baptist churches. We both struggled to combine marriage and career. Raynal had taught English in a junior college and was now teaching at Dallas Baptist College. Her descriptions of DBC piqued my interest. Ten years older than I, with an M.A. in English and working toward her Ph.D., Raynal became my mentor and model. Even if feminism's advice on avoiding the "superwoman" syndrome had been out at this time, Raynal probably wouldn't have heeded it. Her internal tapes about her proper roles played even louder than mine.

Raynal confided that she often felt she had to make up for her work outside the home by trying even harder to prove herself as a wife and mother. Raynal had three young children and a lawyer husband, a conservative Southern gentleman who encouraged her academic pursuits but at the same time expected her to perform all the traditional roles of wife and mother. Raynal described to me a common scene at their dinner time: she'd be scurrying to cook dinner, with children tugging on her and crying, while Will sat oblivious in the den reading the paper. Then she'd struggle to set the table and get the children settled at the table before serving the plates and pouring the milk while Will stood chivalrously holding out her chair for her to sit down. Raynal laughed indulgently about Will's actions, but I felt the unfairness of this situation and told her so.

Raynal's academic acumen and indefatigable energy propelled her through the most demanding tasks. She fulfilled family responsibilities while teaching a heavy load of English courses at DBC and commuting to Fort Worth to take a full load of doctoral courses at TCU; on top of all this, she garnered the "Teacher of the Year Award" and made A's in all of her graduate courses. She was superwoman par excellence, and I took notice.

Two other women influenced me as I worked toward my M.A. degree at TCU. Sarah Gordon, like Raynal, was a brilliant student in the doctoral program. I got to know Sarah in several courses that counted toward both the M.A. and Ph.D. degrees. Sarah and I also discovered political affinities. Together we supported George McGovern, participated in several anti-Vietnam War rallies at TCU, and went to local Democratic Party meetings. Sarah helped me begin moving beyond my Baptist provincialism. A Presbyterian who had recently converted to Catholicism because she found it more aesthetically appealing and because her beloved Flannery O'Connor was Catholic,

Sarah expanded my understanding of the Christian faith. Sarah introduced me to Catholic theologian and mystic Thomas Merton; his *Seven Story Mountain* and *Seeds of Contemplation* intrigued me with their descriptions of a meditative spiritual practice I'd never heard of in Baptist churches. Along with Sarah, I was drawn to Flannery O'Connor, a Southern Catholic fiction writer, whose stories "A Good Man is Hard to Find" and "Revelation" revealed the meaning of grace and redemption more powerfully than most sermons I'd heard. Sarah and I spent hours sitting in the basement snack bar of the TCU student center, drinking coffee and eating jelly donuts while also savoring the intricacies of Merton's contemplative practice and the spiritual profundity of O'Connor's symbolism.

Sarah's singleness challenged me beyond some of my conventional assumptions about the importance of marriage to a woman's worth. In Sarah I had found a woman approaching forty, unattached and unanxious to find a man, secure in her independence and confident in her abilities.

The other influential woman was Ann Gossman, one of my Renaissance literature professors who later became the director of my Ph.D. dissertation. In the fall of 1969 I took her course in John Milton as part of my M.A. program. Dr. Gossman's dazzling intellect and rapid, somewhat eccentric speech pattern at first overwhelmed me to the point that I could hardly take notes. Looking around at my classmates nodding their understanding and busily writing, I felt even more intimidated—as though I had landed on another planet surrounded by creatures somewhat like me but more highly evolved in intellect and language. Dr. Gossman paced back and forth, noteless, in her baggy dress and thick glasses, in front of the blackboard upon which she occasionally scribbled something as hard for me to decipher as her speech. As I grew accustomed to her speech and writing, understanding dawned, and with it the realization that I had never before met anyone with such an incredible memory as well as analytical and intuitive abilities. She quoted long passages not only from Milton but from Shakespeare, Spenser, and many other authors, as well as from literary critics who wrote about these authors.

The first time I took a course from her, she was Dr. Gossman; the next time she was Dr. Landman, having just married and taken her husband's name. Several years later she divorced and became again Ann Gossman. A few years later she became Ann Ashworth, taking her mother's maiden name because she felt closer to her mother than to her father and because she liked the sound of "Ashworth" better than "Gossman." To some of her students, this metamorphosis in her name was simply another of her idiosyncrasies or an overidentification with the characters in Ovid's *Metamorphoses,* to which she often alluded in her lectures. To me, it brought into question for the first time the convention of a woman's changing her name when she married. It seemed overcomplicated and unfair, especially for a woman with a professional identity in one name to have to change that name because she married. Dr. Ashworth gave me a vivid picture of a woman who claims her own power to name. The subtler evolution I made in my name would come later.

LBJ at First Baptist Church, Minden

I took time away from my studies that fall of 1969 to attend a historical event, unlike any Minden, Louisiana, had ever seen. Former President Lyndon Baines and Lady Bird Johnson came to celebrate the 125th anniversary of First Baptist Church, founded by Lyndon Johnson's great-grandfather, George Washington Baines. On Sunday morning, October 26, when David and I arrived at the church, the steep steps leading up to the sanctuary and all entrances to the church swarmed with Secret Service agents and over 300 members of the news media. Johnson was making his first public appearance since leaving office in January of 1969. Members of First Baptist (including those who hadn't come in years) and guests from all over the country overflowed the sanctuary. Anne and

I agreed that this was one of those rare occasions when it was great to be "PKs" (preacher's kids). Families of former pastors were given the enviable seats in front. Anne and her husband Bill, David and I, and Mother sat on the third row of pews on the right side of the sanctuary. We couldn't have had a better view. Lady Bird and LBJ entered through the side door just a few feet from us.

During the worship service the chairman of the church's historical committee presented the former president a leather-bound copy of First Baptist's history, written by longtime member Major DePingre. The history includes an excerpt from the minutes of the organizing congregation describing the first pastor, the Reverend Baines, as "a gentle and quiet man, soft in speech and modest in everything." When the former president boomed out his acceptance remarks, I couldn't help noticing the contrast between him and this description of his great-grandfather. Johnson delighted the congregation with comments about himself as a "member of the great society of the unemployed." He went on to say, "I am very appreciative of the efforts of this committee in the recognition given to my great-grandfather. Mrs. Johnson and I are grateful to the people of Louisiana for their friendship to us through the years and particularly the hospitality today." Lady Bird sang along on all the hymns, but Lyndon didn't join in until we came to the Doxology.

The worship service that day proved Martin Luther King, Jr.'s statement that "Sunday morning at 11:00 A.M. is the most segregated hour of the week in our country." Although pastors and Baptist leaders from around the country came to the service, no African-American pastors or Head Start directors were there to greet the president who had risked disfavor of Southern Democrats to champion the Civil Rights Bill of 1964. I don't know whether or not they were invited. If they were, it was obvious that they didn't feel welcome at the service or the lunch that followed. PK privilege didn't get me into the lunch, but I heard about it from Mother, who sat by LBJ and Press Secretary Bill Moyers. At the lunch LBJ asked about meeting with B.F. Martin, the pastor of Minden's St. Rest Baptist Church, an African-American congregation founded shortly after the Civil War by freed slaves who had been members of First Baptist. Reverend Martin had written to Johnson, requesting a meeting of local black leaders with the former president. It saddens me that the meeting finally took place at the Minden Municipal Airport, shortly before LBJ and Lady Bird departed, instead of at First Baptist.

Messages about Wifely Roles

By the time I was finishing my M.A., David's earlier words, "Aldredge, you're Ph.D. material," had faded into a faint echo. Though I admired Raynal and Sarah and at times wanted to follow in their footsteps, their trepidation as they approached the Ph.D. comprehensive exams filled me with doubt about my intellectual capacities. If these women, whose minds I considered far superior to my own, had concerns about passing comps, then there was no way I could jump this hurdle. I had relished the year and two summers of graduate study, feeling much more at home with myself than in the high school classroom. And meeting the challenge of rigorous academic study massaged my ego.

But no matter how much I achieved, I was always plagued by self-doubt and fears of failure. Although I don't remember direct statements of women's inferiority from the pulpit, I saw no women in church leadership as I was growing up. And I often heard Mother put down her intelligence in comparison to Daddy's. From watching her I got the impression that women could make up for our defects by working as hard as possible. My memory is filled with pictures of Daddy watching TV and lying down on the sofa in the music room listening to classical records. But Mother rarely stopped. She did church work almost full-time without pay, while doing the family finances, housework, and most of the child-rearing. Her model of "superwoman" strongly influenced me.

From Mother and Minden culture I internalized messages about my role as wife. David never discouraged me from continuing my academic studies, but neither had he reiterated his remark about my being "Ph.D. material." He had finished his seminary master's degree the May before I completed my M.A. in August, and he had taken a job as audio-visual director of the Baptist General Convention of Texas, headquartered in Dallas. We moved to Dallas that summer of 1970, and I took my last two M.A. courses at Southern Methodist University. It never occurred to me then to commute from Dallas to Fort Worth, only about thirty miles, to take those courses at TCU. I wanted to be fully supportive of David in his first full-time job. At this time in our marriage we divided our roles along conventional gender lines. Even though David liked to cook and was very good at it, having his dad as a model, I had dismissed him from the kitchen the summer after we married, saying "thank you, but no, I can handle everything just fine." No matter what else I excelled in, I had to do well in cooking and cleaning the house to validate my womanhood. Mother may never have articulated this value to me, but she demonstrated it. To me, being a good wife meant not only performing domestic chores and moving with my husband, but also taking care of his ego. Somewhere deep down in my psyche lurked the fear that if my academic achievement exceeded David's, it might make him feel bad and thus hurt our marriage. Although David had never so much as hinted this feeling, I heard a Minden tape in my head, "Don't beat boys; let them win."

A competing message from Sunday School lessons and sermons on the parable of the talents ran, "Be a good steward of intellectual abilities and educational opportunities." Having already discovered my limitations as a high school teacher, I determined to find a college teaching position. With the M.A. degree, I believed I had a better chance of getting a job at a junior college than a four-year college or university, so I applied to the four schools in the Dallas County Community College system. I quickly learned that a degree in math or science would have been much more marketable; each English position had around 500 applicants.

Racism, Sexism, and Southern Drawl Prejudice

I remembered Raynal's glowing descriptions of teaching at Dallas Baptist College, but thought I had little chance of getting a position there. DBC had recently made the transition from junior to four-year college, and financial struggles had forced the school into a hiring freeze. Nevertheless, I filled out an application and called for an interview. Ed Lacy, chair of the humanities department, told me that it would be a waste of time to come for an interview because there were no English positions open. Several weeks later, I called back, and he told me the same thing. The third time I called, about a month later, I insisted on an interview, and he relented.

As I drove up the winding hill to the college and saw seven buildings regally overlooking Mountain Creek Lake, I knew in my soul that this was where I was meant to be. All I had to do was convince Dr. Lacy.

Everything in his office, including Dr. Lacy himself, seemed too large for this small space. Overstuffed with books and papers and furniture, the office did not feel inviting of visitors. But he smiled and spoke warmly as he cleared off a chair for me. "Welcome to Dallas Baptist College. Pardon my mess here, but we have very little office space. I hope to move to a larger office in the Learning Center soon."

"Thank you for agreeing to see me. I'm glad I got to come out and see the college. It's really beautiful. It looks as though it would be a wonderful place to work. And I'd love to teach at a Baptist college." I started to launch into a discussion of my strong Baptist heritage, but Dr. Lacy politely stopped me.

"You seem to have a great deal of enthusiasm. But I have no English positions available. In fact, we're not hiring any new teachers in humanities. The school barely has the money to pay the salaries of the teachers we have. We've even had to make some cutbacks this year."

Undaunted, I continued. "Perhaps fall enrollment might be greater than you expect and you would need more freshmen English teachers."

"I really don't think so. In fact, we think enrollment will be down with so much competition from the junior colleges and their low tuition fees."

"I'd even consider a part-time position or just teaching a few courses. I really do believe I'm supposed to teach here," I replied, surprised by my assertiveness and self-assurance.

"Well, I appreciate your feelings, but I absolutely cannot hire any more English teachers. However, while you're here, you might as well meet the chair of the English department, Dr. Gusta Nance." He led me into Dr. Nance's office across the hall.

A small but imposing woman, Dr. Nance held out her hand and greeted me in a businesslike tone. "Good morning. Please sit down right here." She pointed me to a chair directly in front of her desk as she sat down behind it.

"Thank you for seeing me," I began. "I appreciate the opportunity to talk with you about possibilities for me here in the English department."

"I suppose that Dr. Lacy told you that there are no available positions. We have received over a hundred applications from English teachers, many of whom have advanced degrees from prestigious universities. I've reviewed your résumé and see that you've just completed your M.A. My goal is to set the highest standards for our English department. When we can hire another English teacher, I'll look for someone with a Ph.D."

Feeling my confidence draining, I ventured, "I thought perhaps you might need teachers at the M.A. level for freshmen English classes."

Dr. Nance politely told me that although several members of the English department had only the M.A. degree, she preferred teachers with Ph.D.s for all English courses. I thanked her and left, somewhat discouraged but still with an inexplicable feeling that I would someday teach at DBC.

Freshmen enrollment that fall exceeded predictions by several hundred. A few days before classes started, Dr. Lacy called and asked me to come out to the college. Roy Austin, dean of students, met me and began giving me a tour of the new Learning Center that housed the library, high-tech video equipment, and some faculty offices. Dr. Austin casually pointed to one of the offices and said, "That's your office." Agape, I stepped into a spacious office with a built-in desk and bookcase and a large picture window through which I saw a magnificent view of the lake and the wildflower-bedecked hill. Later I learned that, despite Dr. Nance's preferences, when it became clear at the last minute that the college needed another English teacher, Dr. Lacy chose me because he wouldn't have to pay me as much as a Ph.D. and perhaps also because of my persistence in pursuing the job.

At only twenty-four, sitting high in my new office on the second floor of the Learning Center, with all the books I loved and with my good friend Raynal just a few offices away, I felt that I had arrived. Mother expressed pride in my academic accomplishment, but seemed even more pleased that I was teaching at a Baptist college. David proudly told his colleagues at the Baptist Convention that his wife taught at Dallas Baptist College.

My students, all 180 of them in five classes, sat in rapt attention as I lectured effusively about the literature I'd assigned them. Not until I began to read their first test papers did I realize that I wasn't in Eden. They looked so much smarter than they wrote. Many of my students' grammar was worse than that of my Paschal High sophomores. But my DBC students seemed so highly motivated that I spent hours meticulously grading their papers and tutoring some individually. Many students felt that I demanded too much. One young man, who planned to be a preacher, came to my office and told me, "I didn't have no time to study for your test 'cause I was busy 'bout the Lord's work. You shouldn't ought to give me this low grade. And besides, I don't know if I want all this highfalutin' Queen's English 'cause it might put me above the people I'm preaching to." I assured him that he need not fear that happening.

That fall of 1970, DBC participated in the federally funded Career Opportunity Program (COP), which paid tuition for students in exchange for service in the public schools as teachers' aids. At DBC this program attracted mainly middle-aged African-American women. Two of my classes had COP students. Most of these women were single parents, and some held other jobs in addition to being teachers' aids and taking college courses. I admired their motivation and courage, and I felt good about helping them achieve some long-deferred goals. The wealth of their life experiences made their English compositions livelier than those of my younger students, but their writing skills suffered from inattention. I found myself struggling as I graded their papers in a way I didn't struggle over my white students' papers. My white guilt prompted me to try to make up for past injustices these black women had suffered. I'm sure that I overlooked errors on papers and passed some of their work that I wouldn't have passed if it had come from my other students. I so much wanted these COP students to succeed. Even so, one of them, who thought she deserved higher than a C on a paper that probably should have been a D, accused me of racism. That stung. I redoubled my efforts to prove I was fair, grading their papers even more leniently and offering them more hours of tutoring. I came to realize that I was discriminating against them by expecting less of them than of my white students just as surely as if I'd expected more.

Another dose of reality that first year of teaching at DBC came while I sat in English department meetings that seemed interminable. Dr. Nance held forth for over two hours at each meeting. It became clear from the beginning that she wanted to dictate everything, including the curriculum of each of our courses, the tests we gave, and our speech patterns. Retired from the English department at Southern Methodist University, she had come to DBC to create a first-rate department at this struggling new college. She approached her mission with the zeal of an apostle.

The youngest and newest member of the department, I became Dr. Nance's pet project. I had known from the beginning that I was not her choice and that she had reservations about my qualifications. But she could tell that I was highly motivated, so she set to work on me. My Southern drawl seemed to bother her the most. One day she said to me, "I know you're intelligent, but you don't sound like it. You've got to get a tape recorder and work on your enunciation. You especially need to work on the word 'get'; you're saying 'git.' Also you leave the 'r' out of some words, like 'understand.'" I didn't try to explain to her that such pronunciations were all that I heard growing up in Minden, Louisiana, and that my eighth-grade English teacher had, in fact, taught us that "hard" and "hod" were homonyms. When I had questioned Ms. Starr, saying "hard" and "hod" don't sound alike, she had responded, "Yes they do: "hod" and "hod."

Dutifully, I got busy working to get rid of my Southern drawl with the help of a tape recorder. I also asked Raynal's help, and she replied, "Oh, Jann, your Southern accent is part of your personality. I think it's charming. Don't worry about Dr. Nance; she thinks we all need changing." Dr. Nance did work on the others as well, correcting colloquial usage and pronunciation in department meetings and putting notes under our office doors detailing errors she'd heard us make.

That first year at DBC I heard rumors that women teachers didn't make as much as our male counterparts. Raynal made passing comments about this inequity, but she was too consumed with her doctoral work to take on the issue. The administrative line was that men needed higher salaries than women because men had to support their families. I bought this line. It never even occurred to me at that time to challenge this sexist belief, and no one questioned the legality of this practice.

"A Boy, Even!"

"It's in the water," Raynal remarked the next fall when I told her that I was pregnant. I was the third English teacher in less than two years to have a baby. Always wanting to structure my life, I had planned for the baby to come right after I completed the spring semester in May. Chad arrived June 17, 1971, according to his schedule, not mine. For a month I'd been trying to coax him out, even by riding a bicycle up and down the hilly streets around Raynal's house. My niece DeAnne, seven years old at that time, said, "The baby might want back in when it gets out." Chad suffered from colic the first three or four months and cried so much that I began to think DeAnne might be right.

The day we took Chad home from the hospital, I felt overwhelming love and awe as I looked down at this tiny, perfect new life I held in my lap. David drove, and I sat in the front seat of our royal blue Dodge Dart with Chad, dressed in the baby blue suit I'd picked out for this occasion and wrapped in a blue blanket. Proudly, I looked over at David and quipped, "Now that I've given you a male child, I've proved my worth." David laughed, and I laughed along with him. Although it's hard for me to admit now, at some deep level I did feel better about myself because I'd given birth to a son rather than a daughter. Later when I read physician Christiane Northrup's book *Women's Bodies, Women's Wisdom,* I realized that this comment had its origin in centuries of disparagement of females. Northrup tells of countless times she's heard new mothers in the delivery room apologize to their husbands when the baby was not male. She finds these experiences staggering, but confesses:

> Yet when my own second daughter was born, I was shocked to hear those very words of apology to my husband come right up into my brain from the collective unconscious of the human race. I never said them out loud, and yet they were there in my head—completely unbidden. I realized then how old and ingrained is this rejection of the female by men and women alike!

Recently my sister Anne handed me a letter I'd written her when her first child, David, was born. I stared, appalled, at my writing on the envelope while Anne sat grinning beside me.

"Can you believe I addressed this letter to 'Mr. and Mrs. William Taylor Herring' and 'Mrs. Truman Aldredge'?" I asked. That was 1963, my junior year in high school. Mother had gone to Baton Rouge, Louisiana, to help when Anne and Bill brought David home from the hospital. I opened the letter and read out loud: "Congratulations, a BOY even! And he weighed six whole pounds! It won't be long till he's big enough to play football!" I'd written the word "boy" about four times bigger than my other words, and had underlined "boy" not once, but four times. "You've come a long way, Jann," Anne laughed. "Who could've imagined that the seventeen-year-old who wrote that letter would grow up to be a raving feminist?" It never occurred to me when I wrote that letter how I had exalted maleness and devalued my own gender. My attitude had not changed much eight years later when I had Chad.

The summer of 1971 I stayed home with Chad, as I had planned. It didn't take long for my ambivalence about motherhood to ruffle my nest. I remembered a statement David had made several years before: "When we have children, I want you to be able to stay home with them." Other messages about what it meant to be a "good mother" bombarded me from church, from advertisements, from baby magazines in my pediatrician's office. I had heard plenty of Mother's Day sermons setting up self-sacrifice and self-denial as ideals of motherhood. Mother had stayed home with Anne and me, so that must be the way things should be. And after all, one of the main reasons I had chosen a teaching career was that it could give me enough flexibility to put mothering first. My college teaching job, I thought, especially afforded me this flexibility. I planned to give my full attention to mothering that summer and then to teach only part-time for the next few years.

David and I both believed that childcare was primarily a mother's responsibility. He "helped" with Chad when he came home from work. But I did most of the less desirable tasks, like middle-of-the night feedings and diaper changing. Laboring under the common assumption that nurturing babies came quite naturally to mothers, I felt unnatural in that I struggled. Nursing certainly didn't come easily, probably because I had too much nervous energy to sit placidly. Attempting to occupy my restless mind, I would read as I sat and rocked Chad for hours. That summer I read a novel I later loved teaching, C.S. Lewis' *Till We Have Faces.* As I rocked Chad, I also read books on child psychology and development: books like *How to Give Your Child a Superior Mind,* which mapped out an elaborate list of things to do from conception until the child entered first grade. I wanted to be the perfect mother. But I found myself scrambling to satisfy his basic physical needs, with little energy left for tasks the book prescribed to give him a superior mind. Even though I believed I should be grateful for the opportunity to stay home and take care of Chad, I questioned my suitability for the task. Especially since Chad cried so much, I felt myself sadly lacking in a role that I was supposed to cherish. Instead of questioning gender stereotypes, I lived with the nagging fear that something was wrong with me. Sometimes as I rocked Chad, I cried along with him.

When the fall semester came, I felt relieved to return to the adult world. I taught three days a week and stayed home with Chad the other two. My part-time teaching turned out to be less than advantageous for Chad or for me. It threw him off schedule, and it slowed down my career progress since my years of part-time teaching did not count toward academic promotion and tenure. Also, because of committee work and conference hours and a heavy load of paper grading, I often felt that I was working full-time for part-time pay.

Living Up to Unhealthy Standards

In the fall of 1973, I went back to a full teaching load, trying to shut out guilt-inducing messages directed toward working mothers, especially those who didn't "have" to work. I tried to prove that I could still be a good wife and mother while pursuing a career. Raynal showed me that a woman could do it all. I looked up to her, even though there were days when she walked into my office, exhausted, saying, "I just want to lie down right there on the floor." There were times when I wanted to join her, although I had only one child to take care of then and no doctoral courses to work on. It did, however, feel as if I had two full-time jobs—one at DBC and the other at home.

From the time I got home, around 4:00 or 5:00 P.M., until Chad went to bed, around 9:00, I didn't sit down. And on Saturdays when I wasn't taking care of Chad, I cleaned the house. David often cooked and loved to play with Chad. But we both agreed that I was the main person responsible for Chad and the house.

Now I cringe when I remember that I became a model of a "superwoman" for another friend. One weekend Martha Lou, Gene, and Kennedy Kirkpatrick visited us. Martha Lou confided in me the difficulties she was having balancing her music teaching job and her mothering of Kennedy, who was Chad's age. David and Gene sat in the den watching TV while Martha Lou and I cleaned up the kitchen after dinner and took care of the babies. She watched me holding Chad in one arm while clearing the table and loading the dishwasher with the other.

As I bathed Chad, Martha Lou said, "You make all this look so easy and effortless. How do you do it—and with your teaching too?"

"Oh, I guess I don't think about it much—I just jump in and do what needs to be done," I said glibly.

"Gene thinks I make too big a deal over everything. He wants me to take notes from you."

The pride I felt over Gene's approval of me now makes me feel sad and ashamed. Martha Lou came up lacking when measured by the standard I set, no matter how unhealthy that standard was. I had thoroughly imbibed the message that women who dare to pursue their own goals must work doubly hard to perform well in traditional domestic roles, and without complaining.

Another Boy, Another Degree

By the time Brett was born, March 27, 1975, I had perfected the art of juggling responsibilities. Not considering staying home this time or even cutting back my load, I delivered Brett during spring break and resumed my teaching two weeks later. I had carefully prepared two weeks of lectures on audiotapes so that my classes wouldn't miss a beat. DBC would probably have granted me a maternity leave, but by this time I wanted to prove that having a baby wouldn't slow me down. Since Brett's birth came long before the Family Leave Act, David couldn't consider paternity leave. Every morning he put Chad and Brett, infant seat and diaper bag and all, in the back of his red MG and took them on his way to work to Cliff Temple Baptist Daycare Center. The boys thrived there, and I didn't have time to listen to any negative messages about mothers who leave their children in daycare centers.

"Come on back to TCU and get your Ph.D.," Dr. Ann Ashworth had been saying to me since I had completed my master's degree. I heard also from DBC administrators, especially from Dr. Nance, that if I wanted to have credibility in academia, I must have a Ph.D. It was the union card. When Rosalie Beck, professor of church history at Baylor University, interviewed me years later for an oral history project, she asked, "Why did you go back to do your Ph.D.?" I laughingly replied, "All my life I've been trying to be legitimate." I went on to explain to Rosalie that even as I began the Ph.D., I had a nagging doubt about its power. The words of my friend Paula Latimer, who was finishing her doctorate as I began, echoed in my mind: "Now I'm not just dirt; I'm Dr. Dirt." Paula's feminist consciousness had been thoroughly awakened to see the devaluation of women. It took longer for me to better understand the lengths women go to "prove" our worth in a culture that says there is something fundamentally inadequate about us.

In the interview I also told Rosalie that at the time I wrestled with the decision about working toward the Ph.D., I was into "fleeces." Like Gideon, in the biblical book of Judges, who put out a fleece of wool and asked God to wet it as a sign that Israel would be delivered from the oppressive Midianites, I asked for a sign from God. Beginning the doctorate seemed right for me professionally, but I wondered about the timing for my family. Brett was only five months, and Chad was four years old. DBC would grant me a leave, but could offer no paid sabbaticals, because of its financial struggles. I had decided I didn't want to teach full-time at DBC while working on the doctorate, after I saw how exhausted Raynal had been doing both. So I prayed, "If it's right for me to go back now, show me that the children will be fine and that I won't be a financial burden to the family."

Signs appeared, first in the form of a Christian Education Fellowship from the Baptist General Convention of Texas and then a teaching fellowship from TCU. Brett and Chad flourished in the daycare center, and David encouraged me to continue my education. So in the fall of 1975, I plunged in. At the end of September, the full confirmation of my choice came in the form of my first two checks. It was uncanny. The checks from the Christian Education Fellowship and from the teaching fellowship equaled almost to the penny my monthly checks from DBC.

This providential "sign" gave me reassurance that I would not be hurting my family financially or any other way by pursuing the Ph.D. Even so, at times guilt drove me into trying to overcompensate at home. Especially after a big test or paper, I'd dash frenetically into housecleaning and into planning special activities for the family.

As I approached the completion of my Ph.D. courses, the comprehensive exams loomed before me like Pike's Peak. I'd watched several of my friends, whom I thought smarter than I, fail these exams. Raynal passed, but told me that she vomited before every test and felt that she'd jump off a cliff if she didn't pass. I was trying to tell myself not to put my whole identity on the line, but I didn't sound too convincing. From the end of the spring semester in mid-May until I took the exams at the end of July, I studied more than ten hours a day.

I'd planned to take the exams in August. When I learned that Ann Ashworth, my major professor, scheduled them for July, I drove frantically to Raynal's house. She saw how distraught I was and jumped in the car with me as I drove up and down the hilly roads around her house.

"Raynal, Dr. Ashworth says I have to take comps in July," I moaned. "I can't be ready by then. You know I'd planned to study eight hours or more every day between now and the end of August. Now I'll never make it."

"Can't you tell her you want to wait until August, that you don't have enough time between now and July?" Raynal commiserated.

"I tried. She's adamant. She said she never liked the month of August."

"That's it? Just that she doesn't like August? You must be kidding."

"No, that's what she told me. She left no room for negotiating. What can I do?" I cried.

"I guess you'll have to take comps in July. You can't get crosswise with your major professor. But this is just another hurdle you can jump. You can do it!" Raynal encouraged.

As the date for my comprehensive exams approached, David also became my cheerleader. He took Chad and Brett to the daycare center and played with them many nights so I could study. About a week before the exams, David insisted that I go with him to the movie *Rocky*.

"Thanks," I said, "but I can barely take time to eat. How do you think I can stop to go to a movie?"

"But this isn't just any movie. It's what you need now. It'll help you with the exams. I promise."

Reluctantly, I went with David to see *Rocky*. He was right. I did get pumped up with confidence and determination to conquer the marathon-like exams. Each morning as I was getting ready to go to Fort Worth for the tests, David played a recording of the theme song of *Rocky*. Every time I hear that song now I feel a surge of energy and of appreciation for David's loving attention. I passed all the exams. As I wrote nonstop for six straight hours on three successive days, I drew upon every power within me and some outside. Several times I even had something similar to an out-of-body experience, looking down on myself sitting at that old wooden desk in the small, windowless office and writing as fast as I could.

That August my sister Anne told me she had filed for a divorce. Maybe Dr. Ashworth was right about the month of August. Regardless, I felt grateful that I'd completed my comprehensive exams in July so that I could be more available to my sister that August.

During the next year I wrote my Ph.D. dissertation while I taught full-time at DBC. I still remember twinges of guilt that came when Chad asked if he could sit in the front bedroom where I wrote my dissertation if he'd be quiet. He just wanted to be near me, he said. And I felt a heart tug when Brett crouched, frightened, under my desk every time he heard the shrill whistle of the train passing near our house. I was caring for them, I tried to reassure myself, while at the same time modeling the importance of education.

On a cold December evening, several weeks before Christmas, I drove to Fort Worth because Dr. Ashworth wanted to talk with me about my dissertation. It was the end of the fall semester. I'd completed my dissertation, even though it wasn't due in the graduate office until early spring for my proposed May graduation. My fear of failure along with my compulsive personality made me the opposite of a procrastinator. I'd gotten the dissertation to my faculty committee months earlier than required. Now Dr. Ashworth wanted to tell me the outcome of their reviews.

I thought it strange that she asked me to come over in the evening and to her house instead of to her office on campus. But I had become accustomed to her eccentricities, though not always comfortable with them. In fact, I often felt unnerved as I'd sat in a creaky chair in her kitchen that fall reading portions of my dissertation and straining to hear her raspy voice over the sounds of the tea kettle and her stirrings around to find a clean cup and saucer amidst the clutter. But her failing eyesight, like that of John Milton whom she identified with, led her, she said, to hold classes and sessions with graduate students in her home. Her brilliant mind and legendary presence at Texas Christian University won the dean's indulgence of her whims.

With trepidation I entered her dark den that December evening, shivering from the cold and the fear of her pronouncements on my work. She'd been mostly affirming, it's true, but she had a reputation of erraticism, and I'd experienced several doses. She greeted me and insisted that I have tea and cookies left over from a party she'd given for students the night before. Since I'd not been able to attend and apologized profusely, I felt obliged to sample her treats.

Her puttering in the kitchen seemed endless. The slow heating of the water in the tea kettle held me in gripped suspense. Finally, cup and saucer in hand, she poured the tea and passed me an array of cookies and cakes. I took several sips too fast, almost burning my tongue, trying to wash down the bites of cookie that stuck in my mouth.

As the shadows deepened over her dining table, Dr. Ashworth went into her bedroom and emerged with my dissertation. I held my breath and tried to read her eyes behind her thick glasses. Finally she spoke, "Your dissertation is outstanding. Every member of the committee gave complete approval. Now all you have to do is defend it, and I'm certain it will pass."

The words "it's outstanding . . . complete approval" rang in my ears as I drove away from Dr. Ashworth's house. I rounded the corner onto University Street, and could hear Dr. Marjorie Lewis's words from the day before, "Your research is fine, and your prose sings." I entered the ramp to I-30 and picked up speed as I joined the other cars on the highway. Dr. Neil Daniel's words joined the others: "Of all the things you do well, writing stands at the top!" I'd been sitting in his campus office several weeks earlier, filled with the anxiety that often plagued me that my work didn't measure up, that I deluded myself into thinking I could write a Ph.D. dissertation.

As I drove down I-30 in my royal blue Dodge Dart, with the Fort Worth Christmas-lighted skyline in my rearview mirror, I turned on the radio. The "Hallelujah Chorus" filled my car and my soul. My hard efforts had been rewarded. And all heaven rejoiced. A choir, more magnificent than the one who'd sung the "Hallelujah Chorus" at Daddy's funeral, sang to me now. I could hear Daddy's baritone voice singing his approval; his "hallelujahs" joined the choir. Turning the volume up on my radio, I sang along, "Hallelujah . . . Hallelujah . . . Hal-le-e-lu-jah."

When I look back at my dissertation, entitled "Love Descending: A Study of Spenser's 'Fowre Hymnes' and Milton's 'Nativity Ode,'" I'm disconcerted by my use of exclusively masculine language for humanity and deity, as well as by the theology that pervades my interpretation of these poems. If I were to read the "Fowre Hymnes" and the "Nativity Ode" with my now-converted feminist eyes, I would see the Love portrayed in these sensuously lyrical poems not only as descending from on high, but as dwelling within and among us.

As I walked across the stage of TCU's cavernous Moody Coliseum to receive my diploma and navy velvet hood, I felt only the relief and exhilaration of accomplishment. On that evening in early May of 1978, I felt as fully abloom as the marigolds and impatiens along the walk to the Coliseum. My family also surrounded me with approval. As Dr. Jim Corder, chair of the English department, "hooded" me, I heard applause and "way to go" from the first balcony on my right, where David, Chad, Brett, Mother, Taylor, Anne and her children David and DeAnne stood cheering. Mother had been walking three-year-old Brett around the stadium to keep him happy. They arrived back with the group for this moment.

I had jumped another hurdle and landed safely. Or so I thought.

I was not prepared for the "post-Ph.D. depression," which I later learned others suffered. At the time I couldn't understand why I should feel down after finally achieving the doctorate. Perhaps it hit with David's teasing words when he saw me down on my hands and knees scrubbing our kitchen floor a week after my graduation: "I'm glad to see nothing's changed. Even though you've got a Ph.D., you still scrub floors!" I gave a less than wholehearted laugh as the disillusionment sank in.

I had held the romantic notion that the Ph.D., for which I had labored so long and hard, would forever change my life. But nothing changed. I continued to play "superwoman," juggling heavy loads at home and at work. Not until several years later did I get any salary raise or promotion at DBC. A few weeks after my graduation, I began a long summer of teaching, with demanding new preparations for courses in world literature and big classes that produced stacks of papers to grade. My nadir came as I taught Henrik Ibsen's *The Wild Duck*. One of the main themes of this tragic drama is that most of our ideals are merely "life-illusions," or "life-lies." As I stood teaching *The Wild Duck* to fifty lackadaisical sophomores in a crowded storage room made-over into a classroom on the third floor of the Learning Center, my ideal of life as a college professor seemed like a "life-illusion."

A Matter of Conscience

In the fall of 1979, W. Marvin Watson became president of Dallas Baptist College. Watson had been an executive with Lone Star Steel Company in Daingerfield, Texas, before becoming one of President Lyndon Johnson's top lieutenants. He served as special assistant to the president from 1965 to 1968 and then as postmaster general until LBJ left office in 1969. Realizing the truth of the frequent reference to DBC in the local news media as "the financially-strapped college," the trustees had decided to hire a businessman/politician for a president, thinking he'd be a better fundraiser than the former presidents, who'd been preachers. Since Baptists were in a fray between the fundamentalists and the moderates, Watson's political savvy might also prove helpful.

Although Dallas Baptist College had been more closely aligned with moderate than fundamentalist Baptists, President

Watson soon recognized the expediency of changing the college's theological stance. W.A. Criswell, one of the nation's most outspoken champions of fundamentalism, pastored First Baptist Church of Dallas. This largest and wealthiest Southern Baptist church in the world stood Vatican-like in downtown Dallas. Among the members were billionaire businesspeople like H.L. Hunt and Mary Crowley. In addition to trying to gain support from these rich and powerful local Baptists, Watson was politically astute enough to predict the fundamentalist victory in the national Southern Baptist Convention battle. And he wanted to be on the winning side, where the power and money were. In 1979 Criswell became chairman of the Dallas Baptist College board of trustees.

Another step Marvin Watson took to curry favor with the fundamentalists came in the spring of 1980. He required that all faculty members sign a statement of faith that included the beliefs that Adam and Eve were the historical parents of the entire human race and that Scripture was "verbally inspired by God and inerrant in the original writings." Those who refused to sign this statement would not receive a contract for the following year.

I felt stunned by Watson's demand because it smacked of creedalism, which Baptists had always vehemently opposed. Signing any creed was onerous to me, especially this one with its affirmations of creationism and biblical inerrancy. I found it ridiculous to deny all scientific knowledge on evolution and to believe in a Bible totally without error in scientific and historical, as well as religious, matters. "It wasn't intended to be a book of science," I told my friend Raynal, who now chaired the English department. "I'm going to do some research on my theological position and then meet with Watson to explain why I can't sign that creed."

Marvin Watson stood behind his large mahogany desk, trying to look as imposing as possible when I walked in his office. He stretched his five-foot-eight frame as tall as it would go and sucked in his stomach that otherwise lapped over his belt and the edge of his desk if he got too close.

"Take a seat," he commanded. Still standing, he glared out over his gold-rimmed glasses at me. "Now, just what is it you wanted to see me about?"

"Thank you kindly for seeing me today, Dr. Watson," I began, giving him the benefit of his honorary degree and my most gracious tone. "I know how busy you are with so many important matters. I hate to bother you, but it's about signing the—well—signing the statement—you see—it's a matter of conscience for me, sir." In spite of being dressed according to the current standards for successful career women—navy blue suit, starched white blouse, and navy pumps—I felt my voice and power sink down into the cushions of the overstuffed brown leather chair in which I sat.

"You do believe the Bible, don't you? I just want to know if you believe the Bible, Dr. Clanton!" He sat down behind his massive desk and glared at me.

"Well, yes sir, of course, I believe the Bible, but you see, sir, there are many interpretations and theories of inspiration of Scripture. You're asking us to sign a creed affirming a literalistic interpretation of Scripture and a theory that God dictated a Bible free of errors. Now, in the first place, I don't believe in creeds, and furthermore, Baptists historically have not believed in creeds." I felt my voice growing stronger. "And second, I read Scripture as a rich blend of symbols and metaphors, not a literal statement of historical or scientific fact. And third, I've done extensive research on the various theories of biblical inspiration and have decided that I can't believe God dictated Scripture word by word, but that it reflects the human personalities and cultures of those who wrote it."

I watched his eyes glaze over as though I'd been speaking Greek, which I tried to tell him was the main language of the original manuscripts of the New Testament, and because these manuscripts are no longer extant, the whole question of inerrancy is moot. Although I kept trying to explain my position, it became obvious that we spoke different languages.

Standing up again, Watson bellowed, "I don't want to hear all your liberal rationalizations and explanations. I want to know if you believe the Bible, the inerrant Word of God." His borrowed fundamentalist rhetoric irritated me.

He began to take a few steps out from behind his desk and over toward me. I felt my heart pounding up from the pit of my stomach into my ears. I knew what I risked. Watson had made his pronouncement that all professors at DBC must sign the creed. I feared the loss of a teaching position that was more than a job to me. It was a vocation, a calling. But the call of conscience sounded more loudly.

"Well, sir, as I was trying to say, I don't use the term 'inerrant,' but—"

"There you go, mincing words again!" By now Dr. Watson was standing over me. "What I'm saying to you is that you must sign the creed."

Moved by indignation up from my chair, I looked him straight in the eyes and said, "I must do what I believe is right."

Ushering me to the door, Dr. Watson said coldly, "I know you'll follow my authority."

As I walked out of his office, I replied with a boldness that surprised me, "I will follow my conscience."

Trembling and fighting back the tears, I started toward Raynal's office. On the way I ran into Larry Braidfoot, the only religion professor who had stood up against Watson's mandate.

"You look like you've just come from the battlefield," Larry said knowingly.

"I've just had a meeting with Watson, and I tried, really tried hard, to explain why I couldn't sign that creed."

"You can't expect Marvin to understand or care. It's all political to him, not theological," Larry said. "What I decided to do was strike out the statements on inerrancy and creationism and write out my position. Not that Marvin will read it, but I want to go on record in case he tries to distort my views, as he probably will."

I mumbled something to Larry about admiring him for taking a stand, and then tried to get away, but he kept expounding on the choice that each faculty member would have to make after weighing all the risks. He quoted Aristotle on choosing battles carefully and finding balance between extremes.

Standing there on the steps of the administration building, I felt I was about to lose my balance as an uncertain future spun out before me. Aristotle and treatises weren't enough to steady me. I had to get to Raynal.

Panting and crying, I ran into Raynal's office. Calmly closing the door, she asked, "That bad, huh?"

"You just wouldn't believe!" I wailed.

"Oh, yes, I know." And Raynal did know about Watson and his power plays. As chair of the English department, she had sat through long administrative meetings in his office and had listened to his harangues.

"What am I going to do?"

"You told him you wouldn't sign, didn't you?"

"Not exactly, but I told him I must follow my conscience instead of his authority."

"I bet he liked that!"

"You probably think I'm making too much of this whole thing. You know I don't want to lose my job. But I don't see how I can sign," I lamented as I looked out the half-open picture window down the hill of bluebonnets across to the misty lake. I loved this campus, especially in the spring.

"They're always more options than we see at first. We'll solve this problem, just like we have others." Raynal reminded me of the time I came whizzing into her driveway, honking, pleading for help, when Dr. Ashworth capriciously moved my Ph.D. comprehensive exams from August to July.

"On the way over here I saw Larry Braidfoot," I said, "and he told me that he's striking out the two most objectionable statements on inerrancy and creationism, and then writing a position paper on his beliefs."

"Do you think you might do something like that?" Raynal pleaded. She had wrestled with her ethical dilemma over signing the creed. Although she didn't believe in signing, she believed even more strongly that she was supposed to keep teaching at DBC.

I struggled and prayed over my decision, waking up from fitful dreams in which I saw myself walking alone down the flower-decked hill away from the college, wandering aimlessly around the streets of the city, carrying a heavy suitcase crammed with books and papers. Finally, after a restless week, one early morning before dawn I took the creed from my briefcase, struck out the statements on inerrancy and creationism, and signed it. Then I wrote out five pages on my theology of creation and biblical inspiration. Before I could change my mind, I stapled the papers and sealed them in an envelope addressed to Dr. Watson.

Contracts came out according to schedule two weeks later. Every faculty member received a contract except Larry Braidfoot and me. Raynal, incensed, marched to Watson's office and demanded to see him immediately. His watchdog secretary tried to stop Raynal before she charged through the door. Startled, he quickly got off the telephone.

Bypassing all formalities, Raynal blurted out, "Why didn't Dr. Clanton receive a contract?"

Watson rose from behind his desk and tried to gather himself. "You know, Dr. Barber, that I made it perfectly clear that only those professors who signed the statement of faith would receive a contract."

"But she did sign; she signed according to her beliefs and took great pains, more than you'll ever know, to act on her beliefs."

"I know, I know. She came by and told me all about HER beliefs. And I instructed her to follow my authority in this matter. I am the president of this college, the one God has placed in authority here."

Watson's God-talk further infuriated Raynal. "I will not stand calmly by while you fire one of the best professors in the college, for nothing more than following her conscience."

Watson didn't like being challenged, especially by a woman. I'm sure he would have dismissed Raynal from his office, but he knew she had power at the college. Many times the students had voted her "Outstanding Professor," and she'd held every office on the Faculty Council, including president.

Trying to pacify Raynal, Watson began, "Well, perhaps we can make an exception with Dr. Clanton. After all, she's not teaching in the religion department, so maybe her beliefs will not get out to the impressionable minds of our students."

"You should pray that her beliefs would influence our students." Raynal refused to back down.

"All right. Dr. Clanton will receive a contract, but I'll request that she not discuss her religious views with students."

Raynal came right over to my office to give me a full account of her meeting with Watson. She looked relieved, but tired. I told her how grateful I was to her for saving my job.

"Well," she said, "it was partly selfish. I want you to stay here not just because you're a good friend, but because I need you in my department."

I received my contract for the school year 1980-81, and signed it. Marvin Watson began using the statement of faith to play to the fundamentalists, hoping to draw students and financial support. He ran advertisements in religious publications, stating that the entire faculty believed in creationism and in the inerrancy of the Bible. Once again I struggled with my conscience. My beliefs were deliberately misrepresented.

In the midst of my dilemma, I dreamed again that I was walking down the hill away from DBC. This time it was winter, and the hill was covered with dry, gray-brown brush. Patches of ice and snow, where the bluebonnets had been, made my way slippery. My fingers stung with cold, and my arms ached with the weight of the suitcase filled with books and papers—all the contents of my office.

Chapter Five

Testing the Waters of Ministry

Several years before I finished my Ph.D., David brought me a book called *All We're Meant to Be* by Nancy Hardesty and Letha Scanzoni. David had not read the book, and neither of us could have imagined the revolutionary effect it would have on me. The words of "Amazing Grace," which I'd long sung— "was blind but now I *see*"—became reality for me. I'd never questioned the biblical interpretations that told women we were to be submissive at home and at church. I hadn't objected to designations of David as the "head" of the house and of me as "Mrs. David Clanton." And it never occurred to me to question the divine right of men as church leaders. As I read Hardesty and Scanzoni, I discovered more than enough biblical support for the equality of women and men in marriage and in church leadership. In addition, this book introduced me to the radical notion that God might not be male. Although Betty Friedan's *The Feminine Mystique* had come out in 1963, I'd never heard of the book or raised any questions about women's traditional roles. The call to gender justice could reach me only through the Bible and interpretations of it.

With great enthusiasm, I bought additional copies of *All We're Meant to Be* and gave them to the leaders, all men, at our Baptist church. I naively thought that the book would also open their eyes to new revelations, that the copious scriptural evidence and the clear theological reasoning that had so thoroughly convinced me of the rightness of gender equality would persuade them as well. The chairman of the deacons graciously accepted the book and later told me that he thought it was "interesting." Since I knew him to be a man who tried hard to please everyone in the church and to avoid conflict, I shouldn't have been surprised by his noncommittal response. I also gave a copy of the book to the pastor. He never said a word to me about it. His only acknowledgment was telling David to tell me that he had read it. The pastor's response was especially disillusioning, because I still held an idealistic view of pastors, mainly because of the respect I had for Daddy. I knew Daddy would have been open-minded and fair-minded enough to consider the validity of these new interpretations of passages traditionally used to keep women in subordinate roles, and I longed to discuss them with him. Now I missed Daddy more than ever.

I should have known that the pastor of Calvary Baptist wouldn't have appreciated *All We're Meant to Be* because he'd made it clear that he didn't believe women were meant to be that much. Even though Raynal had a Ph.D. and headed the English department at Dallas Baptist College, Calvary Baptist did not allow her any leadership roles except that of teacher of a women's Sunday School class. Raynal's husband Will was a deacon in the church. Raynal had told me her frustration over deacons' Christmas parties: "Jann, you just wouldn't believe it. The pastor asks all the men to come into this meeting room and tells the wives to wait outside in the dining room. The men meet for over an hour, and then come out for the party. It's like they have some secret fraternity that's off limits to women. Why can't they have their meeting some other time, rather than get us all up here and keep us waiting?" What upset Raynal even more was the pastor's practice of inviting only the men and boys to the altar for prayer at the end of worship services: "I guess he believes that men and even little boys are more spiritual than any woman, no matter how saintly or wise she may be!"

My dissatisfaction at Calvary Baptist grew, as I devoured Pat Gundry's *Woman, Be Free,* Paul Jewett's *The Ordination of Women,* Harry Hollis' and Sarah Frances Anders' *Christian Freedom for Women and Other Human Beings,* and other books that championed gender equality based on cogent interpretations of the Bible. At that time I was leading children's church at Calvary Baptist and becoming more and more upset that women were allowed to lead children but not adults in worship. No matter how this discrepancy was justified by torturous scriptural interpretations, it became increasingly clear to me that it derived from the devaluation of women and children. Children, contrary to all the rhetoric, were not that important in the church, so women could lead them.

Feminist Consciousness Raised Higher

When I heard that Cliff Temple Baptist Church was ordaining Martha Gilmore, I knew I had to go. By now I had become convinced that women should have equal opportunity in the church. But all the books and biblical interpretations and theological debates paled in the light of my experience at Martha's ordination. Witnessing Martha kneeling to receive this blessing, I felt, for the first time, the sacred value of women. Epiphany flooded my soul. And I vowed to work toward change in the church so that women could have freedom to follow God's call.

Shortly after Martha's ordination, our family joined Cliff Temple Baptist. And I began spreading my new revelation not only concerning women in ministry but concerning the worth of all women. I subscribed to *Daughters of Sarah: The Magazine for Christian Feminists,* a quarterly publication with this defining statement: "We are Christians. We are also feminists. Some say we cannot be both, but for us Christianity and feminism are inseparable." I photocopied articles from

Daughters of Sarah to give to my colleagues at DBC. I joined Southern Baptist Women in Ministry, National Organization for Women (NOW), and Women's Equity Action League.

Anne and I went to several local consciousness raising meetings and rallies for the Equal Rights Amendment. We covered ourselves with buttons that had slogans like "A Woman's Place is in the House—and in the Senate" and "ERA YES!" In July of 1978 we went to a gathering of about 500 women and 50 men in a large banquet room at the Hilton Hotel in north Dallas. In February of that year NOW had declared a State of Emergency to win congressional support of a deadline extension for the ratification of the ERA. That July an ERA Extension March drew more than 100,000 supporters to Washington, D.C. At the local simultaneous rally at the Hilton Hotel, Anne and I stood for several hours listening to impassioned speeches and shouting with the crowd, "ERA! ERA!"

But I was still teaching the generic "he" in my English classes at DBC. Anne had just begun work toward her Ph.D. in psychology and had read feminist psychologists' arguments about the importance of inclusive language. She challenged my sexist language:

"Jann, you can't still be teaching the so-called generic 'he' and 'man.' That never has been generic. It came out of a patriarchal culture that sees men as the norm and women as deviant."

"Well, you know I don't believe that, Anne. But I have to teach correct grammar. It's just a matter of pronoun-antecedent agreement. I can't teach students to write 'a person should know their own mind,' and it's awkward to say 'a person should know his or her own mind.'"

"Better awkward than sexist. It's a justice issue. With all that masculine language, you're saying that women don't exist or we're not worth much. You of all people should know the power of language. Just by teaching inclusion of women in language you can make a powerful contribution to justice."

"Anne, you're absolutely right!" I was an instant convert, not only because Anne had always had great influence on me, but because her argument for inclusive language brought sudden recognition. I did indeed believe in the power of language. After all, I was a language teacher. From that time on, teaching inclusive language became part of my mission for gender equality. I taught ways to avoid exclusively masculine pronouns while avoiding awkwardness, such as changing antecedents to plural form so that the pronoun "their" would be grammatically correct. Another possibility, I said, was to alternate the use of "she" and "he," as in some articles published by professional journals in the behavioral sciences that had begun to reject any submissions with exclusive language.

My DBC students were not the only recipients of my teaching. With evangelistic zeal I spread the gospel of inclusive language at church, at home, and anywhere else I found a receptive mind. My preschool son Brett responded most enthusiastically to my message. Changing sexist language became a game for him. He talked about the "postperson" and "repairperson." Although I suggested the term "police officer," Brett preferred "policeperson." He loved catching me in a reference to a "congressman" or to a doctor as "he."

The winter of Brett's first-grade year, he came home one day saying, "Mom, today Ms. Burns passed out sheets for us to color."

"Yes, Brett, let me see."

Showing me his paper, he said, "Ms. Burns called this a snowman, and I said, 'No, that's a snowperson.' She looked kinda funny at me and said, 'It's a snowman.' But I told her, 'My mom says 'snowperson.'"

I couldn't remember ever using the term "snowperson," but I was glad that Brett had inferred it from all my other inclusive references. Beaming with pride, I answered, "Brett, you're right. This is a snowperson, and I like the way you colored it. One day Ms. Burns will know 'snowperson' is the right word."

As my conscience wrestled with the ethics of staying at a college that misrepresented my beliefs, my feminist consciousness continued to awaken. Vocational choices expanded into fields I'd never dreamed possible for women. I learned of women in a variety of ministerial roles. Martha Gilmore supervised ministry interns at Perkins School of Theology. I met several women who served as hospital chaplains. I heard that churches in some denominations had female pastors and associate pastors. In the back of my mind were my friends' statements: "one day we'll be going to your ordination" and "maybe your next calling is the ministry." One Sunday evening at Cliff Temple I "went forward," according to Baptist tradition, to dedicate myself to some kind of calling. I had no idea what kind.

Evangelism Explosion

The pastor of Cliff Temple Baptist Church suggested that I explore my call by participating in a program called "Evangelism Explosion." It required months of seminars and on-the-job training with a mentor. When I had passed the written tests, I went out with my mentor, door to door as I had peddled Girl Scout cookies in the second grade. We knocked on our first door, fully armed with Bible verses, questions, and openers. A man answered the door and politely invited us in. Then a woman entered, and he introduced her as his wife.

"That's a beautiful clock there on the mantel. It looks like it's hand-carved," I ventured, hoping my mentor would approve of this opener.

"The clock's been handed down for generations in my family. It was carved by my great-grandfather," the woman explained with pride.

"Do you ever get the feeling that time's passing too quickly? Do you ever think about what might be after this short life?" My mentor jumped in, worried that I might take too long to get to the punch line.

The woman nodded courteously, while her husband squirmed in his chair and gave me a look that begged for escape.

Then came "Evangelism Explosion." My mentor blew up

the question right there in that small living room: "If you were to die tonight and stand before God, and he were to say to you, 'Why should I let you into my heaven?' what would you say?"

The husband, who had bent down to stroke the blond cocker spaniel lying at his feet, gasped and dropped his tea glass on the dog's head. The dog howled, jumped up, and ran around the room, shaking off the cold liquid.

Settling the dog down, the wife said, "I would tell God that I've tried to live a good life, treat people right, and go to church. Of course, I haven't been perfect, but I hope he'd let me in."

I smiled and gave a response I knew my mentor would approve, "That's all very well, but that won't get you into heaven."

The husband, visibly ruffled, busied himself drying off the dog. My mentor and I, righteous and sure, continued to explode our truth upon them.

Finally, the husband had all he could take and shouted at us, "Who do you think you are, coming in here and questioning the holiness of my wife?" She sat there in tears, looking out the window. "She's the most decent person in this world, and you have no right to question her. She's going to heaven, all right, but I'm not sure about you people. Take your preaching somewhere else." He opened the front door for us.

That evening I walked away, not from ministry but from the exclusive, intrusive forms it often takes. I became more and more aware of the connection between metaphor and method of ministry. "Evangelism Explosion," "Bold Mission Thrust," "Pioneer Penetration," "On Fire for the Lord," "Prayer Warriors," popular images in my tradition, carry connotations of violence and coercion. Several also suggest masculine sexuality. Again I realized the power of language to create reality.

Slowly Claiming My Own Voice

My call gradually took on clarity as I listened to a persistent internal voice: "I'm not only supposed to support women ministers; I'm supposed to be one. I've got determination and intelligence. I've got a genteel Southern accent and personality that might help people hear me and open their minds to women in ministry." This voice scared and excited me.

Having finished my Ph.D. degree just two years earlier, going to seminary didn't seem feasible. I learned about Clinical Pastoral Education (CPE), an on-the-job ministry training program that paid a stipend. This program sounded promising because it would allow me to explore professional ministry for a year. When I talked with the CPE supervisors at Baylor University Medical Center in Dallas, they told me that a seminary degree was usually a requirement for this internship program, but they said, "Some nuns without theological degrees but who've been teaching in parochial schools have been accepted into CPE programs. You've been teaching in a Baptist school, so we can offer you an internship." Although I thought it curious that they put me in the same category as nuns, I didn't question their rationale. Also, they were impressed with my Ph.D. Even though my Ph.D. had little money-making power, I was beginning to appreciate its worth in gaining the respect of some people. I remembered Raynal's telling me, "Use the doctorate any way you can, because it's never going to make you rich." Several times she had used her title "Dr. Barber" to get in to see hospitalized friends after hours.

When I told David I was considering Clinical Pastoral Education, he responded, "You'd be throwing away your Ph.D." I tried to explain that I wouldn't be throwing anything away, but would be using everything I had learned and experienced thus far. Even though David knew how conflicted I'd recently felt about working at DBC, he had difficulty understanding how I could even think of leaving academia only two years after finishing my Ph.D. It didn't help that David had a disquieting experience in a summer unit of CPE in a Houston hospital. David, naturally reserved, had not appreciated supervisors' prodding him in an Interpersonal Relationship Group to reveal his feelings. David asked me, "Why would you want to do CPE? It's such an intrusive, confrontational program."

Raynal tried to support my call to ministry, but she wanted me to stay at DBC. "Can't you be a minister here?" she pleaded. "Heaven knows, this school needs some ministering." My conscience tugged both ways. I'd already signed my contract for the year 1980-81, and after all, Raynal had suffered a confrontation with Marvin Watson so that I could have that contract. I turned down the Clinical Pastoral Education internship and stayed at DBC that year, but with little peace about my decision. Claiming my own voice above that of others, especially those dearest to me, did not come easy.

Watson continued to steer DBC toward fundamentalism, mandating that we open every class with prayer and Bible readings so that he would have another sign of our "holiness" to advertise in religious journals. The call to leave DBC and move on to a new vocation grew stronger and stronger. But I had to put out a "fleece," just as I had before my decision to pursue a Ph.D. The sign I asked God for this time was that I'd have another opportunity to do Clinical Pastoral Education at Baylor. Since I'd turned down the internship the year before, I wondered if the supervisors would consider me again. I went through the arduous application and interview process once again and soon received my letter of acceptance. I could no longer question the divine call. Taking a year's leave of absence from DBC, I began a chaplaincy internship at Baylor University Medical Center, the fall of 1981. Raynal had convinced me to take the leave of absence rather than resign, just in case I might want to come back to teach.

Token Woman

At 7:30 Wednesday morning of the first week I was at Baylor, I proudly pinned my new badge that read "Jann Clanton, Chaplain Intern" on my navy suit jacket and hurried to my first Pastoral Care Department staff meeting. Although I knew I was the only woman on staff, entering that room filled with twenty men made my stomach do flips like it did when I rode the Ferris wheel at the State Fair. Baylor University Medical Center, an institution supported by the Baptist General Convention of Texas, had always had white Southern Baptist male chaplains. Although Clinical Pastoral Education was a national, ecumenical program that encouraged diversity, Baylor had had mostly white Southern Baptist male interns as well. I was only the second female chaplain intern. That morning in staff meeting the phrase "token woman," which Anne and I had heard at consciousness raising gatherings, became my reality.

In one of the first meetings of the chaplain interns, one of our supervisors distributed an article on the dynamics of a group that had only one woman. The article delineated various roles the woman might assume, such as "Iron Maiden," "Seductress," "Mother." Naively, I felt that I could avoid all these labels. The message I got from the article was that if I fell into any one of these roles, it was my own fault, not that of the men in the group. My consciousness was not raised high enough at that time to understand that men and women bear equal responsibility for relationships.

A month before entering the chaplaincy internship, I began writing sermons to preach in chapel services. The part of the job description of a chaplain intern that had most intimidated me was preaching in chapel. I'd never had a preaching course nor even heard a woman preach. No wonder I felt anxious: I would be the first woman I'd ever heard preach a sermon.

But I'd written a dissertation and had taught principles of composition for years, I told myself. How much different could it be to write a sermon? That August before I began my internship I sat at the desk in our bedroom and typed out ten sermons, with Chad and Brett running in and out of the room. I'd read that Bach put the letters "JH" ("Jesus Help") and "TGBG" ("To God be the Glory") at the beginning of his musical compositions. If Bach needed such inspiration, I certainly did. So I wrote "JH" and "TGBG" in the top right-hand corner of the first page of each of my sermons.

That fall when I saw the preaching schedule, I was dismayed

that my name was left out. The four male chaplain interns were scheduled to rotate chapel services. I immediately went to the chaplain who made the schedule and asked, "Why am I not on the chapel schedule?"

He replied, "I think the administration has a problem with women preaching. The only other time we've had a female chaplain, the CEO made it clear that she wasn't to preach. She did a Bible study for some of the secretaries in the hospital instead."

"I don't think that's fair to the other chaplain interns nor to me," I asserted. "Chapel services are part of the training program. Preaching will be especially valuable for me because I'm trying to explore every aspect of ministry."

He said, "Well, okay, I'll go to our department director and see what he says about this." The director gave permission for me to preach.

With the other interns I rotated the weekday and Sunday chapel services. One Tuesday morning, shortly after I'd begun my internship, I rushed down from seeing a pre-surgery patient to Penland Chapel. Bible and notes in hand, I walked to the massive pulpit in the center of the platform. Taking a deep breath to gather myself, I looked out at my congregation: one person on the front-row pew and another on the third row. The other thirteen pews stretched back long and empty. It's not me, I told myself. Weekday services don't usually bring many people. And I took heart from the memory of Daddy's saying that if he reached only one person with a sermon, he hadn't preached in vain. He preached most of his sermons to hundreds of people, so I realized my odds weren't as good as his of reaching one person. But I drew up all the fervor of my fresh calling and began my sermon entitled "The Blessing of Forgiveness" with an illustration from my teenage years.

Like all the other teenagers in my hometown I looked forward to my sixteenth birthday so that I could get my driver's license. I was so excited when this time came, believing it to be my ticket to fun and freedom. But I soon discovered that my chances to drive would be few. My parents were reluctant to let me take the one family car because they needed it most of the time and also because my father, especially, was very particular about the car. One Saturday afternoon, however, shortly after getting my license, they let me take the car to my friend Waynette Farrington's house. I was elated to get this chance and carefully drove the car off. When I was almost to Waynette's house, I turned a corner too sharply and ran right smack into a large, solid street signpost. Trembling, I got out of the car to examine the damage. The whole right front of the car was dented in; the right front door wouldn't even open. How could I face my parents now? What would my father say when he saw the condition of our almost-new white Buick? Would I ever get to drive the car again? I lashed out at myself for being so careless. Crying so hard I was afraid I'd have another wreck, I slowly drove home. I crept out of the car and into my room. I started looking through my desk drawers for my savings bonds. Maybe I had enough to pay for the repairs. My mother came into the room and found me sobbing, holding my savings bonds. It took me a while to compose myself enough to tell her what had happened. Finally I confessed my carelessness and told her I wanted to pay for the repairs. She immediately hugged me and forgave me, saying, "Thank God, it's nothing worse." When I told my dad about the accident, he was not so sure there could be anything worse than wrecking the car. But he too forgave me. That night I experienced the load-lifting blessing of forgiveness.

About an hour after I finished preaching "The Blessing of Forgiveness," I saw two of the other chaplain interns.

Chuckling, one asked, "So how much did it cost to repair your parents' white Buick?"

"What did your dad really say when he saw the dents in the car?" the other laughed.

Startled, I asked, "How did you find out about that?"

"We have our sources," they teased and walked off.

A little while later I saw another intern at a nurses' station. He waved me over and asked, "Were your savings bonds enough?"

"Enough for what?" I demanded.

"Oh, you know, enough to pay for the car repairs."

Recognition dawned, and my cheeks burned red with the anger I'd learned not to express. I had preached that sermon oblivious to three of the chaplain interns lurking just outside, ears pressed close to the small crack between the chapel doors. A few days later in a group meeting, I managed to tell them that if they had wanted to hear my sermon, they should have come on in the chapel instead of sneaking around behind my back. I didn't have the nerve to tell them I thought they were teasing me because they'd never before heard a woman preach. But I knew I had to forgive them. In my sermon, I had asked the question, "Having experienced the blessing of forgiveness, shouldn't we bless others by offering our forgiveness?" I had to practice, so soon, the sermon I had preached. But I also needed to learn the kind of forgiveness that gives room for justified anger.

The chaplaincy training program included Interpersonal Relationship Group (IPR), that met once or twice a week for several hours. The five interns with at least one of the supervisors sat in a circle for the purpose of "getting in touch with our feelings" and learning to express these feelings honestly so as to enhance our relationships. The philosophy was that ministers need understanding of ourselves and awareness of our own emotions in order to relate to other people in the most helpful ways. The most common remark supervisors made to trainees was, "I don't want to know what you think but how you feel about that." I approached IPR with some ambivalence. It made sense to me that ministers need self-awareness and training in relationships since our work takes us into the most intimate moments of people's lives. I had already discovered how important it was to recognize the psychological dynamic of transference when I was called to the bedside of a dying man around the age of my daddy when he died. And since all my education had emphasized cognitive development, I welcomed the opportunity to grow in the emotional dimension of my personality. On the other hand, I had heard tales from David and others that IPR at times invaded personal privacy. There were things in my background, like my anorexia, that I didn't want to tell the group.

When I told Anne, in the middle of her psychology internship at the time, of my apprehension about IPR, she said, "Jann, we don't have to go through anything like that in our training program. We're required to do some individual therapy, but that's different—private and confidential. I wouldn't want to talk about my personal life in a professional setting. Remember that you don't have to reveal anything you don't want to."

One afternoon during the second month of my internship, I sat in a small, windowless room with the four other chaplain interns and one of the supervisors. By this time I'd gotten used to being the only woman in any chaplains' meeting and had tried hard to avoid token woman roles, like "Seductress" and "Iron Maiden," cautioned against in the article the supervisor had given us. So that afternoon I sat in the IPR circle feeling confident about my growing identity as a minister and about my relationships with the pastoral care staff. One of the interns began to talk about how he'd grown in his acceptance of women ministers. He said, "I've never known a woman minister before I came to Baylor. I used to believe it was unbiblical for women to be ministers. But now I'm much more open-minded. Seeing you in ministry here, Jann, has shown me that God does call women as ministers."

I responded, "Thank you for saying that. It helps confirm my call. I'm glad you're open to women ministers now."

Several of the other interns talked about struggles they'd had accepting me as a peer in ministry. They were members of Baptist churches that had no women pastors, deacons, or worship leaders.

The supervisor broke into the discussion: "You're all in your head. Talking about whether or not you approve of women ministers distances you from Jann. I don't want to know what you think about Jann as a minister, but how you *feel* about her."

"Well, I feel she's doing a good job here."

"Yes, I feel she's a competent minister."

"No, no, that's not what I mean. How do you *feel* about Jann as a *woman?* It's obvious that Jann's not just one of the boys. It's time to lay our feelings right out on the table," the supervisor demanded.

The five men stared at me. I was sure they could hear my heart drumming in my ears and see my blood rushing up into my face. Finally, they began to lay out their feelings.

"I find Jann attractive."

"Yes, I think you're pretty, Jann, but my feelings toward you are more like brother for sister."

"I find myself liking you. You're a very sexually attractive woman."

"I like you too, Jann, as a mothering person. You're caring and nurturing."

Another one of the interns grinned at me and said, "Jann, you turn me on. You're a good-looking woman. If I weren't married, I'd really go after you."

"Never mind that I'm married," I thought, wondering if I were supposed to respond to these expressions of feelings about me as a woman.

If I told them how uncomfortable this discussion made me feel, I was afraid they'd label me prudish, or heaven forbid, an "Iron Maiden." If I just sat there silently, I knew someone would prod me to respond. If I told the intern who said I turned him on that he didn't turn me on, I was afraid I'd hurt his ego and thus our professional relationship. If I got up and bolted out of the room, as I really wanted to do, I would be breaking a cardinal rule of IPR. And I wanted desperately to succeed in CPE, which I thought was my only door into ministry. I felt trapped and totally drained of the self-confidence I'd felt just a little while before.

I stuttered out, "Well, thank you—you know—I'm fond of

all of you too, that is, I'm glad for this chance—for this opportunity—to work with you." Several of the men tried to get
me to say more, but Anne's wise words echoed in my mind,
"You don't have to reveal anything you don't want to."

Five years later, I received a call from a reporter for the
United Methodist news journal. She told me that she was in-
terviewing women ministers for an article on sexual harassment suffered by clergywomen. Another article had just been
published citing a surprising number of Methodist clergywomen who had been harassed by clergymen, and she wanted
to report on the experience of clergywomen in other denominations as well.

She asked me, "Have you ever experienced sexual harassment in your role as a clergywoman?"

Without hesitation, I responded, "Oh no."

The reporter tried again. "You're in a denomination in
which male clergy vastly outnumber clergywomen. Have you
ever been made to feel uncomfortable in any way by clergymen?"

"Well, some have tried to convince me that what I'm doing
is wrong, but I'm not sure that's what you mean."

"Have any clergymen made sexual innuendoes, or have you
been in any settings in which clergymen made you feel uncomfortable sexually?"

"No, nothing like that. I can't believe clergymen would do
anything like that," I glibly answered and hung up the phone.

More years would have to pass before I came to an understanding of sexual harassment, especially in its more subtle
forms. When I did, the memory of that afternoon in Clinical
Pastoral Education, feeling trapped in that cramped room surrounded by five men telling me how they felt about me as
a woman, came flooding back. Also, I remembered clergymen
in other settings calling me "baby" and "darling" and telling
offensive jokes. But I couldn't have admitted to the reporter,
or even to myself, that I had been sexually harassed by clergymen because Daddy was a pastor and I had profound respect for him.

The incident in CPE occurred two years before Baylor's first sexual harassment policy and ten years before Professor Anita Hill's accusations against Judge Clarence Thomas brought sexual harassment into public awareness. Even when I became conscious of my own experience, I tried to minimize it because the CPE program had been of great value to my ministry and because I felt profound gratitude to the supervisors. Also, cultural voices of denial sounded strong within me: "Oh, you're too sensitive. You're just overreacting. You're exaggerating. Nobody would believe you. It's your fault because you flirted with the men. You might lose your job if you accuse clergymen of sexual harassment, or your family might be hurt." I realized the strength of the forces against women's speaking out about harassment.

Another kind of putdown came one day when I was a chaplain intern visiting patients on Baylor's oncology unit. One of the nurses ran up to me in the hallway and said, "You remember Mr. Bradley in room 723?"

"Oh yes, I had a good visit with him yesterday."

"Yes, I know—that is—right after you left his room, I went in to give him some medication. He said to me, 'The chaplain was just in here, and it was a woman!' I told him, 'Yes, I know, and she's quite a good chaplain.' Then he said, 'I guess so. We have a new lady associate minister at our church. She reads Scripture and prays in our services. She does okay, but I guess you could teach even a chimpanzee to read Scripture!'" I tried to laugh along with the nurse, who found this story hilarious, but inside I screamed.

Becoming a "Real" Minister

Several months later, I noticed a man standing in the elevator beside me, staring at my badge that read "Chaplain Intern" under my name. Unable to contain his curiosity any longer, he asked as we stepped off the elevator, "Are you a *real* minister?" Years later, my sister, by that time director of psychology at

Texas Scottish Rite Hospital for Children, told me she came close to tears as she tried to convince her supervisor that I was a "real" minister. Anne had casually mentioned that her sister was an ordained Baptist minister, to which the supervisor replied, "That's impossible. She can't be a real minister."

"But she is. She's a chaplain at Baylor."

"But she can't be an ordained minister. Baptists don't ordain women. It's unbiblical." And the supervisor proceeded to quote texts traditionally used to exclude women.

Anne quoted a few in refutation, and then repeated, "She is ordained. I went to her ordination service. She is a real minister."

No wonder I suffered from what psychologists have termed the "impostor phenomenon." This condition is especially prevalent among high-achieving women who live with the fear that we will be "found out." No matter how much we achieve, we feel we constantly have to prove ourselves. Though psychological factors play a part in the "impostor phenomenon," it's easy to see the sociological roots. Questioned as to whether or not we are "real" ministers or "real" doctors, women may work twice as hard as our male counterparts and still feel nagging self-doubts. Anne told me about an accomplished surgeon who agonized because she felt "so inadequate." The question "Are you a real minister?" lingered in me for many years, even after I had more than enough professional certifications.

The year I did the chaplaincy internship I discovered that my Ph.D. was not enough to make me legitimate in my new vocation. My gender was not the only challenge to my identity as a minister. From time to time patients would ask, "Where did you go to seminary?" Others questioned, "Are you ordained?" That spring I took the first step by requesting Cliff Temple Baptist Church to license me to ministry.

Individual Baptist churches, not a group of bishops or a denominational assembly, can license and ordain anyone they wish. Traditionally, all one had to do to be licensed was to state a call to ministry—and be male. A boy in his teens could be licensed, but not a woman of any age. Churches licensed young men when they first felt a call, but often didn't ordain them until after they completed seminary. For Baptists, the distinction between licensing and ordination is not always clear. With a license comes the authority to perform marriage ceremonies and to preach. Ordination carries the highest blessing of the church. Ordination usually gives ministers more opportunity to pastor churches and more power to perform the rituals of baptism and communion. Many Baptist churches ordain men who have no education beyond high school. The majority of Baptist churches still won't consider licensing or ordaining a woman, no matter what her level of education or how sincere her call. Since Cliff Temple Baptist had ordained Martha, I knew this church was different.

During a Sunday evening service, the pastor handed me a certificate with these words inscribed: "This is to certify that Dr. Jann Clanton who has given evidence that he possesses gifts for the work of The Gospel Ministry was licensed to preach the Gospel as he may have opportunity, and to exercise his gifts in the work of the Ministry by Cliff Temple Baptist Church at Dallas, Texas on the 14th day of February, 1982." Since I wanted so desperately to believe that Cliff Temple was an egalitarian church, I tried to tell myself that the only certificates available in Baptist bookstores had masculine references to ministers. But my belief in the importance of language to define reality and to assign roles in society grew even stronger. Because I could never be the "he" designated in my license, some people would refuse to recognize me as a minister. Even though I had a license to preach, because I was a "she" I had few opportunities to preach and none to pastor a church.

Cliff Temple treated women so much better than Calvary Baptist did, so at first I thought Cliff Temple was an Eden of equality. The church, after all, had women deacons—five out of a hundred. Like the majority of church members, I felt pride in this representation, somehow convincing myself that it was equal. Because the church had ordained Martha Gilmore, I expected to hear her preach at Cliff Temple. She had preached once before we joined the church. The pastor, receiving pressure from a few critics, never asked her to preach again. Women seldom had any visibility in worship services. When I volunteered to usher for services, the head usher looked at me as though I'd said I planted a bomb in the sanctuary. I felt gratitude, prematurely, to the pastor for allowing me and a few of my women friends to usher on Sunday evenings. The first time we gathered at the altar before taking the offering, he relieved his tension by joking, "The ushers are better looking tonight than usual!"

My transition into a new vocation included changing the way I talked with my family about work. The year I did my chaplaincy internship, Brett was six and Chad was ten. Brett liked to surprise his friends with "My mom's a preacher," and Chad thought it exciting that I carried a beeper. Chad wanted to hear all the gory details of my calls to the emergency room, but I told him only generalities because I didn't want to exacerbate his already precocious fear of death. And because of David's skepticism about my ministry, I didn't bring home tales of my work as I'd done when I was teaching. He had a hard time affirming my chaplaincy work because of his experience in Clinical Pastoral Education and because it seemed so strange to be a minister's husband. I could tell he didn't want to hear any stories of Interpersonal Relationship Group or about dying patients. So I trusted my deepest feelings about my work at the hospital to the IPR Group.

One of the experiences I told the group about occurred when I was on call and the emergency room supervisor beeped me to come quickly. When I got to ER, I saw paramedics running through the hall with a stretcher carrying a young man, trailing blood on the floor. The triage nurse told me that this twenty-three-year-old man named Tom had been riding a motorcycle when a truck crashed into him. Not wearing a helmet, he had suffered massive head injuries and probably wouldn't survive. The nurse took me to the family room, where I found Tom's mother and girlfriend, hysterical.

The mother grabbed my arm and pleaded, "Chaplain,

please tell us . . . please . . . please tell us. Tom's going to be all right, isn't he?"

"He's been in a very serious accident and—"

"No, no!" she screamed. "Don't tell me he's going to die!"

"The doctors and nurses are working hard to save his life. We just don't know yet."

"Chaplain, do something . . . please . . . oh, please pray that he'll be okay."

Right in the middle of my prayer, five husky men burst into the room. "Where is Tom? Take us to him," they demanded. Tom's motorcycle buddies filled what little space remained in the family room. When they threw off their black leather jackets, their massive, tattooed arms protruded from tank tops. The air reeked of beer and cigarettes and fear, so that I could hardly breathe.

A physician came in and said that Tom had sustained such traumatic injuries to his head that he probably had no brain activity left. A ventilator was all that was keeping him alive. Two by two I took Tom's family and friends into the trauma room. I could hardly stand to look at Tom's dark purple, swollen face with blood seeping out his nose and ears, and respirator tube jutting out his mouth. But more heart-rending was trying to comfort Tom's mother as she bent over him, hugging and kissing him, crying out, "Oh, God, not my baby, not Tom. Please, God, not Tom. Tom, can you hear me? Please, Tom, don't leave me. I love you so much, Tom."

When I took two of his friends in, one yelled out, "That's not Tom," and then collapsed to the floor. I squatted down and put one hand on his shoulder and one on his arm, while his friend got on the other side and tried to pull him up. Several security officers ran over and helped us get him into a chair. Finally, he came to, stammering, "Did I pass . . . pass . . . out . . . or something? Sorry. I just . . . can't believe . . . no way . . . this can't be happening." He jumped up and ran over to Tom with the other friend, officers, and me close behind. "Oh, Tom. Come on, man! Come on, Tom. Dammit! You can do it . . . keep fighting . . . you can . . . " His tears choked off his words.

Two days later Tom died in ICU, in spite of the most aggressive efforts to save his life. I stood close by Tom's mother, father, girlfriend, brother, and sister as they watched the waves on the heart monitor shorten and then dissolve into a straight line. Embracing Tom on either side, his mother and girlfriend sobbed out their grief, while his father, brother, and sister wept silently. I took deep breaths and tried to blink back tears. The ICU nurse, stoical, gave me a look that said, "Pull yourself together; you're supposed to be supporting them."

Tom's family and motorcycle buddies spilled out of the ICU family room down the hall, disturbing other patients and families with their outbursts of grief. I led them down to a larger family room by the Pastoral Care office. I stood in the center of the room, surrounded by about thirty people—family members and big burly friends—all weeping, looking at me, waiting for some word of comfort. I felt small and overwhelmed. What could I say that could make any difference? How could I answer their questions when I had so many? A memory of an incident Daddy had told me flashed through my mind. He had gone to comfort a family after they'd received news that a son had drowned. They grieved loudly and uncontrollably for what seemed hours, he said. Finally, he started quoting the Twenty-third Psalm, and they began to quieten. So I began quoting the psalm, voice quivering, but growing stronger as I got to "Yea though I walk through the valley of the shadow of death, I will fear no evil, for thou art with me." The words I'd memorized as a child in Vacation Bible School now reached like comforting arms around me and all the grieving people in that room.

Later that day in our Interpersonal Relationship Group, my tears came flooding out, in spite of my efforts to squelch them. The other interns said they had felt the same sense of helplessness and identification with grieving families. But I hadn't yet seen any of them cry in the group, and I felt embarrassed and mad at myself for crying in front of them. The supervisors assured me that tears were appropriate as long as they didn't get in the way of my ministry. But in this group of men, I felt in a double bind when it came to my emotions. Sometimes it seemed that they expected me to cry, and then judged me for crying.

Becoming More Legitimate as a Minister

In May of my internship year, David got an offer from Baylor University in Waco, Texas, to serve as director of public relations. By this time I had decided to go back to school. I had come to the realization that without a seminary degree, I would always have two strikes against me—my gender and my lack of theological education. Although the director of Baylor's Pastoral Care Department explored with me possibilities of serving as a lay chaplain, I knew in such a position I'd never have full credibility as a minister. Also, I welcomed the challenge of studying theology. I chose to go to Southwestern Baptist Theological Seminary in Fort Worth, even though the Methodist seminary in Dallas, Perkins School of Theology, was closer to our home. As a woman and a Perkins graduate, Martha Gilmore had been doubly suspect to Baptists. Idealistically, I believed that with a degree from the best-known Baptist seminary and my disarming Southern accent, I could break down the Baptist prejudice against women ministers. My only reservation in pursuing another degree had been the effect it would have on my family. And now that David had this new opportunity in Waco, how could I go to seminary in Fort Worth?

I'd grown in strength to claim the importance of my own vocation as equal to David's. But I also wanted to support his creative growth. David expressed excitement about the public relations position in Waco, and I couldn't stand in his way, although I struggled with questions about my future. He had hoped that my venture into ministry had been only a phase I was going through and that I would go happily to Waco and settle into an English-teaching job at Baylor University. When I told him I'd decided to go to seminary, he said, "I can't believe you really want to do that! I thought hospital chaplaincy and CPE would have showed you how good you had it as a college teacher." My affirmation of his career move, however, helped him support me. We worked out a compromise. David would commute from Dallas to Waco for one year, while I went to Southwestern Seminary. He rented an apartment in Waco, where he stayed three weeknights. Chad, Brett, and I stayed in Dallas, while I took classes at Southwestern and went back to teaching English full-time at Dallas Baptist College. I believed that since my career was as important as David's, I carried equal financial responsibility for the family. I was grateful to my good friend and English department chair, Raynal Barber, for arranging my teaching schedule around my seminary classes.

That fall of 1982 as I stepped onto the campus of Southwestern Baptist Theological Seminary, posed regally on the highest hill in Fort Worth, my heart skipped with excitement and a sense of history. The cracked sidewalk on the way to the Scarborough Administration Building was probably the same one that Mother and Daddy had walked; perhaps it had even been there more than sixty years before, when Grandmother and Grandpa Hickerson graduated from Southwestern.

On my way to register for classes, I saw Dr. T.B. Maston, retired ethics professor who at that time was in his eighties, moving slowly on his cane toward Roberts Library to continue his research and writing. Mother had graded papers for Dr. Maston when she was a student at Southwestern and later had received flak from some of the members of First Baptist in Minden when she taught Dr. Maston's book *The Bible and Race*. Published in 1959, this was one of the first religious books challenging not only Baptists but people of all faiths to repent of racial bigotry. Deep in my soul, I felt the rightness of my decision to study theology at Southwestern.

In the first meeting of evangelism class, the professor announced, "You're all invited to a reception at our home to welcome new students. Please bring your wives, and come to our home at 7:00 P.M. this Thursday evening." Shocked, I looked around at the other women—about a fourth of the class—who obliviously wrote this invitation in their notebooks. Did these women have wives? Why was I the only one who seemed to notice the professor's comment? During the whole semester this evangelism professor never called on a woman to lead in the prayer at the beginning of class and never called on a woman to answer a question. It was as though women were invisible, as Ralph Ellison laments about African Americans in *The Invisible Man*. How could the seminary of Dr. Maston, that great voice for justice, have a professor so insensitive?

One of my favorite courses was Philosophy of Religion. Professor Yandall Woodfin used the Socratic method to engage students in discussion of the textbook he'd authored. His theology seemed progressive, and he did call on women students. But reading his book, one would conclude that God, ministers, philosophers, and all humanity were male. I circled all these references, gathered my courage, and went to his office to tell him my feelings about this language.

Dr. Woodfin responded, "Thank you for taking time to come by and point this out to me. You're right, and I'll change these references in the next edition. I had a woman read the manuscript before it was published, and she didn't say anything about the language."

"Unfortunately, not all women understand the importance of our being included in language. But thank you for understanding, and I appreciate your willingness to change," I said.

In Old Testament class I sat on the front row by a young man in his early twenties with slicked-back blond hair and a jaw set tight in his unquestioned theology. Noticing that I was obviously older than the few other women in this large class and that I wore a wedding ring, he interrogated me.

"So why are you here in seminary?"

"Because I'm studying theology."

"I can't help noticing your wedding ring. I guess you're not here for the MRS. degree, like most of the women here," he said with a forced chuckle.

Not amused, I responded, "No, I'm a serious student of theology, just as I assume you are."

Now his voice grew stony. "Well, what do you plan to *do* with your theology degree?"

"God has called me to ministry," I said, and growing bolder, I heard myself say for the first time, "I'm preparing to be a pastor."

"It is unbiblical for women to be pastors," he declared, looking down at his Bible placed on top of his Old Testament textbook.

I couldn't let this young man rest in his smug ignorance. I found this blatant sexism at Southwestern easier to confront than the subtler kinds I'd experienced. I began pouring out all the theological and biblical support for women in pastoral leadership that I could marshal from the books I'd been reading the past few years. He continued staring at his Bible, and I finally realized that I was wasting my energy. My presence and statement of call could stand as my best defense. He said nothing more to me the whole semester.

There were no women professors in theology at Southwestern Seminary and only a few in music and religious education, even though these fields had been more open to women in Baptist churches. During the three years I studied at Southwestern, I never had a female professor. Some of my professors, however, gave me more affirmation than many of the female or male students. Scott Tatum, my preaching professor, was among the most supportive. Perhaps his regard for women came from having a strong daughter, whom I remembered from high school student council conferences. She had been the first girl ever elected as student council president of the largest high school in Shreveport, Louisiana.

My preaching class included only one other woman among thirty students. She told me that she took the class so that she could help her preacher husband-to-be with his sermons. When I told her that I was there to learn to preach myself, she stared in disbelief.

My anxiety kept rising as the day approached for me to preach in class. Although I'd preached in chapel at Baylor Medical Center and lectured to classes daily at Dallas Baptist

College, I still felt intimidated by the word "sermon." It had such an aura of holiness and maleness. I'd never heard a woman other than myself preach a sermon. And I supposed that the men in my preaching class had as little or less experience of women preachers. For weeks I worked assiduously on my sermon entitled "Faith in the Middle of the Storm." My text came from Matthew 14, the story of Jesus' walking on water to the disciples out in a boat amidst a storm. I carefully wrote out my scriptural interpretation, illustrations, and applications. Then I memorized the sermon and practiced delivering it without notes. I even worked on gestures, standing in front of the mirror in our bedroom.

As I preached the sermon, I felt poised and confident, believing that I, like the disciples in my text, received supernatural aid to calm my fears. I delivered the sermon without any lapse in memory of words or gestures, even though I could see Dr. Tatum and the students writing their evaluations as I preached. After I finished, Dr. Tatum invited students to make comments to me while I stood at the pulpit.

One man began emphatically, "She was obviously very well-prepared, and I can't find anything wrong with her content. But her delivery was unnatural."

Another student agreed, continuing the third person references to me, although he was supposed to be addressing me: "Yes, she seemed stilted and affected . . . yes, she looked unnatural."

Several others nodded their heads in agreement. Dr. Tatum, sitting on the front row, stood and faced the students. "How many of you have ever heard a woman preach before today?" he challenged. A few of the men, other than the ones who criticized my delivery, raised their hands.

"Then how can you possibly judge what is natural or unnatural for Jann?" Dr. Tatum continued. "The reason you find Jann's delivery unnatural is that you feel it's unnatural for a woman to preach."

Although Dr. Tatum's defense and the A at the top of his glowing written evaluation of my sermon helped my feelings, the words "unnatural" and "affected" battered my fledgling confidence as a preacher.

Restored assurance of my call came through a letter from Mother. I had sent her a copy of the sermon I'd preached in Dr. Tatum's class. She wrote me a piece of her story she'd never told me before. Before she had children, Mother had prayed for a child who would grow up to be a preacher. After all, she was the daughter of a Baptist preacher, the granddaughter of a Baptist preacher, the sister of a Baptist missionary preacher, and the wife of a Baptist preacher. So she thought it only appropriate that she also be the mother of a Baptist preacher. After having two daughters and then a miscarriage, Mother and Daddy decided not to have any more children. So Mother forgot her prayer, thinking God had not answered it. As she was reading my sermon, God brought back to her memory that prayer she had prayed many years ago before I was born. She suddenly realized that God had indeed answered her prayer, though certainly not in the way she had expected.

Following David to Waco

After my first year of seminary, I knew we needed to move to Waco. David had grown tired of the ninety-mile commute from Dallas to Waco. We had received a good offer on our house and found a house we liked in Waco. Yet I had made A's in all my seminary classes and wanted to finish my degree at Southwestern Seminary, in spite of the sexism I'd experienced there. At that time I'd never heard of dual-career couples working in separate cities, and David had proved more progressive than most men by commuting for a year. Although I questioned the fairness of cultural expectations that a woman should move with her husband, I wanted to support David in his new position. So I began to explore options for me in Waco. There was no seminary in Waco at that time, but I thought that I might transfer my courses from Southwestern to a graduate degree in religion at Baylor University, while I taught English at Baylor instead of Dallas Baptist College. Things didn't work out so conveniently. I learned that my Southwestern Seminary courses would not transfer to Baylor and that it was the seminary degree that I needed for pastoral ministry. I had interviewed for several chaplaincy positions in Waco, but I didn't qualify because I hadn't completed the seminary degree. Also, there were no openings for English professors at Baylor.

After hearing only disappointing news from both the director of graduate studies in religion and the chair of the English department at Baylor, I met David and his boss for lunch. David asked me a few questions about the interviews and could immediately hear in my voice that they had not gone well. His boss, unaware, sat there smiling and extolling the city of Waco, like a Chamber of Commerce agent. Then he insisted on driving David and me around and showing us the sights. David sat in the front seat with his boss, and I sat alone in the back seat.

The boss seemed especially proud to show me all the shopping opportunities in Waco. "There's our new shopping mall—Richland Mall—it just opened a few months ago," he pointed to his left, looking over his shoulder at me. "I know you'll enjoy shopping there, Jann. My wife loves to go there. Of course, I have to keep a tight rein on her, or she'll spend all my money," he said, chuckling. He didn't seem to notice my lack of enthusiasm for shopping or the way he talked about his wife.

As we drove back to Baylor campus, I let David respond to his boss's comments. All I could think of was holding myself together until I could get back to my car and my decision about what I was going to do with my future. All of a sudden I was jarred back by the boss's pointing at a billboard and saying, "Jann, maybe that's your next calling!" He laughed raucously as I looked up at the huge picture of a woman clad in the skimpiest of bikinis, breasts spilling over the top, leaning forward seductively, advertising her dancing at a local night club. He didn't notice my silence nor the tears that began streaming down my face. David didn't laugh either.

After school was out that May of 1983, we moved to

Waco. Chad, eleven, and Brett, eight, sat crying amidst all the boxes stacked in the den. I sat down in the floor with them as they talked about how they were going to miss all their friends and their school. Tears welled up in my eyes as I tried to comfort them but also thought of all I was leaving behind. The prospect of living in Waco seemed bleak even ten years before David Koresh and his Branch Davidians made this Central Texas city infamous.

A few weeks after we moved, alone in the house, I finished unpacking the last boxes. As the finality of the move settled over me, so did the realization that I had not decided what I was going to do that fall. Feeling bereft and dislocated, I lay down on the floor in the study and cried out for direction. I had been getting mixed signals, I told God. I had felt confirmation of my call to ministry and had successfully completed a year of seminary education, but I believed I was supposed to support David in his new job in Waco, where I'd found no opportunities to continue my calling. Did I have to choose between my vocation and my family? It didn't take long for the answer to come. I'd never believed that I, or any other woman, should have to make such a choice, so why should I raise this question now? I would continue my seminary education and continue supporting my family. I jumped up from the floor, believing that I could somehow do both.

When I told David that I planned to commute to Fort Worth to finish my seminary degree and to keep teaching at Dallas Baptist College to help support the family financially, he responded, "That's ridiculous and impossible!" Inside, I was also wondering about the practicality of this plan, but I believed so strongly that it was right and knew I had to convince David that it was possible.

"What about the boys? The boys need their mother," he pleaded.

"I'll still be there for them. And it'll be a wonderful experience for you. You're already a great father, and this will give you the opportunity to grow even closer to them," I said.

"I know, but the mother's role is most important," he

responded, probably thinking about the close relationship he had with his own mother.

"I believe the father is equally important." I would have continued, but realized from the look on David's face that this wasn't the time to get into a debate on gender roles.

Instead, I started talking about the logistics of my plan and everything I would do to make sure things went smoothly at home. I told David that I had already worked out rides for Chad and Brett to and from school. I would take them for dental and medical check-ups that summer. And since they rarely got sick, he'd probably not have to take them for doctor's appointments the next year. I planned to spend only two nights a week away from home. Since Southwestern Seminary held no classes on Mondays, on Tuesdays I would leave around 5:30 A.M. and drive to Fort Worth for morning and early afternoon classes. Then I would drive to Dallas to teach late afternoon and evening classes at Dallas Baptist College, spending Tuesday nights in the women's dormitory at DBC. Wednesday mornings I would drive to Fort Worth for more seminary classes, and then drive back home to Waco in the late afternoon. Thursday mornings I would get up early again and drive to Fort Worth for more seminary classes and then on to Dallas to teach afternoon and evening classes, staying in the dormitory Thursday nights. Friday mornings I would drive to Fort Worth for seminary classes, and then drive back home on Friday afternoons. By squeezing in as many seminary classes as possible, I could finish in just two more years. And with Raynal's help, I could work a full-time teaching schedule around seminary and commuting. I would make tapes of seminary lectures and play them in the car during all this commuting, so that I wouldn't have much studying to do when I was home. Thinking about this elaborate plan now, many years later, I feel dizzied and exhausted.

At that time, I tried to laugh off any doubts, quipping to David, "Instead of *A Tale of Two Cities,* one day I'll have a tale of three cities." David looked more anxious than amused.

A Tale of Three Cities

When I began classes at seminary and at DBC that fall of 1983, David seemed somewhat reassured to see me continuing to do so much with and for the family. When I came home, I tried to hide my fatigue. I'd rush in and start cleaning up the house while talking with Chad and Brett about all their activities. On weekends David and I often went with the boys to Spenco Athletic Center, where they loved to play tennis and swim. Also, I'd take them shopping for clothes, school supplies, and groceries. Monday evenings I usually made their lunches for the rest of the week. David had always enjoyed cooking, so he gladly prepared other meals. He also took the greater share of responsibility for Chad and Brett during the week. But I realized that I was trying to overcompensate at home, in ways that David never did the year before when he spent three nights away from home. I remembered Raynal's saying to me when she was trying to juggle doctoral work, teaching, and family, "Women have to make up for giving attention to our own careers. It's almost like we have to justify our self-development. Men never feel they have to do this." Shortly after our move to Waco, I couldn't help saying to David, "Marriage is not a good deal for a woman."

One way I survived those years of commuting and studying and teaching, while trying to be a good mother and wife, was to teach Chad and Brett independence. Anne had used the phrase "benign neglect" for her successful parenting of David and DeAnne while she completed her graduate degrees. I took her theory to mean encouraging self-reliance in children. From the time Chad and Brett were nine years old, they did their own laundry. In fact, Brett took this domestic chore more seriously than I ever had, meticulously separating white from colored clothes. One day he saw me dumping some of his white T-shirts in with colored towels and shirts, and expressed horror. He never again let me close to his clothes.

One day Brett came home from his best friend's house and said, "You know, Mom, I saw Jeremy's mom washing his clothes and even packing them for camp. Can you believe that? How would she know what he wanted to wear? Isn't that weird?"

Both of my sons had always packed their own clothes for trips. I wanted Brett to think he was the norm, although I didn't know many nine-year-olds who did their own laundry. "Yes, that's strange to me," I said. "You're perfectly capable of taking care of your own clothes."

Sitting in the grove at Ole Miss years later, watching Brett receive a master's degree he'd earned while teaching for two years in an "underresourced" school in the Mississippi delta, I felt the rightness of my mothering philosophy. Whether called "benign neglect" or fostering independence, it had worked. Beside me sat Chad, who'd received his master's degree in public affairs at the University of Texas two years before. Both sons had chosen careers of public service and had big dreams of changing the world. Both had become magnificent human beings indeed. As the sun shone down on that hot May graduation day in Oxford, Mississippi, I beamed with pride. But I knew I couldn't take too much credit for Chad and Brett. David had become one of the most involved and caring dads I'd ever seen. Added to our parenting were heavy portions of grace, their own good choices, and the influences of wonderful teachers, grandparents, aunts, uncles, and cousins. I also believe that by choosing to grow in my vocation, I gave Chad and Brett freedom and inspiration to develop their talents. I learned from my own experience that women, like men, can choose both career and family.

As I drove back and forth between Waco and Fort Worth and Dallas, the word "Ebenezer," from an old hymn, kept coming to mind. Growing up, I had loved singing, "Here I raise mine Ebenezer; hither by Thy help I'm come," not knowing what in the world an "Ebenezer" was. Later, I discovered that these lines in the hymn "Come, Thou Fount of Every Blessing" referred to the prophet Samuel's raising an altar between Mizpah and Jeshanah and naming it "Ebenezer," a Hebrew word meaning "Stone of Help." As Samuel was grateful for divine help in the battle against the Philistines, I felt supernatural aid in surviving two years of commuting over 520 miles a week while juggling roles of full-time teacher, full-time student, wife, and mother. At times I was so exhausted that I had to fight desperately to keep from falling asleep at the wheel. I drank coffee and Big Red and tried more creative methods of staying awake, like holding my left foot up for as long as possible. Also, I'd sing hymns, vociferously. But sometimes my eyes got heavy, and I felt the car weaving over to the shoulder of the highway. I believed angels of help kept me from having a wreck. Another major miracle was that I never got a speeding ticket, although I often drove over the speed limit. And I never had car trouble during the entire two years of commuting. Often I thought about stopping somewhere on Interstate 35 between Waco and Fort Worth and placing an altar with the sign "Ebenezer."

As I approached graduation from Southwestern Seminary, I could find no opportunity for ministry in Waco. There were no openings for chaplains and no Baptist churches that would even consider a woman in a pastoral role. It didn't seem to matter that I had made straight A's at Southwestern, poured so much energy into preparation for ministry, and felt such a strong sense of divine guidance. I felt betrayed by the religious tradition that had encouraged me to answer God's call to ministry and endorsed me to go to seminary. After challenging me all my life to follow God's call wherever it might lead, Southern Baptists now gave me nowhere to fulfill my call. The placement office at Southwestern wouldn't even try to place women in pastoral roles. A young man in my church music class had tried to persuade me to let him copy my summaries of assigned articles. This man already had a position as pastor of a church. I was incensed that a man who cheated had more opportunity as a minister than any woman. No matter how well a woman did in seminary and no matter how skilled she might be in preaching and pastoral care, she had little opportunity in the Baptist tradition.

Often I fantasized about standing before an assembly of

Southwestern Seminary administrators and theology professors, all male, delivering a powerful sermon denouncing these blatant injustices. I would boldly demand, like the prophet Amos, "let justice roll down like waters, and righteousness like an everflowing stream." Always more courageous in writing, I put my complaints in a letter to the president of Southwestern: "It is deceptive and unconscionable for the seminary to train women for ministry while at the same time placing barriers to the fulfillment of our calling. Instead of following and sanctioning the gender injustice in our culture, the seminary should be prophetic in proclaiming the liberating truth of the Gospel." In my letter I quoted biblical passages, such as "there is no longer male and female; for all of you are one in Christ Jesus" and "your sons and your daughters shall preach." I never received a response.

Gradually I had to let go of my need for male validation. Growing away from my need of David's approval was especially slow and painful. David had a hard time supporting my vocational change. I had to develop enough inner strength and autonomy to do what I believed I had to do, regardless of his opinion.

David came to hear me preach one Sunday evening in the spring of 1985 at our church in Waco, Seventh and James Baptist. It was the first sermon I had preached in a church setting and the first with David in the congregation. When I stood in the pulpit and looked out at David on the back row, my knees trembled more than they ever had in preaching class or in chapel services at Baylor Medical Center. All I could think of was a remark David had made several years before: "A woman may give a good speech, but she'll never preach. Preaching is a male form." I'd countered, "Just because it has been, that doesn't mean it always will be." Now I stood in the pulpit, trying not to feel too much pressure to prove my words. Somehow I got through that sermon, feeling much the way I did when I took my Ph.D. comprehensive exams, outside my body observing myself. After the worship service, people came by to shake my hand, according to Baptist tradition, and to commend my sermon. As I greeted people, I looked around for David. After the last person had come through the line, I still couldn't find him. Disheartened, I walked to the car. He was sitting behind the steering wheel. Not until we started on our way home did David comment, "That was a damn good sermon!" For the first time I felt David's affirmation of my pastoral vocation.

David's close bond with his mother also contributed to his growing support of my vocational change. Evelyn had given me wholehearted acceptance from the moment she met me and now applauded my new ventures. Evelyn knew what it felt like to be a woman in a nontraditional profession; she had been DeRidder High School's first woman band director in the 1930s. Back then in Louisiana, women had to quit teaching not just when they got pregnant, but when they married. Although she had established herself as an outstanding band director and music teacher, she lost her job when she married "Hoss" Clanton, a local car dealer. She held every volunteer church position allowed to women while her three sons— David, Mike, and Mark—were young. She even served as the choir director for First Baptist Church in DeRidder. But the church didn't pay her, and wouldn't consider her for the position of minister of music. In fact, she was not allowed to direct congregational singing. When he was about ten, David asked her, "Mom, why is it okay for you to direct the choir but not the whole church? It's all right for everybody to see your back, but not for you to turn around and let them see your front?" Evelyn told me this story when I was in seminary, and the affinity between us grew stronger. David's respect for his mother, along with his growing understanding of discrimination against women, strengthened his appreciation of my calling. Also, he became a staunch advocate for pay equity for the women in Baylor University's Public Relations Department, which he directed.

In Systematic Theology class that last semester, as I studied complex doctrines of the Trinity established by church councils during the first five centuries of Christian history, I slowly realized that all our language for deity is metaphorical. I understood that those early church councils formulated the Trinity in an attempt to articulate the richness and fullness of the divinity they had experienced. The question came to me, "If God can include three persons, can't God include two genders?" This question would later become a chapter title in a book on God-language and gender equality. But at that time it came as a personal revelation of great power and freedom. I realized that it was just as appropriate to call God "She" as "He." But what would it feel like to call God "She" and "Mother"? The first time I prayed, "Our Mother," I trembled. Would I be struck by lightning? Instead, a deep sense of affirmation began to flow through me. Praying to God as Mother helped me feel that She was on my side and just as incensed over discrimination against women as I was.

Driving home to Waco from seminary one Friday afternoon, I sang one of my favorite hymns to keep awake. But instead of "He leadeth me," I sang, "She leadeth me," beginning softly and timidly but then gaining strength: "She leadeth me! O blessed tho't! O words with heav'nly comfort fraught! Whate'er I do, where'er I be, still 'tis God's hand that leadeth me! She leadeth me, She leadeth me, by Her own hand She leadeth me: Her faithful foll'wer I would be, for by Her hand She leadeth me." Approaching home, now singing "She leadeth me" to the top of my voice, I looked up and saw a glowing rainbow arched over the city of Waco. The bright colors— emerald, turquoise, yellow, orange, scarlet, rose, magenta, purple—beamed down from the sky into my soul, assuring me that there would be creative opportunity for me in Waco.

Family in Minden parsonage, 1951. Eva, Jann, Anne, Truman.

Flossie, the "church dog," 1956.

Jann, Church Mission
Organization Queen, 1958.

Family in front of First Baptist Church, Minden, Louisiana, 1959.

Truman Aldredge in pulpit of First Baptist in Minden, 1960s.

Grandmother Hickerson, Mother Eva, Daddy Truman, Grandpa Hickerson, 1954.

Top Ten in Minden High School Class of 1964. Valedictorian Jann on top.

First runner-up to Miss Minden, 1964.

Homecoming Maid Jann, 1964.

Runner-up in Miss Peach Pageant, 1967. Jann at right.

*Jann and David at Phi Mu
Sorority Formal, 1966.*

*Jann as majorette in
Louisiana Tech Band, 1965.*

Jann and David's wedding, First Baptist Church, Minden, 1968.

Papa and Mimi Aldredge, Jann, David, Grandmother Hickerson, 1968.

Family in DeRidder, Louisiana, 1976. (Back row) David, Jann, Mike Clanton, "Hoss" Clanton, Mark Clanton; (front) Chad, Brett, Debbie Nichols Clanton, Evelyn McPhail Clanton.

David, Brett, Jann, Chad, 1977.

Family in San Angelo, Texas, 1977. Taylor Henley, Eva, Anne, DeAnne Herring, David Herring, Jann, David, with Chad and Brett in front.

After Jann's ordination, Seventh & James Baptist Church, Waco, 1985. Eva, Martha Gilmore, and Jann.

Jann in pulpit of St. John's United Methodist Church, 1980s.

After wedding of JoAnn Bristol and Jim Pettit in Muir Woods, 1989.

Taylor, niece DeAnne, and Jann, before officiating at DeAnne's wedding, 1988.

Opening doors to a new perspective. This photo accompanied an article about Jann's ministry, Waco Tribune-Herald, *August 3, 1985.*

ASKING QUESTIONS OF GOD'S IMAGE

Dec. 1, 1990

A new book portrays a God above gender.

By DOUGLAS WONG
Tribune-Herald staff writer

When Jann Clanton was a student at Southwestern Baptist Theological Seminary in 1982, she began to question the use of male pronouns in reference to God.

Those questions led her to study the historic image of God in Christianity. Clanton puts her findings in her newly released book, *In Who's Image? God and Gender.*

"The thesis of the book comes from Genesis 1:27, that all are created in God's image, both male and female are created in God's image," Clanton said. "So if male and female are in God's image, well then God's image must include something of the female as well as the male."

"I try to show how the biblical material in both the Old and New Testament shows a God above gender, an unlimited God, but a God with both masculine and feminine images," she said. "I also try to show how Christian historians have also included the feminine in their image of God. They have not been able to get away from that. To me, that is a sign of a fuller God continuing to break through history."

It took Clanton four years to write her book and have it published. Crossroads Publishing Company is distributing the book nationwide, and several local bookstores will soon have it on their shelves, she said.

Although giving God human characteristics makes him a more tangible figure, Clanton said, it also limits God. She said viewing God with both male and female qualities may provide a better understanding of what God really is.

"Ultimately this will help us get to a transcendent, unlimited idea of God," she said. "I think we can go more easily from an androgynous view of God to a spirit image of God than from a masculine to a spirit image."

The issue of viewing God with both female and male qualities came to a head recently with the release of the New Revised Standard Bible. The NRS Bible uses inclusive language, that is it refers to God as a parent rather than father, and the translators tried to remove any reference to gender whenever possible.

However, Clanton said, searching for the androgynous God is nothing new.

"Way back in the Middle Ages, this fuller concept of God was breaking through," Clanton said. "There was a male theologian, St. Anselm of Canterbury, who talked about God as our mother and Jesus as our mother: 'You also, Jesus, good Lord, are you not also mother? Are you not mother who are as a hen who gathers her chicks under her own wings?' He was going from the biblical passage in Matthew where Christ compares himself to a mother hen and using that image fully.

"There were a lot of theologians throughout history. For instance in the reformation, Luther and Calvin both talked about the mother aspects of God. It's not a recent thing at all. I think there is more attention given to it recently because there are a lot of female theologians and male theologians that have seen the importance of this."

Since society is changing, and the media and literature use inclusive language on a more frequent basis, Clanton said, the church also must begin using inclusive language or be viewed as archaic."Men and women must stand equally before God in the ministry and society," she said.

"I see a lot of positive changes that can come by an unlimited theology that then will empower both women and men in the church."

Viewing God with feminine qualities gives the Lord a birthing, life giving, creating type of image, both in the old and new testaments, she said.

"That can be a very powerful, motivating force for religious people to save creation," she said. "If we believe God is the creator of this world, and we are stewards of creation and if we can incorporate the feminine into that too, not only does that empower women, but also gives some legitimacy to things that have often been called feminine issues for men.

"In addition, being able to see an androgynous and a transcendent God will help us claim androgyny among our ownselves. Being in an image of God means that being of one gender, we still have characteristics of both and we can become whole people as we incorporate those characteristics."

Staff photo — Rod Aydelotte

Jann Clanton holds her new book, *In Who's Image? God and Gender*. In it, Clanton explores the use of inclusive language in the worship of God.

Waco Tribune-Herald *article after release of* In Whose Image? God and Gender *(December 1, 1990).*

Brett's high school graduation, 1993. Evelyn Clanton, Brett, Jann, Eva.

Brett after receiving M.A., University of Mississippi, 1999. David, Brett, Jann, Chad.

David, Chad, Brett, and Jann after Chad received his M.A. and Brett, B.A., University of Texas, 1997.

Eva, Jann, Chad at March to Conquer Cancer, Washington, D.C., 1998.

Eva's birthday celebration, 1998. Brett, nephew David, Jann, and Eva.

Eva Aldredge Henley preaching, 2001.

Jann, Eva, and Anne, New Year's celebration, 2001.

Near niece DeAnne's home in Roanoke, Virginia, 2000. Eva, Anne, Jann, DeAnne, Chandler.

Chad in Oval Office, 1999. Author Willie Morris, Chad, President Bill Clinton, Senior Adviser Paul Begala.

Sons Brett and Chad, 2000.

Brett receives Mississippi Press Association Award for story in the Indianola Enterprise-Tocsin, 2000. Brett, publisher Jim Abbott, newswriter David Rushing.

New Wineskins Community, Easter 2002. Steve Lyons, Anne Campbell, Elizabeth Babcock, Elizabeth Zedaran, Anne Morton, Jann Aldredge-Clanton, Pam Oliver-Lyons, Brian Burton.

Chapter Six

Waco's Give 'Em Hell Minister

Several weeks before my graduation from Southwestern Seminary in July of 1985, I received a call from Jay Beavers, pastor of St. John's United Methodist Church in Waco. He said, "I'm looking for an associate pastor, and you've been recommended to me."

After a long pause, I said, "Well, that's good, but you must have the wrong person. You see, I'm Baptist. I'm about to graduate from Southwestern Baptist Seminary."

"That's all right. We don't have anything against Baptists," he laughed.

Reverend Beavers went on to explain that ministers of other denominations were sometimes given special appointments in Methodist churches or institutions. Even though I had joked to David that I might go see James Shuler, our next-door neighbor and district superintendent of the Methodist Central Texas Conference, and ask him if he had any available church positions, this call came as a complete surprise. In my work as a chaplain intern, I had ministered to people of all denominations, and I considered myself to be even more ecumenical now. But I had not known a Baptist church to seek a

Methodist minister, so I wouldn't have expected a Methodist church to consider me.

I'd sung "She leadeth me," and now I felt the full power of those words. I'd never had anyone approach me about a job before I'd even applied. In addition, I learned that Martha Gilmore, who played such a significant part in my call to ministry, and Libby Bellinger, a good friend who was one of the first ordained Baptist women in the country and who now served as chaplain of Waco's ecumenical Inner City Ministries, had recommended me to St. John's. When I interviewed with Reverend Beavers and the Personnel Committee, I knew that this would be the perfect place for me.

But I wondered what David and Mother would think about my ministering in a church other than Baptist. By this time I didn't feel I had to have their approval, but I still wanted it. Mother expressed delight in this opportunity for me to be an associate pastor, but kept asking if I had gone to Calvary Baptist, right across the street from St. John's, to inquire about openings. At that time Calvary Baptist didn't have women deacons or women in any leadership roles. Ironically, thirteen years later Calvary became the first Baptist church in Texas to call a woman—Julie Pennington-Russell—as senior pastor, and I like to think my work at St. John's helped open this door. David tried to share my enthusiasm for the St. John's appointment, but he felt apprehensive—partly because I would not be with our family for worship and partly because of possible political repercussions for him as public relations director of a Baptist university. I tried to explain to David and to Mother that I could maintain my Baptist identity and membership while being associate pastor of St. John's. I joked that I would be like a Baptist missionary to the Methodists.

A "Methobaptist" Minister

I learned to tease people away from religious divisions by calling myself a "Methobaptist." My work at St. John's coincided with my growing feminist consciousness. Gender inclusiveness opened my spirituality to embrace various expressions of faith. I saw myself in a description written by Elinor Lenz and Barbara Myerhoff in *The Feminization of America:*

> The search for a new spirituality is bringing together women of many different faiths who are seeking equal time in their religions for the celebration of the feminine experience. In contrast to the divisiveness of religious sectarianism, the search for this new spirituality is ecumenical in its scope, integrative rather than divisive, crossing over the sectarian boundaries of traditional religion.

After I preached "God of the Unexpected," my first sermon at St. John's, one of the older women in the congregation told me, "You did a great job. It was wonderful to hear a woman preach! It doesn't matter that you're a Baptist because labels don't matter anyway."

On Sunday, July 21, 1985, I began my ministry at St. John's. On Saturday, August 3, the *Waco Tribune-Herald* carried a story about my appointment on the front page of the religion section. "CHURCH OPENS DOOR TO WOMAN MINISTER" stood in bold black letters at the top of the half-page story. To the left of the story was a color picture of me, the full length of the story and two columns wide. Looking more triumphant than holy, I beamed out a full-toothed smile, although I usually tried not to show my crooked lower teeth. But the only unrestrained parts of me in that picture were my smile and my dancing eyes. I was wearing a blue suit with a starched white blouse buttoned up to my neck and a navy blue scarf tied in a bow around the collar—what some women used to describe as a "wanna-be-a-man tie." My naturally curly hair was cropped short enough to lie straight and flat on my head. Holding a black Bible with both hands, I stood in front of the communion rail.

The *Waco Tribune* article, by reporter Debbie Hutchinson, began:

Two months ago, Jann Clanton's chances of becoming a minister looked bleak. In June, while Mrs. Clanton was finishing her work at Southwestern Baptist Theological Seminary, messengers at the Southern Baptist Convention were across town waging war over such issues as the role women should play in the 14-million member denomination.

The article quoted my descriptions of "dark nights of the soul" during the convention and my delight over my new pastoral role at St. John's United Methodist Church.

"My heritage is strongly Baptist. My father and grandfather were Baptist ministers. But what is larger to me is my calling to be a minister. ... I must follow that calling by accepting the opportunities God has given me at this time and in this place. ... I am breaking down cultural barriers."

In the interview, Debbie Hutchinson had asked me about how my career decision might affect my husband's position at Baylor University. I responded, "I am very hopeful that this will not hurt his effectiveness." I also expressed hope that the number of Baptists supporting ordination of women would continue to grow and that "Baptists will apply our radical stand on the priesthood of believers to the ministry of women."

Hutchinson explained that I planned to exercise my call in two denominations.

While she pastors St. John's congregation, Mrs. Clanton is keeping her membership at Seventh and James Baptist Church and is also seeking ordination in the Baptist denomination. The Southern Baptist Convention passed a resolution last year opposing the ordination of women. But, according to Baptist tradition, each church has the option of deciding the issue for itself. Seventh and James has ordained a woman, Terry Brandon, this year and Mrs. Clanton may be the second.

Ecumenical Ordination

Four months later, I did indeed become the second woman to be ordained by Seventh and James Baptist Church. I felt deep gratitude to Terry Brandon for persevering in the midst of some opposition to her ordination. Because she had opened the door, my process toward ordination didn't take as long as hers, and I had complete freedom in planning the ordination service. After the congregation voted to recommend me for ordination, I went for questioning before a council, composed of all the ordained deacons and ministers in the church. Appearing before this ordaining council intimidated me partly because some were religion professors at Baylor, but mostly because all except Terry were men. Before the examination I had carefully studied the doctrinal statements in the *Baptist Faith and Message,* and had reviewed my Systematic Theology and Philosophy of Religion textbooks from seminary. But the council asked more questions about my personal pilgrimage toward vocational ministry than about theology. They seemed curious as to why I would seek ordination and what I planned to do with it. Later, one of the members of the council admitted that with male candidates the questions focused more on theology, and with me they had spent more time examining my personal motivation for ordination. I'd never been to an ordaining council. For me the proceedings had always been shrouded in mystery, like Daddy's Masonic meetings. So I didn't know the difference.

All I could or wanted to feel at that time was affirmation. After the questioning, the ordaining council asked me to leave the room while they voted. In less than ten minutes they called me back in and congratulated me. According to Baptist democratic polity, the chair of the council would have to present to the whole congregation a motion to ordain me. This final step was considered a mere formality, and so the council signed my certificate of ordination.

Looking at my certificate, sixteen years later, I'm noticing for the first time that the number of signatures is twelve, a holy number, like the twelve tribes of Israel and the twelve apostles. Unlike my certificate of license to ministry, the ordination certificate has feminine pronouns in reference to me. It reads:

> We, the undersigned, hereby certify that upon the recommendation and request of the Seventh and James Baptist Church at Waco, Texas, which had full and sufficient opportunity for judging her gifts, and after satisfactory examination by us in regard to her Christian experience, call to the ministry, and views of Bible doctrine, Jann Aldredge Clanton was solemnly and publicly set apart and ordained to the work of the Gospel Ministry by authority and order of the Seventh and James Baptist Church at Waco, Texas, on the 24th day of November, 1985.

One other difference I notice as I compare the two certificates is my name: "Jann Clanton" when I was licensed in 1982, and "Jann Aldredge Clanton" when I was ordained in 1985. The hyphen would come later.

Mike Smith, on the ordaining council, had said to me, "Part of your calling must be to serve as a bridge. You're being ordained as a Baptist pastor to serve in a Methodist church. Also, you're director of the Conference of Christians and Jews. And you're obviously trying to bridge the gap between women and men."

Although I was officially ordained by Seventh and James Baptist Church, the members of St. John's United Methodist ordained me as well. The pastor of St. John's, Jay Beavers, led the Call to Worship at the ordination service, and members of St. John's took part in the ritual of laying on hands. Later Myrt Meador, Bruce Meador, Doris Boozer, Lois Claire Ohlsson, and others from St. John's expressed gratitude for the opportunity to participate for the first time in the laying on of hands. In Methodist tradition only the district superintendents and bishops perform this ritual.

As I knelt at the front of the sanctuary, Catholics and

Presbyterians and Episcopalians joined the Methodists and Baptists in blessing me with their words and hands. It was more ecumenical than any ordination I'd ever seen.

After the ordination service my stepfather Taylor said, "A new day has dawned!" Dan Bagby, the pastor of Seventh and James, told me, "The congregation grew through this." In the ensuing months, seeing services at Seventh and James return to predominantly male leadership and masculine language, I wondered, "Just how did the church grow? What's different? Did the new day awaken and then go right back to sleep?"

A Message from Daddy

Tuesday afternoon after my ordination, I sat in my office at St. John's feeling the natural letdown after a giant hour. Dan Danzeizer knocked on my door. Retired from the Air Force and from his hat business, and an active participant in a senior adult growth group I led at St. John's, Dan came by to see me almost every week when he did volunteer work at the church. Unlike some members who came by for casual conversation or to talk about a problem, Dan always brought up some serious theological issue. Often he wanted to discuss some point I'd made in the children's sermon or the "big" sermon. So it didn't surprise me to see him at my door several days after my ordination.

"Is this a good time?" Dan hesitated at the door.

"Sure, please come on in," I responded, hoping that he wanted to talk about my ordination.

Sitting down directly in front of me, he came right to his point, "Did you understand what I said to you Sunday night at your ordination?"

Hundreds of people had filed by, placing their hands on my head and whispering prayers in my ears. Most of the time I had my head bowed, so I couldn't see the people. How did Dan expect me to know what he had said? I stared across the table at him.

After an uncomfortable silence, he asked earnestly, "Don't you remember what I said?"

The raspy tone of Dan's voice suddenly brought recognition. I did recall a strange blessing—words that sent chills from my head to my bent knees. So it was Dan who had spoken those cryptic words: "I may not be able to help you that much, but I'll help you all I can."

I told Dan the truth. "Now I remember what you said. I felt your blessing, but I really didn't understand what you meant."

"I'm not so sure I did either. That's why I came by this afternoon." Dan began trying to explain his statement, that perhaps he meant that his support of me might be limited, that of course he wanted me to know that he believed what I was doing was right, but that he was getting older and his health might not always be good and he had many family responsibilities. Dan, who usually spoke concisely and always valued logic, rambled on, struggling for understanding. Something had happened that he could not explain. I too felt mystified.

Not until almost seven years later, April 13, 1992, when I stood beside Dan's coffin, leading his funeral service, did the meaning come to me. As I read Dan's obituary, I learned that he was eighty years old—the exact age Daddy would have been. My mind flashed back to all the times Dan had taken my sermons seriously enough to engage me in theological discussions, as I often longed to have with Daddy if he had been living. Now I saw clearly. Daddy had come to me through those discussions. And Daddy had delivered a message to me through Dan at my ordination: "I may not be able to help you that much, but I'll help you all I can." I could give no rational or theological explanation, but I knew. I felt in the depth of my soul that Daddy had sent these words. He had been at my ordination in a way more palpable than through my memories of his cheering support and his familiar words, "Jann, I was busting my buttons!"

I had studied and experienced enough in pastoral counseling to recognize psychological transference when I saw it. Dan was not Daddy. I knew that. In spite of the similarity in age and in some personality traits, they were more different than alike. What I'd experienced couldn't be explained only in psychological terms. Nor as reincarnation. I believe Daddy spoke to me through Dan at my ordination. In the years since, I'd had other numinous experiences of Daddy. He had come to me especially in those trembly times when I took some unpopular stand. There were also times when I needed his help and didn't feel it. I pondered the metaphysical meaning of the words, "I may not be able to help you that much, but I'll help you all I can." What limits are placed on those in another dimension of reality? What lines are drawn between dimensions?

Giving 'Em Hell with a Feminine Flourish

In those early years as a minister in Waco, I had to spend more time on challenges in this world than on wondering about lines between worlds. In my part-time positions as executive director of the Waco Conference of Christians and Jews and counselor at Samaritan Counseling Center, as well as in my full-time job as associate pastor of St. John's, I often found myself bumping up against conventional walls. My personality has always leaned toward avoiding conflict, but my strong convictions on social issues kept me speaking out. Brett, still in his unself-conscious preteens and a child of my feminist-awakening years, could celebrate this side of me more than Chad and David could. Brett enjoyed his friends' comments about my frequent statements in the *Waco Tribune*. One of Brett's friends gave me the label "Waco's Give 'em Hell Minister."

An article in the *Waco Tribune-Herald,* November 21, 1987, almost two years after my ordination, quoted me along with five other clergywomen in our local ecumenical Women in Ministry organization. I spoke openly about the hostility I'd experienced from some male ministerial students at Southwestern Seminary: "At seminary some of these guys wanted to get me into an argument, to prove myself scripturally." I attributed the hostile attitudes to the growing fundamentalist movement and to competitiveness in the ministry. In this article, in contrast to the one published just after I'd accepted the appointment at St. John's, I used the terms "pastoring" and "preaching" in reference to myself. And I condemned the bind that women preachers often feel from cultural stereotypes: "Being emphatic in preaching is seen as trying to copy men. Being quieter is seen as being too meek." I spoke out more strongly than before about the importance of breaking down divisions among faith groups and about the richness I'd experienced through ecumenical relationships. My appearance, along with my words, had become a little freer. In the picture that accompanied this article, I wore a plaid skirt and a solid jacket, instead of a suit. I let out my natural curls around my ears and my neck. But my blouse was still buttoned up to the top, with a half-male tie around the collar.

Less than a year later, August 15, 1988, in a picture with a Q&A article in the *Waco Tribune,* I wore a dress with a lace collar, and my hair waved softly over my forehead and ears. I had entered the woman-is-powerful phase of feminism—comparable to the black-is-beautiful stage of the civil rights movement—claiming the value of my feminine self instead of trying to mimic men. As my appearance grew softer, my words became stronger. The editors of the *Tribune* interviewed me for this article because of my position as director of the Waco Conference of Christians and Jews. In the article, my answer to one of the editor's questions boldly challenged religious institutions to integrate: "It's past time for churches in Waco to integrate. I think for churches and synagogues to preach on justice and equality, that we're all God's children, and to have all segregated churches and synagogues is hypocrisy." To a question concerning religious tolerance and intolerance, I answered: "I don't believe there should be intolerance for different interpretations of the Bible. But I have preached that there are some things we should not tolerate—racism, sexism, injustice of any kind." A sidebar with the article listed personal information about me, and noted that a famous person I most admired was Barbara Jordan.

Debating the Ordination of Women

That summer of 1988 I emphatically called for the ordination of women in an article in a national Baptist publication, *Baptist History and Heritage*. Several months earlier I had debated Dorothy Patterson on this issue at the annual meeting of the Southern Baptist Historical Society in Nashville, Tennessee. Dorothy, an intelligent woman with a doctorate in theology from New Orleans Baptist Seminary, epitomized the traditional female role of "power behind the throne." Her husband, Paige Patterson, along with Houston lawyer Paul Pressler and Dallas First Baptist Church pastor W. A. Criswell, had begun the fundamentalist takeover of the Southern Baptist Convention, but many people believed that Dorothy orchestrated the movement from behind the scenes. It seemed strangely contradictory that a woman with so much leadership ability and theological education would spend her energy advocating against full participation of women in the church. The contradiction reminded me of the articulate lawyer Phyllis Schlafly, who traveled all over the country lecturing women to stay home.

The debate with Dorothy Patterson took place in a large meeting room in one of the imposing buildings of the national Southern Baptist headquarters. David and I had flown to Nashville the evening before. I felt pleased that David had come to support me, but also anxious as I thought of his being in the audience when I delivered my confrontational message. We arrived early to learn the order for the debate. I was scheduled first to read my paper "Why I Believe Southern Baptist Churches Should Ordain Women," and then Dorothy would read her paper, "Why I Believe Southern Baptist Churches Should Not Ordain Women." We had twelve minutes each. Although we had read each other's papers prior to the debate, we were to make no rebuttal of each other's points until both of us had finished. Then the audience could direct questions to us, and we could respond to them and to each other.

I sat on the platform beside Dorothy, a tall, big-boned woman who wore a high-necked, long floral-print dress with her hair pulled back in a bun under a wide-brimmed hat adorned with pink and yellow flowers. Dorothy always wore a hat as a sign that she submitted to male authority, just as the Bible told her to do, she said. I felt small and shaky as I listened to the moderator introduce me.

When I stood at the pulpit and looked out at the sea of male faces, my knees shook so hard I felt I might collapse. I was glad that I'd chosen for this occasion what Brett called my "power suit": a tailored teal jacket with a straight black skirt. My voice began softly and tentatively but gained power as I referred to the biblical story of Gamaliel, who counseled religious leaders not to hinder the apostles' work because "if it is of God, you will not be able to overthrow them. You might even be found opposing God!" I swiftly drew the parallel, "Southern Baptists cannot overthrow the ordination of women because it is of God." I moved confidently into my theological arguments, heavily buttressed with scriptural passages.

Also appealing to Baptist history, I cited examples of Baptist women preachers in England as far back as 1646 and told of a leading Presbyterian minister's accusing Baptists of tolerating "she-preachers." In eighteenth-century America, Eunice Marshall had suffered imprisonment for not obeying an order to stop preaching. When I spoke of history's providing many more "examples of Baptist women who have felt so strongly the call of God that they surmounted formidable cultural obstacles to answer that call," I felt, in the grandiosity of that moment, that I might be one of those women. Inflamed by my passionate conviction in the rightness of my position, I delivered my concluding call to action.

As in the issue of equality of the races, Southern Baptists have failed to take a prophetic stand on the equality of men and women. Not only have we failed to be a redemptive force in society, but also we have impoverished our churches by placing restrictions on the ministry of women . . . over half our members. If we follow the steps of Christ and of our Baptist forebears, we will repent of past sins and ordain all women, along with men, whom God calls to ministry.

Dorothy clapped along with the audience and gave me a strained smile as I sat back down beside her. She rose and walked slowly to the pulpit, adjusting her hat and putting on her glasses. Instead of beginning with her paper, according to the agreed-upon procedure, she couldn't refrain from making several impromptu comments about my paper. She questioned the legitimacy of my biblical interpretation and the orthodoxy of the theologians I referenced. And then in the midst of her paper, she made an offhanded comment about "women whose need for power led them to seek positions in denominations other than Baptist." It was obvious that she wanted to discredit me by implying that I was not a true and loyal Baptist because I had taken a pastoral appointment in a Methodist church. Inside I seethed, but I tried to sit there on the platform looking pleasant and professional.

Sweat started trickling down my back as Dorothy proceeded to muster all the biblical passages traditionally interpreted to exclude women from ordination. She spent the longest on a few verses in 1 Timothy that state that women should "learn in silence with full submission" and should not "teach or have authority over a man." These verses had fueled the 1984 Southern Baptist Convention resolution against the ordination of women, and as I listened to Dorothy expound on them, I wondered if she had written that resolution. In my paper I had commented on the 1 Timothy passage, using what I believed to be responsible contextual and historical principles of biblical interpretation. I said, "Those who take the statement concerning women's silence in church as an eternal principle must also take as a literal command for all time the preceding statement forbidding women to wear braided hair, gold, pearls, or costly attire." As I remembered making this point, I looked up at Dorothy and noticed, with satisfaction, that Dorothy wore several large strands of pearls. But I couldn't tell if anyone in the audience had made the connection.

My irritation grew as Dorothy went over her allotted time, continuing even after the moderator called "time" twice. Because I had worked diligently to shorten my paper so that I could read it in the prescribed twelve minutes, I felt it unfair for Dorothy to go on for almost twenty minutes. Some people in the audience looked perturbed as well.

An earnest young man directed the first question to her: "Dr. Patterson, if you believe, as you stated so strongly, that women are not to teach or to have authority over a man, why is it that you have come here today to teach us, an audience of mostly men?"

"That's a good question," she began. "I've come here only by the permission and under the authority of my husband, Dr. Paige Patterson. By the way, he regrets very much that he could not be here today, but he gave me permission to speak to you. As you probably know, I wear this hat as a symbol of my submission to the authority of my husband." I could see David on the back row of the auditorium about to burst out laughing. Others also looked tickled.

One man asked me why I had taken a position in a Methodist church, but I could tell by his tone that his question was not so much a challenge as an invitation to defend myself against Dorothy's charge. Confidently I answered that although I'd like to have an opportunity to pastor in my Baptist tradition, my call to ministry took precedence over denominations. He responded by lamenting the loss of talent and creativity Baptists suffered by excluding women from ministry. Many people in the audience nodded in agreement. Even though this was not a formal debate, with judges of who won, I could tell that the audience leaned in my favor. But I realized, sadly, that this group, so open to my message on the ordination of women, did not represent the majority of Southern Baptists.

After the program, Dorothy and I exchanged polite compliments. Then she opened her Bible to Genesis and redoubled her efforts to prove that, from the beginning of creation, God had ordained women's subordinate role. I had to admire her tenacity; she had not succeeded in convincing that audience, but somehow she still believed she could convince me. I countered that hers was only one interpretation of the passage and proceeded to reiterate mine. Pointing adamantly at the verses, voice rising, she insisted, "But this is what God says, right here! Can't you see?" As we went back and forth, I glanced up and saw David waiting patiently, a big grin on his face. I finally broke loose from Dorothy and walked back to meet David. He laughingly said, "I can't believe you stayed down there trying to convince Dorothy."

"She kept trying to persuade me that her interpretation was not an interpretation at all, but the literal word of God, and that's scary! But she did invite me to come to her home in Dallas."

"Maybe she wants to hold you captive!" David quipped.

Baptizing Brett

David continued to grow in his support, or to "adapt," as he often called it. But it would have been more difficult, I knew, for him to accept my new vocation if I were pastoring a Baptist church where he had membership. With me at St. John's Methodist and in community ministries, he escaped the unconventional label of "preacher's husband." And Chad and Brett, I was glad, did not have to be "preacher's kids." A teenager, Chad understandably had found it easier to tell his friends that his mom taught college English. When Brett asked me to baptize him at Seventh and James Baptist Church, Chad questioned, "Why don't you just let Dan Bagby baptize him?" I replied, "Because Brett wants me to." But I felt for Chad as I remembered how embarrassed I'd been as a teenager by some of the things my mother and daddy did.

As in most Baptist churches, the baptistry at Seventh and James stands in a prominent place in the sanctuary. The placement of the baptistry symbolizes a distinctive Baptist doctrine: believers' baptism by immersion. At Seventh and James the baptistry rises high above the choir loft at the front and center of the sanctuary. The baptistry includes a large basin about six feet deep, ten feet long, and six feet wide, and, rising above it, a twelve-foot-tall stained glass window depicting John the Baptist baptizing Jesus. Several weeks after I'd begun as associate pastor at St. John's Methodist, Pastor Jay Beavers asked me if I would bring in the baptistry at the service the coming Sunday. Shocked, I exclaimed, "You've got to be kidding!" I had images of carrying some massive structure, the only "baptistry" I'd ever seen. When he showed me the small baptismal font, I laughed and teased, "Oh, you call that a baptistry." But I knew that, as I had begun to expand my images of God, I needed to broaden my experience of spiritual symbols.

Before Brett's baptism, I went to the pastor's dressing room behind the baptistry. I had heard Daddy describe the "waders" he wore under his white baptismal robe to keep his pants dry while performing baptisms, and had laughed at stories of his clomping out before a congregation in waders to wait for the baptistry to fill up with water. But I'd never seen waders. Dan Bagby, the pastor of Seventh and James, had graciously offered his waders to me. I knew Dan was over six feet tall, but the black rubber waders hanging in the dressing room looked to me like the boots of the giant in "Jack and the Beanstalk." I had to sit on the floor and lay the waders down in front of me to slide my legs into them and then take several big jumps to stand up. When I pulled the waders up, they came to my armpits. I tried to fasten the suspenders over my shoulders, but they kept falling down. When I tried to walk, I had to take several steps to move an inch. If Chad and his friends had seen me, they would have thought me weird indeed. With frustration I decided that I would just have to get wet, and I struggled out of the waders. I knew that since ordination certificates for women had only recently become available, it would be a while before I could expect waders for women.

When I stepped into the baptistry, my stomach and knees quivered. But my voice grew strong as I declared that the ritual of baptism symbolized the reality of God's grace and proclaimed the mystery and miracle of the resurrection. While Brett and I stood in the baptistry, David and Chad stood at the pulpit reading Brett's statement of the meaning of this experience for him. Then I baptized Brett in "the name of our Creator, our Redeemer, and the Holy Spirit." Brett, almost as tall as I, helped by bending his knees and leaning back into the water, so that I didn't have to bear all of his weight. Even so, I got almost as wet as Brett.

The symbolic water held transforming power for me just as surely as for Brett. The water flowed through my being, restoring my hope in new life. I stood there suddenly aware that I was the first woman ever to perform this holy ritual in that baptistry, and that I had spoken a new word from that high place, changing the traditional Trinity (Father, Son, and Holy Spirit) to an inclusive Trinity (Creator, Redeemer, and Holy Spirit). Instead of being upset that I'd changed the sacrosanct Trinitarian formula as I had feared they might be, people with tears in their eyes told me how profoundly moved they were by my presence and my words in the baptistry. Then Brett, Chad, David, and I hugged, and the experience of grace felt complete. By including David and Chad and me in his baptism, Brett brought us all together in a new bond of loving acceptance.

West Texas Cowboy Preacher

At St. John's United Methodist Church I led a Sunday night series on expanding images of God to include the feminine. For several years I had been studying this subject, now getting up each morning around 5:30 to write for a little while before dressing for work. Only my passionate belief in the urgency of my message got me staggering up at that dark hour to sit in front of our small Apple computer, working on the manuscript that would become *In Whose Image? God and Gender.* Pat McClatchy, at that time pastor of St. John's, wholeheartedly supported my Sunday night series. The congregation, at first, seemed to welcome the discussion of inclusive language. Like some of the Seventh and James congregants at Brett's baptism, some in St. John's expressed a deepening of their spiritual experience through a new naming of the divine. But others felt torn between their positive feelings toward me and their discomfort with my teaching. They spread the rumor that "Jann's been infected with some liberal Methodist theology. She's too sweet to have those ideas." I found it curious that they blamed my "liberal" infection on their own Methodist denomination.

In the first two sessions of the series, I had delineated numerous biblical references with feminine divine images. The third Sunday night I explored applications of inclusive theology to equitable human relationships. At the conclusion of this session, one man rose, visibly agitated, and demanded, "You do believe Mary was a woman, don't you?"

Surprised by such a question, I answered, "Why, of course."

"The Bible says she's a virgin, so God has to be a man," he continued smugly, as though he had just solved the riddle of the Sphinx.

I stood there before the small congregation gathered in the chapel, too flabbergasted to reply. Had I heard him correctly? I looked back at the third pew where he still stood, waiting, a man in his sixties. I might have expected such literalism from a ten-year-old.

Finally I stammered out something about God's mysterious, miraculous work unlimited by our experiences of human sexuality.

Helen Danzeiser rose more boldly to counter the comment about Mary and God: "That's ridiculous! That sounds like something out of Greek mythology—Zeus copulating with some mortal woman to get her pregnant. Surely our theology has progressed beyond that. If you can believe in a virgin birth, you don't have to conjure up some kind of male God to take the place of a human man, do you?"

The next day Pat McClatchy said to me, "If I, an old West Texas cowboy rancher preacher, could understand what you've been saying about new ways to talk about God, then I don't see why everybody else can't. I couldn't believe that guy who said God had to be a man because Mary was a virgin! My grandson would know better than that. But you and Helen set him straight."

Messages of Life's Transience

Helen Danzeiser participated in the senior adult growth group I led at St. John's each Tuesday. One morning the group gathered in the church parlor to discuss a book on medical ethics. The issue of individual choice in health care stimulated the most energy. In the midst of the conversation, Helen bluntly announced, "I've just been diagnosed with cancer, and I've decided not to have chemotherapy." Everyone in the room, except her husband Dan, sat shocked by this news. To me, Helen had always seemed larger than her slight 100-pound weight and five-foot height. Now as I stared at her, she looked frail. I fought back tears, as I tried to offer words of hope and support. She had been one of my biggest supporters, not only on inclusive language, but on enrichment projects for neighborhood children and every other project I'd initiated at St. John's. Others in the group began to implore her to undergo cancer treatment, telling her stories of people they knew who'd done well with chemotherapy. I struggled between my desire for her to do everything to fight the cancer and my respect for her personal choices. Helen went on to tell the group that her doctor had explained that there was only about a twenty percent chance that chemotherapy would extend her life and that it would, of course, have side effects. She had chosen quality over quantity of life, just as we'd been discussing.

One of her good friends replied, "That was different when we were talking about some abstract ideas in a book. But this is your life we're talking about now. We can't just sit by and let you do nothing about the cancer!"

Adamantly, Helen replied, "Why is it that all our lives in church we've talked about how wonderful heaven is and then when it comes time to go, everybody tries to hold me back? We all know that this life's not all there is, that there's something out there so wonderful we can't even imagine it—that's the faith we celebrate every Sunday. This life's only a breath, only a fleeting moment compared to eternity."

We all sat still and silenced by Helen's eloquent sermon, not wanting to dispute it but longing, nonetheless, to hold her here on earth. Suddenly, the church secretary, Paula, burst through the door, yelling, "The space shuttle just exploded! I heard it on the radio." It was January 28, 1986, around 10:40 A.M., by our time, an hour later at Kennedy Space Center. The *Challenger* shuttle exploded just seventy-three seconds after liftoff on its historic mission with the first school teacher to fly in space. Paula brought a radio to the church parlor for us to hear the news reports of the explosion. After our initial exclamations of disbelief, we all gathered solemnly around the radio. A surrealistic feeling enveloped me. There could have been no more graphic illustration of the words Helen had just spoken on the transitoriness of life than this tragic accident. I felt a special affinity for Christa McAuliffe, the enthusiastic teacher-astronaut, and for Judith A. Resnik, who in 1984 became the second woman in space. Both were about my age and had also chosen nontraditional paths. That evening as I watched the images on television—of these two women and the other five crew members, pulsating with life and exuberance, smiling and waving as they got on the space shuttle, and then of them all, only moments later, vanishing in giant puffs of smoke in the sky—I knew the truth of Helen's words. But, like the others in the St. John's group, I didn't want to face the transience of this life.

Helen remained alert and assertive and active until about

a week before her death. She lived longer than anyone expected, even without chemotherapy. Her funeral had an air of unreality, much like that January day when she had announced her cancer and the *Challenger* shuttle had exploded. As I gave the eulogy, comparing Helen to Deborah and other strong biblical women, I could feel her presence and hear her voice, proclaiming, "There's something out there so wonderful we can't even imagine it."

Proud to be a Baptist Woman Preacher

On June 11, 1988, I challenged those gathered in San Antonio, Texas, for the annual meeting of Southern Baptist Women in Ministry to "imagine what is yet to be" in this world, instead of the next. I'd felt honored, but scared, by the invitation to preach at this national gathering. Since Martha Gilmore's ordination, when I'd vowed to support women in ministry, I'd been attending these annual meetings. At my first meeting I applauded the courage of ordained Baptist women, like Nancy Hastings Sehested, who preached so passionately about the importance of following God's call in spite of opposition. But I couldn't imagine myself preaching.

As I stood that Saturday morning in June of 1988 at the pulpit of Manor Baptist Church in San Antonio, surrounded by people looking eagerly at me, I began, "A little girl wrote God, 'Dear God, what's it like to die? P.S. I just want to know. I don't want to do it.'" I confessed that the first time I went to the ordination of a woman I had "just wanted to know what a woman minister was like. I didn't want to be one." But I stood there, I said, "a woman minister, in a prophetic role." Continuing my sermon entitled "Prophesy by Faith," I urged all gathered that morning—more than 150 women and about 20 men—to see themselves as prophets.

We are all prophets because we can imagine what is yet to be. We all come today with prophetic visions. I envision the day when Southern Baptists recognize that God distributes gifts according to grace, not gender. When women and men stand side by side in ministry, including the pastorate. When we see women and men serving equally on all our boards and agencies. When we can go to Southern Baptist Convention meetings and thrill to the rich harmony of male and female voices from the pulpit as well as the choir. When we can open a state Baptist newspaper and see pictures of women as well as men, and read stories of women using their gifts in the ministry. When we can walk into any Baptist church and be greeted by deacons, female and male, black and white. When we teach our girls that they are just as truly in the image of God as boys.

This statement of my visions appeared almost verbatim in the *San Antonio Express-News,* the *Fort Worth Star-Telegram,* the *Waco Tribune-Herald,* and the *Baptist Message.* I felt especially gratified that the *Message,* the weekly newspaper of Louisiana Baptists, ran the story and referred to me as "Jann Aldredge Clanton, a native of Minden." For many years Daddy wrote a column called "Parson to Person" for the *Baptist Message,* and when he died, both the editor and the associate editor wrote glowing eulogies. I hoped that people who read the article on my sermon at the Women in Ministry meeting would recognize me as Truman Aldredge's daughter and would see me as following in his prophetic footsteps. The *Baptist Message* story also quoted my statement that "the very existence of Southern Baptist Women in Ministry is prophecy—a challenge to male domination." When I read this story, I gained hope in the fulfillment of one of my visions—that state Baptist newspapers would publish stories on women using our ministry gifts.

On Sunday night following the Saturday morning I'd preached, my friend Libby Bellinger delivered a sermon called "Going Home by a Different Way" to the Southern Baptist Forum. Libby, one of the few other ordained Baptist women in Waco, had been a model and confidant to me. In addition to serving as chaplain for Waco's Inner City Ministries, Libby was president of Southern Baptist Women in Ministry. The Southern Baptist Forum had begun several years before to provide a moderate alternative to the fundamentalist Southern Baptist Pastors' Conference. Along with Southern Baptist Women in Ministry, these two groups met that weekend before the Southern Baptist Convention began on Monday. While the Forum ostensibly affirmed the equality of women and men in the ministry, Libby was the only woman preaching at the Forum.

A full-bodied woman, Libby stood confidently in her hot pink suit at the pulpit of First Baptist Church, San Antonio, preaching to a crowd of around 3,000. From where I sat, near the back of the center row of pews under the balcony, I could see three Libbys—the flesh-and-blood Libby on the center stage and two much larger images of Libby projected on screens set up on both sides of the imposing sanctuary. There could have been no more powerful feminine image than this trinity of Libbys, bold and bright pink, preaching in that holy place. Libby declared, "Now, it is a miracle that I'm here tonight to preach this word to you. I should be silent if some people have their way, but the age of change is blowing through our convention. It is a spirit of change that is going to require us to go home by a different way." Libby alluded to the Magi's going home by a different way to keep King Herod from finding and killing the baby Jesus, and referred to a James Taylor song about this event. She called on the congregation to resist "the Herods in our midst" who seek to destroy Baptist traditions such as priesthood of all believers and the autonomy of the local church. Libby made me proud to be a woman preacher.

No Escaping Labels

For many months St. John's had been making plans to merge with two other smaller inner city Methodist churches. The merger plans included the appointment of new ministers to the newly formed Central United Methodist Church. The bishops' cabinet reassigned Pat McClatchy to a church in Brownwood, Texas. Since I was not an official Methodist minister, I knew I would not be automatically reappointed. The district superintendent, now Ed Otwell, came to my office at St. John's to encourage me to begin the process of transferring my ordination to the Methodist denomination, as Martha Gilmore had done several years before. Then I could be appointed to pastor a Methodist church. I understood Martha's changing denominations and seriously considered transferring to the Methodist denomination, so that I could pastor a church. If I remained Baptist, there might be no ministry opportunities for me. I could not stay at St. John's after the merger in September of 1988.

I struggled with this decision about denominations for several months. I still believed my call was much larger than Baptist or Methodist or any denomination, remembering the woman at St. John's who told me after I preached my first sermon, "Labels don't matter anyway." But I knew that I couldn't escape a denominational label if I wanted credibility as a minister.

Either Mother's constant prayers that I would return to the Baptist "fold" or the stories Methodist clergywomen told me of inequities they also suffered led me to seek a ministry within my Baptist tradition. When we first moved to Waco, the director of pastoral care at Hillcrest Baptist Medical Center had told me there were no openings for chaplains. But now, the time was right for Hillcrest and for me. No more than a week went by between the time I left St. John's and the time I learned I had a chaplain's position at Hillcrest. I got the bonus of the month of October off to get ready for my new job. Since St. John's paid me through October, I never missed a month's paycheck. In November of 1988 I became the first female chaplain at Hillcrest.

Members of St. John's gathered in Fellowship Hall to give me a send-off party and a tall oak bookcase with a gold plate at the top with this inscription: "In Love and Appreciation, St.

John's United Methodist Church, September 25, 1988." My voice cracked as I tried to express my gratitude to these dear people. In just three years they'd taught me more about being a pastor than I could ever learn in a seminary. They gave me abundant affirmation and opportunities to preach, to conduct funerals, to perform weddings, to lead worship, to teach, to develop urban ministry programs, even to test out my budding feminist theology. I felt sad to leave these people and also to leave local church ministry. Thank God, no one asked me why I was leaving the ministry, as some of my chaplain friends had been asked. They'd explained, with some frustration, that chaplains are just as much ministers as pastors of local churches and that in fact this specialized ministry required even more preparation—Clinical Pastoral Education in addition to a seminary degree and ordination. As a chaplain, I would still be a pastor, but with a hospital instead of a church as a parish. I could still marry, bury, preach, lead worship— all the pastoral functions I'd been doing. Even so, I left St. John's with mixed feelings.

Several months later, across the top of the front page of the religion section, the *Waco Tribune-Herald* ran this headline: "FEMALE CHAPLAIN ADDS VITALITY TO HOSPITAL." Underneath was the subtitle: "CLANTON BROADENS MINISTRY AT HILLCREST." David teased, "You're not that broad!" The newspaper article quoted the director of pastoral care as saying that Hillcrest had not hired a female chaplain before because "there just haven't been that many qualified people." How often women, along with minorities, have heard that justification. It disappointed me to read his statement. Religion reporter Sandra Gines added: "Testing sex stereotypes is not new to Clanton, who said she was the only female chaplain while training at Baylor." Gines quoted me on the importance of women and men working side by side in ministry to break down gender stereotypes: "We need to realize that women can be strong as well as tender, and men can be tender as well as strong."

Posing for a Pathfinder Award

Also in November of 1988, I received the Waco-McLennan County Pathfinder Award in Religion. The awards banquet, sponsored by the YWCA, took place on November 14 in the Barfield Drawing Room of the Bill Daniel Student Center at Baylor University. I felt proud when I read this description in the program: "Pathfinders are outstanding women from the Waco-McLennan County area who have distinguished themselves as being 'first' in their chosen field, having shaped their surroundings so that other women may follow in their path." The program cited me as the first woman to serve as chaplain at Hillcrest Baptist Medical Center and the first woman executive director of the Waco Conference of Christians and Jews, a position I was glad I could keep when I began work at Hillcrest.

The YWCA organizers of the banquet asked the recipients of Pathfinder awards to come several hours early to practice. I couldn't understand what there was to practice, so I arrived only an hour early. When I entered the large meeting room on the second floor of Baylor's Student Center, I found, to my amazement, women taking turns walking up to a platform on the arms of county judges serving as escorts and then standing and smiling under the glare of bright spotlights while large slides of themselves were projected on a screen behind them and a narrator read a script of their accomplishments. For a moment I thought I had stumbled into the wrong place. The scene before me looked like some strange combination of style show and beauty pageant. When I saw that most of the other women wore semi-formals, I felt underdressed in my tailored navy blue dress.

After dinner Vivian Castleberry, women's editor of the *Dallas Times Herald* for twenty-eight years and founder of Peacemakers, addressed the gathering, and I forgot about my attire. Vivian spoke about Peacemakers' recently completed project, "Global Peace—From Vision to Reality: An International Women's Conference," which drew into Dallas 2,000 women from all over the world. I sat mesmerized by her passion for creating a more peaceful, just world. I jolted to the announcement that it was time for the presentation of Pathfinders, but was glad that we went alphabetically by categories instead of by names and that my category was "Religion."

My turn, however, did come, and I, like some demure debutante, took the arm of my escort, Judge Ray Matkin. I stood on the platform in the blinding spotlight for what seemed hours as slides of me in various ministerial roles flashed across the large screen behind me and the narrator read a script based on an interview I'd given several weeks before. I tried to smile and stand daintily, as I'd been taught as a teenager in a Mr. Lynn modeling course I'd won as runner-up to Miss Minden. But an overwhelming feeling of incongruity came over me as I heard the narrator read the statements I'd given the interviewer. On women generally: "We have a long way to go before there's justice and equality for women." On women in the ministry: "It's biblical, it's right for women to be ministers. Beautiful things can happen in a church when women are in positions of leadership." On Baptists: "Baptists should be among the first to accept women in the pulpit because of our theology of the priesthood of all believers—but, we're not." On Waco: "Waco would be better if it gave more attention to the inequities of opportunities and salaries for women, and it would be better if the churches did what is long overdue—integrate." It seemed as if this program, planned by and for women, inadvertently perpetuated inequities by disconnecting women from our voices. Why couldn't I have preached my own words instead of having to pose while someone else read them?

"Rose Among the Thorns"

Being the first or the only woman often felt more like a burden than an honor. I soon learned the wisdom of the advice of one of my Methodist clergywomen friends, "You don't have to accept every invitation to preach or to sit on some committee. I used to think that if I didn't accept, then women wouldn't be represented. But I soon learned that I can't be everybody's woman."

Shortly after I became chaplain at Hillcrest Baptist Medical Center, I became the only woman pastor at the monthly meetings of the Waco Baptist Pastors' Conference. Hillcrest chaplains hosted these luncheon meetings in a banquet room at the hospital, so I couldn't get out of attending. At my first Pastors' Conference, I learned that the few other women in the room were secretaries or wives of pastors. The moderator of the conference introduced me: "I want ya'll to meet the rose among the thorns. Please stand up, Jann. This is Jann Clanton, a new chaplain here at Hillcrest. She sure does improve the looks of the chaplaincy staff around here, don't you think?" Everyone laughed and applauded, as I stood blushing and praying that my beeper would call me to some hospital emergency. Month after month, at the Pastors' Conference, I had to listen to the moderator comment about me as "the rose among the thorns."

I found a way, however, to stop one pastor from calling me "darling" or "baby," whenever he saw me at the hospital or at the Baptist Pastors' Conference. One day he walked into our Pastoral Care Department office, and in front of the other two chaplains and the secretary and several other pastors, I called him "darling" first. They all laughed, while he blushed. From that day on he called me Chaplain Clanton or Dr. Clanton.

"Like an Abused Woman"

My ambivalence toward my Baptist tradition did not go unnoticed by Rex Lewis, the facilitator of my interview for membership in the College of Chaplains. Learning that Hillcrest Baptist Medical Center required chaplains to be certified by the college, I sent in my application materials and scheduled the interview. I had not relished this additional professional hurdle to leap. But I'd heard that this certification process wouldn't take as much effort as what I'd put into

Clinical Pastoral Education and American Association of Pastoral Counselors. So I confidently drove down to Brackenridge Hospital in Austin for the College of Chaplains interview.

I found the drab, windowless meeting room, and met the two women and two men who formed my interview committee. Rex, the chair of the committee, read his summary of my background and pastoral theology. Then Sister Sigrid Simlik jumped in: "I could tell from reading your theory of ministry that you've explored feminist theology. Would you talk to us about ways you're integrating this theology into your pastoral care?" She had offered me the golden scepter, and I felt free to speak the truth I was discovering. I talked about the writing I was doing on Feminine Divine images and the ways I had brought this theology into my work as chaplain. Barbara Holloway, a Baptist woman serving as chaplain in another Austin hospital, enthusiastically joined in our discussion, encouraging me to complete my book. Visibly agitated during this conversation, Rex finally broke in with a question to me: "So why are you still Baptist?"

Startled by this non sequitur, I hesitated. "I . . . I don't . . . I don't quite follow you."

"Let me try to clarify," he continued. "You're obviously quite steeped in feminist theology. So how can you be a Baptist and a feminist?"

"Well, you see, Baptists have always valued soul competency," I began, trying not to sound as shaky as I felt. "That is, individual freedom of conscience, in other words, the priesthood of all believers—a major Baptist tenet—means that I have the freedom to interpret Scripture," I continued, giving biblical references for Feminine Divine images and quoting feminist theologians, hoping that he would not point out that none of them were Baptist.

Rex interrupted, "You're just like an abused woman who won't get out of a marriage. That's why you stay Baptist!"

Blood began to rush to my face, and I could feel myself on the verge of tears. Sigrid and Barbara tried to take the interview in a different direction, and Dan Fry, the other committee member, offered a few words of support. But Rex kept goading me for a response to his accusation.

All I could say was, "Well, that's not how I see it."

The interview ended abruptly. Rex asked me to leave the room while the committee voted on whether or not to recommend my certification as a "fellow" in the College of Chaplains. Outside the room, I tried to tell myself that membership in the college really didn't matter that much to me and that surely I could convince the administration at Hillcrest that I didn't need it. The irony of having to become a "fellow" to be legitimate at Hillcrest hadn't escaped my notice.

When Rex called me back in the room and told me that the committee had voted unanimously to approve me, I felt dazed. Driving back home to Waco, I played over and over in my mind his words, "You're just like an abused woman who won't get out of a marriage." I continued trying to develop justifications for staying Baptist. Also, I tried to tell myself that Rex was probably just a disgruntled Baptist or perhaps jealous that he had been left out of the conversation on feminist theology. But the words "you're just like an abused woman . . . like an abused woman . . . like an abused woman" reverberated from my head to the pit of my stomach, where they sat like stones. I knew I had a long way to go to explain to others, as well as to myself, how I could be a feminist and a Baptist.

Back at Hillcrest Baptist Medical Center, now a certified chaplain, I found myself more and more reluctant to wear the label "Baptist." When patients asked my denomination, I diverted with the response, "I minister to people of all faiths." Some would question, "Are you ordained?" When I said "yes," they'd press on, "Well, what denomination ordained you?" Cornered, I'd confess, "Baptist." I never said "Southern Baptist." My resistance to owning my Baptist tradition was often justified. Some people, either with a tone of curiosity or criticism, would say, "I didn't know Baptists ordained women." Others put on me all their negative impressions about Baptists, especially about the wrangling between fundamentalists and moderates. Even worse, some people sighed with relief, assuming that, even though a woman chaplain, I wasn't one of "those liberals." Since I was Baptist, they thought that I must share their conservative viewpoints on all manner of issues like abortion and homosexuality.

Denial Accommodates Feminist Pursuit

In spite of David's ambivalence about my growing feminism, I pressed ahead. Like many genteel Southerners who never learned to deal directly with conflict, David and I glossed over the tension. Denial, I knew, had helped other Southern marriages survive, but usually at the expense of wives. I learned, however, to use our avoidance to accommodate my feminist pursuit. I just plowed forward, putting my energy into my work without stopping to ask David how he felt about it. And he rarely told me how he felt—that is, not directly. One day while I was working on *In Whose Image? God and Gender,* I left to run some errands. At the top of our Apple computer screen were my words: "To speak of God in masculine images alone is unbiblical and idolatrous." When I came back, I found these words underneath, "But it's true!" I laughed, but twinged inside as I felt David's discomfort with my ideas underneath his joking.

Along with his humor, David would say that his flexibility helped.

Many times David has said that he's been adapting to me throughout our marriage. I have to admit that he married a traditional Southern woman who at first told him when he came into the kitchen, "Thank you, but I don't need any help." David thought he was marrying a teacher, not a preacher. And when we married, neither of us had ever heard of feminism. It's true that I did more of the changing, and he the adapting to my changes. I usually refrained from telling David the ways I'd adapted to him, because I felt so grateful for his "live and let live" attitude. His mother says that the reason all three of her sons have such "sweet dispositions" is that she rocked them so much when they were babies. Evelyn now has at least one rocking chair in each room of her house and four on the front porch. Maybe that's why, in her eighties, she still has a healthy disposition and body despite a steady diet of sour cream and onion potato chips, Rocky Road ice cream, and Popeye's fried chicken.

Reactions to *In Whose Image? God and Gender*

My book *In Whose Image? God and Gender* came out in the fall of 1990. *Waco Tribune-Herald* reporter Douglas Wong interviewed me over the phone about it. Without asking permission from anyone, I sat in my office at Hillcrest Baptist Medical Center and talked freely "on the record" with Doug. In my unquenchable idealism, I believed people would be convinced of the truth of my words and turn from their patriarchal ways. The two-column picture accompanying Doug's article shows me holding up a copy of the book close to my beaming face, as if to say, "Love me and my book! We'll change your life for the better." Many people probably thought I looked too congenial to be espousing any radical ideas. Others understood the implications of my words: "The thesis of the book comes from Genesis 1:27; male and female are created in God's image. If male and female are in God's image, then God's image must include the female." Several people called the director of the Hillcrest Pastoral Care Department with complaints. Instead of talking directly to me, they wanted a man to get me back in line, just as the pastor of Calvary Baptist had talked to David rather than me about the feminist book I'd given him.

What worried me more than any complaint about my theology was this inaccurate quote in the newspaper: "Although giving God human characteristics makes him a more tangible figure, Clanton said, it also limits God." I had stopped calling God "him" five or six years before, and certainly wouldn't have used this masculine reference when talking about my book that advocated gender-inclusive language. How could Doug Wong have missed my point? My grandiose, naive notions about my book's changing the world began to confront the reality of millenniums of worship of a masculine deity. Doug thought he heard me call God "him" because that's all he'd ever heard. It discouraged me to hear friends, family, Sunday School groups of many denominations who had studied the book—even those who said they loved it—continue to call God "He." One woman even told me she enjoyed my book "In His Image"!

I received the most enthusiastic response when I taught *In Whose Image* to a large Sunday School class at Seventh and James Baptist Church. This group of people prided themselves on their open-mindedness and progressive ideas. But some of them became the staunchest opponents of inclusive language in the worship service. They wanted to learn about inclusive theology at 10:00 A.M. but not practice it at the high holy hour, 11:00 A.M. I soon discovered that theological reasoning could go only so far, that the resistance to change came from deeply ingrained emotions. These feelings still lodged in me, even years later after much more writing and advocating of feminist theology.

One night I dreamed I had a diagnosis of cancer, and I prayed, "Okay, I'll call you 'Lord' or 'Father' or whatever, if you'll just heal me." When I woke up, I felt dismayed over this dream prayer, but more aware of unconscious fears of questioning traditional male authority. Later, Sue Monk Kidd brought increased recognition through these words in *The Dance of the Dissident Daughter:*

> Thousands of years of repression, hostility, and conditioning against a Divine Mother have made a deep impression on us. We've been conditioned to shrink back from the Sacred Feminine, to fear it, to think of it as sinful, even to revile it. And it would take a while for me to deprogram that reaction.

In Whose Image may not have made instant converts, but it did stir some controversy in Waco. Another article in the *Waco*

Tribune, titled "War of Words," lined up several ministers on the side of inclusive language and several against. United Church of Christ minister Paul Kluge's opposition to inclusive language obviously came from his belief in male superiority: "If we just look around at the world, the whole of our world's development is patriarchal. And when I say that, I mean with critters also. The male of the species, it doesn't make any difference if it's worms or coyotes or man, there's a certain innate gift." Richard Freeman, pastor of First United Methodist Church, opposed inclusive God-language with this more sophisticated but convoluted statement: "To change the gender of God is to misunderstand that God does not have gender anyway." Reporter Sandra Gines chose Presbyterian pastor Trish Holland, Baptist pastor Roger Paynter, and me to speak for inclusive language. Gines quoted Trish's article published in *Journal for Preachers:* "Inclusive language affects the way females perceive their own worth. I wish to challenge a 'carelessness' in references to God as male." Roger told of his experience of a worship service conducted by women ministers using all feminine imagery. He said, "I found myself feeling excluded. I could identify with how women might feel having to translate the language from masculine terms to encompass the feminine."

In my interview with Sandra Gines, I was more outspoken than in the one with Doug Wong just after *In Whose Image* came out. I had begun to wonder if I had been too conciliatory, like a good Southern woman; perhaps this was why people had not taken my book seriously enough. In fact, in one Presbyterian class where I'd taught the book a man even asked, "You don't mean we have to change our worship language, do you?" So in this *Tribune* article I didn't mince words:

> Inclusive language is a justice issue, just like racial inclusiveness. Exclusive masculine language devalues females by ignoring them. Women receive the message that maleness—because it's used for references to human beings in general and to God—is worthy of greater respect than femaleness. ... I believe it's unbiblical and idolatrous to refer to God

as exclusively male. ... The tragic thing is that on racial equality and gender equality, the church has followed secular society rather than being a prophetic voice.

My friend JoAnn Bristol, a social worker at Hillcrest Medical Center, immediately championed my book. She said it made her embrace her full power. JoAnn was already one of the most powerful women I knew, but I celebrated the idea that my book could help her feel even stronger. A tall, big-boned woman with a copper Afro that stood out about four inches all over her head and a voice like Barbara Jordan's, JoAnn commanded attention. JoAnn did everything with great gusto and originality. For example, she kept two Vietnamese pot-bellied pigs in her back yard, flew me to San Francisco to perform her marriage ceremony to Jim Pettit under a giant red-wood in Muir Woods, swept into my office one day and completely redecorated it in less than an hour, came to our house and pulled old pictures out of closets to transform our den, and gave me her discarded purse to replace one with peeling plastic I'd had for years. Sometimes I thought she saw me as her "project." After she read *In Whose Image,* she said, "Jann, I knew there was a wild woman under your sweet Southern Baptist facade; I could tell by the gleam in your eyes. Now she's out!"

Whether I chose to be "out" with everyone around the hospital or not, JoAnn loved to introduce me by saying, "This is one of our chaplains who calls God 'She.' Isn't that great?" When JoAnn had back surgery, she asked me to come to the "holding area" to pray with her. At this time I'd just begun to explore the biblical image of *Sophia* (Greek word for "Wisdom"). JoAnn asked me to pray to Sophia for her physician. When he came by, she said that I'd asked Sophia to guide him. He looked perplexed and then stammered, "Oh ... *sophos* ... philosophy ... oh yes, thank you."

By this time David had left Baylor University and developed his own public relations business, but he still had mostly Baptist agencies as clients. Although he tried to be supportive,

In Whose Image evoked fears in him—fears of my losing my job and of his losing business, as well as other fears he never named but I could sense. On an intellectual level he agreed that God is all-inclusive, but he couldn't understand why I made such a big issue of gender-balanced language. In spite of his close relationship with his mother, he resisted any naming of God as "Mother" or "She." He seemed shocked when I got upset over his beginning a prayer in church with "Our Father."

"You're just being too sensitive," he said.

"When I hear you pray like that, I feel you're negating everything I stand for, and giving the message to people at church that they don't have to take me seriously," I countered with voice beginning to crack.

"Are you telling me how to pray? I don't tell you how to pray."

"I bet you would if I began a prayer in church with 'Our Mother,'" I snapped. My anger dissolved into sadness that I'd set out to change the world and couldn't even change those closest to me.

David surprised me that Christmas with a tape of jazz singer Bobby McFerrin's *The 23rd Psalm,* which begins:

> *The Lord is my Shepherd,*
> *I have all I need.*
> *She makes me lie down in green meadows,*
> *beside the still water She will lead . . .*

These powerful words, sung with haunting beauty by McFerrin, helped move the Divine Feminine from my head to my soul. Whether or not David understood my feminist mission, the gift of this music, more than anything else, helped me see that he was trying. Most of all, it convinced me that he respected my spiritual journey. It reminded me of his gift of *All We're Meant to Be,* which began my feminist awakening, and of his earlier statement, "Aldredge, you're Ph.D. material." At crucial times David had encouraged my growth, perhaps more than he realized or intended.

Others in my family supported me in various ways.

Without reservation, Anne celebrated *In Whose Image* and told her friends about it. Mother staged a book signing at Waldenbooks in San Angelo. She sent out hundreds of invitations to the event and sold books to her friends who couldn't come. When several people who read the book called with concerns, she tried to reinterpret my words to make them more palatable. But she did more than any single person to get the book out. She was an indefatigable agent, and I didn't pay her a dime. That Christmas Chad and Brett, along with their cousins David and DeAnne, recognized my book with a good-natured prank. Equipped with a video camera, they drove out to Sunset Mall in San Angelo on Christmas Eve. Like roving reporters, they stopped people for quick interviews, asking each one to deliver holiday greetings to a member of our family. Amazingly, many people cooperated. Chad, Brett, David, and DeAnne showed a copy of my book to the most macho-looking West Texan they could find, and told him what the book was about. Then they asked the man what he thought about it. He shouted into the camera, "Jann, I read your book, and I don't agree with a damn thing in it!"

Meeting Ann Richards

The previous Christmas, Chad had given me Ann Richards's book *Straight from the Heart,* with her autograph and this inscription, "To Dr. Jann A. Clanton, with thanks for your faith in me." Still tucked away in this book is another treasure—Chad's letter to Ann, written when he was a freshman at the University of Texas:

Dear Honorable Richards,

I hope that you will be able to sign this book to my mother, Dr. Jann A. Clanton. It is my Christmas present to her. We are from your hometown, Waco, Texas. My mother has followed you throughout your political career, and has been a very vocal supporter of yours. She especially loved your speech at the Democratic National Convention; I believe she even videotaped it. You truly are an inspiration to my mother as well as to many other Texans. I appreciate your time in signing this great book.

Sincerely,
Chad A. Clanton

Ann Richards had indeed inspired me to political activism. A native of Waco, she was treasurer of the state of Texas and a contender for governor. Her quick wit and bold stands on social issues won my allegiance. Also, it was exhilarating to see a powerful woman running for office.

In October of 1990 Ann spent several days of her gubernatorial campaign in Waco. She spoke at chapel-forum at Baylor University, her alma mater. Although her audience was largely Republican, Ann received rousing applause, even to her pro-choice statement, "I don't believe that government has a right to dictate to us whether we bear children."

The next day I met Ann Richards at Indian Spring Park on the banks of the Brazos River. She had just delivered a speech, less formal than the one she gave at the Democratic National Convention but equally impressive. She included the famous line from her convention speech: "George Bush was born with a silver foot in his mouth." I didn't want to call Ann my "role model," because this label sounded trite. I'd grown tired of being asked, "Do you see yourself as a role model for women in ministry?" But Ann's influence on me caused me to reconsider the value of models for women. She gave me a feeling of power and confidence in myself as a woman trying to speak out for change. Tough and feminine at the same time, she turned her gender into an asset whenever anyone suggested it might be a liability.

I loved what she said about women at the beginning of her Democratic National Convention speech: "If you give us a chance, we can perform. After all, Ginger Rogers did everything that Fred Astaire did; she just did it backwards and in high heels." Her Southern charm and colloquial expressions helped people to hear even her most controversial statements. She might have chuckled to know that I saw her as a woman preacher to emulate. Persuasively and playfully, like the biblical Lady Wisdom, she delivered her liberating message.

That day at Indian Spring Park, Ann Richards stood in the band shell, surrounded by hundreds of people on tiptoe to catch every word and gesture. Her white suit and matching white hair accentuated her eyes, deep blue and sparkling like the Brazos River flowing along the park. My friend Sally Browder and I had nudged our way to the front of the crowd. After her speech, Ann moved among the people, shaking hands. Sally pushed me toward her, encouraging, "Go on, Jann, you've been wanting to meet her. Now's your chance." I wove in and out of people until I came to Ann. I reached out tentatively and shook her hand, mumbling some words of support and gratitude for her signed book. Then came a spontaneous, quick embrace, followed by my saying, "Ann, God's on your side." For a moment our eyes met, and we smiled knowingly at each other. Then together we declared, "Yes, She is!" Sally stood close by, snapping pictures of us. But even more than the photos, I have treasured the ringing memory of those words we spoke in unison, "Yes, She is!"

Inaugural March

Several months later, Ann Richards became the first female governor of Texas since Miriam ("Ma") Ferguson had come to the office in 1925, after her governor husband was impeached. On January 15, 1991, I took a day off and went to Austin to join more than 20,000 cheering supporters marching with Ann up Congress Avenue to the Capitol for her inauguration. The joyous "People's March" symbolized Ann's pledge to "reclaim this Capitol for the people of Texas."

Early that morning I left Waco for Austin, along with my good friends Sally Browder, Libby Bellinger, and Nancy Chinn. We arrived around 9:00 A.M., thinking we had plenty of time to get to the march that began at 10:00. But cars and marchers already thronged Congress Avenue and the surrounding streets. By the time we found a parking place and ran almost a mile to the site, the march had already begun. We missed seeing Ann walking behind a marching band from Edgewood Independent School District. Later, we got a glimpse of her, radiant and waving, after she'd climbed onto a horse-drawn surrey. The morning sky overhead was as blue as Ann's eyes.

News media swarmed through the marching crowd. A reporter from a Waco TV station came toward us, shouting, "Anyone here from Waco?" Sally and Libby called out, "We're from Waco." And pushing me toward the reporter, they said, "Interview her!"

The reporter asked what should have been obvious from looking at me, "How do you feel about being part of this historical occasion?"

"This is one of the most exciting days of my life! It's electrifying, the energy in this crowd! I'm so thrilled to be part of this! Ann makes me feel that anything's possible. I believe she's going to make some important changes in this state—changes in education and changes that help disadvantaged people. She makes me so proud to be a woman and a Texan and from Waco." Sally, Libby, and Nancy joined my cheer, "Yea, Waco! Yea, women!" I continued, "I think this march is the greatest idea; it demonstrates Ann's belief in the people's participation in government. She's just marvelous! She gives us all hope." I kept raving on, until the reporter finally cut me off.

The crowd grew thicker and thicker. I felt as though my feet had left the pavement and I was being carried forward on a triumphant wave of people. Someone knocked my black purse off my shoulder, and when I stooped to get it, I got shoved under for a moment. When we reached the Capitol, I couldn't get close enough to see Ann, but I heard her inaugural address amplified by loudspeakers around the Capitol grounds. I clapped and cheered when she declared, "Today, we have a vision of a Texas where opportunity knows no race or color or gender—a glimpse of what can happen when we open the doors of the government and let the people in. Tomorrow, we must build that Texas." Chad, now in his second year at the University of Texas, met me on the Capitol lawn holding two box lunches he'd stood in a long line to buy. We sat down on the grass, watching the squirrels play and listening to the rest of the inauguration while we ate our barbecued beef sandwiches and coleslaw.

The next day one of my Waco friends said, "I saw you interviewed on TV . . . Were you on steroids or something? I've never seen you so charged up."

A few months later I sent Governor Ann Richards a copy of *In Whose Image,* with the inscription: "Congratulations! She is indeed on your side! I will continue to pray for you." I received a personal thank-you note from Ann, in which she wrote: "Thank you for sending me the autographed copy of your book, *In Whose Image? God and Gender.* This was a thoughtful gesture and I appreciate it very much. I also appreciate your words of encouragement and support and most of all your prayers."

New Year's Resolution

The victory of Ann Richards recharged my idealism. She made me feel that I could make a difference. In my roles as director of the Waco Conference of Christians and Jews and president of the Waco Ministerial Alliance, I had opportunities, at least locally. Along with Mayor Charles Reed and district judge Bill Logue, I was featured in a New Year's Day *Waco Tribune* article entitled "CITY OFFICIALS TACKLE WEIGHTY RESOLUTIONS for 1991." The article recalled my resolution printed in the paper the year before: "The Rev. Jann Clanton . . . resolved in 1990 to spend more time praying, studying and writing." The reporter pronounced that I had met this "resolution in a big way," as my book *In Whose Image? God and Gender* had been published and I was writing a book for children. I gave this resolution for 1991: "to do more with the Waco Ministerial Alliance and the Waco Conference of Christians and Jews to make peace in the community and help eliminate poverty, sexism and racism." I wonder if I thought about what I'd say the next year if asked whether or not I'd kept this grandiose resolution.

Against sexism, I continued to speak and preach on inclusive theology. The children's book I was writing, *God, a Word for Girls and Boys,* encouraged gender and racial inclusiveness. Against poverty, I led the Conference of Christians and Jews in a tour of Caritas to inspire support of this local agency that gives assistance to the poor. Also, I was one of the chairpersons for the Caritas annual fundraising dinner, "A Feast of Caring." I worked with the Human Rights Committee to challenge McLennan County's bail bond system that discriminated against indigent people. Against racism, I led the Ministerial Alliance in sponsoring Martin Luther King, Jr. birthday rallies. I worked with the Conference of Christians and Jews on a Hispanic issues seminar. At one Ministerial Alliance gathering, I gave a speech in which I stated that the church, instead of following its mission to bring justice, has too often perpetuated racial inequities.

More controversial was my opposition to the annual Cotton Palace Pageant because of its racism. The pageant had become an institution in Waco, which in the nineteenth century was the home of the largest cotton industry in the world. But the pageant celebrated a time in Waco's history when slavery was an accepted practice. Myrtle Thompson, president of the McLennan County NAACP, called the Cotton Palace Pageant "insulting and insensitive to many African Americans." A *Waco Tribune* article, "PAGEANT GLORIFIES REPRESSION, SOME LEADERS SAY," published the day of the 1991 pageant, included this excerpt:

> "I think it is historical in nature and way past its time," said Jafus Cavil, a Waco Independent School District trustee, who is black. "I think it lends nothing to bringing people

together. It just reinforces where we are presently on a two-track existence, and that some people would like to keep it that way. ... It has a negative consequence, just like the Confederate flag. I understand how people need to keep their heritage, but they need to be sensitive to the fact that it does hurt people."

"While I appreciate efforts to preserve our history, the Cotton Palace Pageant focuses on a time in history that important groups in our community cannot celebrate," said the Rev. Jann Clanton, president of the Waco Ministerial Alliance. "As we continue to work to heal and to build race relations, I believe we should move beyond the Cotton Palace Pageant to an event that celebrates the rich heritage of our ethnic diversity," said Clanton, who is white.

Many white supporters of the Cotton Palace Pageant didn't appreciate my speaking against it. The pageant, first held in 1894, is still part of the Brazos River Festival each year.

The Inclusive Worship Community

In 1989 I had joined a small group—including Sally Browder, David Stricklin, Trish Holland, Debra Woody, David Woody, and Betsy Ritz—to initiate a worship community committed to gender and racial inclusiveness. To make our mission clear, we began by calling ourselves the "Alternative Worship Community: intentionally integrated, deliberately inclusive in language, and open to all people." Soon we dropped this unwieldy title and became simply the "Inclusive Worship Community." We met early on Sunday mornings to accommodate those of us who remained active in other faith communities. We attempted to do what Rosemary Radford Ruether advocates in *Women-Church: Theology & Practice*: "Women-Church means neither leaving the church as a sectarian group, nor continuing to fit into it on its terms." But in our hasty enthusiasm for inclusiveness, we had skipped over Ruether's step of a separate community for women to analyze our own specific problems with patriarchy and to develop our own empowering rituals. Unrealistically, as I'd later discover, we thought we could accomplish gender and racial equality all at the same time.

The Inclusive Worship Community met for about a year in the sanctuary of Central Presbyterian Church, predominantly white and socially active, where Trish Holland served as associate pastor. We began getting pressure from some of the church leaders, ostensibly because we didn't always vacate the sanctuary in time for preparations for the church's morning services. But the criticism became more intense after I'd led worship in this church, praying to "Our Mother-Father who art in heaven." I'd overestimated the church's open-mindedness.

We moved to the predominantly black St. Luke African Methodist Episcopal Church. The pastor, Walter McDonald, having discovered the importance of black images of deity through the study of black liberation theology, also acknowledged the need for Feminine Divine images. In a meeting of the Inclusive Worship Community he expressed his identification with an image of Christ as a raped woman. "The entire African-American race has been raped," he lamented. "We've experienced some of the same emotions. Like raped women, I've gone through denial for the sake of survival and then anger from recognition of the violence." He read from one of Rosemary Radford Ruether's books the story of a rape victim's compelling vision of Christ as a crucified woman:

> As she lay transfixed by this vision, an enormous relief swept over her and she realized that she would not have to explain to a male God that she had been raped. God knew what it was like to be a woman who had been raped. . . . Just as women have been able to experience themselves in the crucified rabbi from Nazareth, men must be able to experience Christ in the raped woman.

By the trembling in his voice, I knew that Reverend McDonald did enter into this experience.

We'd hoped that the move to St. Luke AME would increase participation of African Americans in the Inclusive Worship Community. But only a few came. Debra Woody, an African-American sociologist and one of the founders of the Community, had trouble convincing other African Americans that inclusive sacred symbolism was vital to racial and gender justice. The majority of black women and men, she said, dismissed it as a white middle-class women's issue. Again, my idealism had led me to believe that the Inclusive Worship Community would draw us all together to work on common causes of freedom and equal opportunity. I thought there would be many others who, like Reverend McDonald, had experienced the spiritual impact of inclusive images and also understood their political significance. He told me how appalled he'd been when he heard the St. Luke children's choir singing,

> *Who's that dressed in white?*
> *It must be the children of the Israelities.*
> *Who's that dressed in black?*
> *It must be the hypocrites turning back.*

He identified with my struggle to introduce female divine imagery into the church because of the difficulty he was having trying to persuade St. Luke to change from white to black pictures of Christ. It seemed ironic that many African Americans wanted only white sacred symbols, just as so many women clung to masculine symbols. Now I better understood one of the poignant lines I'd memorized from Lord Byron's "Prisoner of Chillon": "My very chains and I grew friends."

The Inclusive Worship Community also labored toward the feminist ideal of breaking down hierarchies. "Constructing a church liberated from patriarchy will require the dismantling of clericalism," wrote Rosemany Radford Ruether, and we agreed. So we had no paid leaders, and we encouraged everyone to take leadership responsibilities. But in reality, the ordained clergy did more of the worship leadership. It was hard for the laypeople to see their gifts as equally valuable. And it was hard for the clergy, including me, to let go of control. I welcomed different styles of leadership and various worship forms, like liturgical dance and guided meditation. The hardest thing for me was when several of the worship leaders continued to use only masculine God-language. Then I felt the conflict between our mission of inclusive language and our mission of inclusive leadership. And I became over-responsible. I wrote six pages of practical guidelines for using inclusive language and gave this document to everyone in the Inclusive Worship Community. But I resisted becoming the inclusive language patrol. I wanted everyone to take responsibility. After several years, and after Sally Browder and some of the other founders moved, our goal of shared leadership seemed even harder to realize. If I didn't lead the services, I had to find someone else to do it. We had fewer people committed to the original mission of the Inclusive Worship Community, but I was determined to keep it going.

Moving On

I continued working with the Inclusive Worship Community, even after I left Hillcrest to become a chaplain at Baylor University Medical Center in Dallas in August of 1992. I commuted to Dallas for a year, so that Brett could finish his last year of high school in Waco and David could have time to move his public relations business to Dallas. It was David's turn to move with me, since I had moved with him to Waco. One of the ways we survived, even flourished, in our dual career marriage was to keep a high standard of fairness and respect for each other's vocations. If I attended business events with David, then he believed he owed me an equal number of appearances at my functions. Because of the time I spent becoming oriented to a new job and the time I spent commuting that first year I was a chaplain at Baylor, I dropped all my Waco activities except the Inclusive Worship Community. I felt strongly about keeping the

Community alive, even though some Sundays we had fewer than five in attendance.

Just as the *Waco Tribune-Herald* had marked the beginning of my ministry in Waco, it marked its ending. On October 5, 1992, the paper published an article headlined "WACO MINISTER CALLED AWAY." The subtitle read "CLANTON MOVING TO DALLAS TO FULFILL MINISTRY AS AGENT OF CHANGE." Some people might have been thinking instead, "Give 'em hell Minister leaving, yeah!" As ever, the paper quoted my lofty sentiments:

> I feel so heavily invested in Waco, but I believe this is something God has called me to do as a change agent. Everything I have been involved in here in Waco has been a part of this calling. And I want to express my hope that things continue to move forward here.

The article listed organizations I'd been involved with, followed by my statement that this participation "shows a desire for peace in the community and a wish to help eliminate poverty, sexism and racism." There they were again—the three big evils I battled. And just in case anyone remembered my 1991 resolution, I was on the record as having wanted, at least, to keep it.

Chapter Seven

The Power of Naming

A new name went with me to my new job at Baylor Medical Center. Now I was "Jann Aldredge-Clanton." I insisted that this name be inscribed on my chaplain's badge, in spite of many objections. The department secretary complained that this name was too long to get on the badge, as well as on department schedules. Some of my colleagues objected that "Chaplain Aldredge-Clanton" was too cumbersome to be used around the hospital. Also they worried that this hyphenated name might be construed as making a feminist statement, and get them as well as me in trouble.

At first David took it as a personal affront.

"What's wrong with 'Clanton'?" he challenged.

"Nothing. After all, I'm keeping 'Clanton,' just adding Aldredge."

"Why do you need to do that, after all these years?"

"You know I've been going by 'Jann Aldredge Clanton,' but the 'Aldredge' keeps getting dropped. And I want to keep that identity. How would you feel if you changed your name?"

"It's just going to cause problems. You'll wish you hadn't done this," David said in an ominous tone.

"This is the nineties, for heaven's sake! Look around.

Many women never change their names, and a lot more hyphenate them. If I hadn't changed my name in the first place, I wouldn't have to worry about all this." I felt myself getting irritated trying to justify myself.

The zealous opposition to the hyphen in my last name, like that to calling God "She," convinced me of its importance. I recalled responses I'd gotten to requests I'd made to balance masculine and feminine references to deity: "You're making such a big deal over a few words. The Creator of the universe can't be limited; He's above male or female." When I agreed and said that there should then be no problem referring to God as "She" as well as "He," I was met with strong negative reactions. No better proof could be found for the bias against the feminine and the need to overcome it by calling God "She." My hyphenated last name also carried power, more than I at first realized, to confront traditional discrimination against women. My colleagues were right. It was a feminist statement, and I was proud of it.

Years before, a woman at an English conference asked me when I introduced myself, "Is that your husband's name or your father's?" I stared at her as she laughed and explained, "I didn't take my husband's name, because I reject that symbolism. But then I realized I still had my dad's name. How can we ever get away from being owned by men?" Ann Ashworth, my major professor at TCU, had tried to escape by changing from her husband's to her father's name and then to her mother's maiden name. Now she had her grandfather's name.

As I was getting used to my new name, Jann Aldredge-Clanton, which I had to admit was a mouthful, I recognized the irony. In trying to reassert my own identity, I now had the names of both my father and my husband. But somehow, at least in my mind, the hyphen made the name my own. My father wasn't "Aldredge-Clanton," and David wasn't changing his name.

Perhaps the hyphen brought back to my personality the shy girl, Jann Aldredge, who had shrunk from public speaking while growing up. Or maybe it did have some mysterious power to reclaim my true nature: every time I take the Myers-Briggs personality test, I come out more introverted than extroverted. In Dallas I didn't get involved in community organizations like I had in Waco, and I stayed away from media attention. I felt drawn toward quieter ways of advocating change, like writing. In Waco I often preached in churches of many denominations when pastors were on vacation, but now I rarely accepted preaching invitations. In fact, I felt relieved that I hadn't been selected as pastor of several churches that had considered me.

Passed Over

At the time, I felt disillusioned and angry over inequities in the selection processes. A year before I took the job at Baylor, Lake Shore Baptist Church in Waco began to look for a new pastor. Several of my friends who were members of the church gave my name to the pastor search committee. The committee had agreed to consider women candidates, although the church had never had a woman pastor. Baptist churches select their own pastors, according to a cherished policy of local church autonomy.

I'd thought this process preferable to that of Methodist churches whose pastors come by appointment of district superintendents and bishops. But Methodist clergywomen told me the appointment method helped them get pastorates more quickly than if they had to wait for churches to be "ready" for a woman. Churches might resist a woman pastor in the abstract for years, but when a woman comes by appointment and begins ministry with them, she wins their support.

The chair of the Lake Shore Baptist pastor search committee called to ask if I were interested. Always wanting a new challenge, I said "yes." I sent my résumé to the committee. I had preached a few times at the church, so the committee didn't ask for a sermon. A few weeks later the chair of another committee to find an interim pastor for Lake Shore came to see me at

Hillcrest. Sitting in the cafeteria over coffee, he told me that I was his committee's first choice for interim pastor. I thought there'd been some mistake. I said, "Thank you, but maybe you didn't know that I'm being considered for pastor. Would that affect my serving as interim?" He told me he hadn't known that the pastor search committee had my name and that the church had decided to keep the roles of interim and permanent pastor separate. I declined the offer of interim pastor so that I could continue to be considered for the permanent position. As it turned out, the interim pastor became the new pastor.

The chair of the pastor search committee sat, red-faced and sheepish, in my office at Hillcrest trying to explain the situation. "I want you to know that the committee was very impressed with you and your credentials. We did consider you and other candidates. But the church had grown to love the interim pastor and voted for him to stay. We didn't plan for this to happen. I'm sorry if you've been hurt."

"The main reason I didn't accept the invitation to be interim was that I wanted to be considered as pastor," I said, trying not to sound too judgmental. He knew the process had been unfair to me and was trying to apologize. I took some consolation in the hope that perhaps I nudged the church a little closer to accepting a woman pastor. Ten years later, the church elected as pastor a gifted young woman, Dorisanne Cooper.

As I was considering the offer of a chaplain's position at Baylor, I also had my résumé with St. Charles Avenue Baptist Church in New Orleans. My friends Sally Browder and David Stricklin were now members of this church and had recommended me. One of the members of the pastor search committee, a medical doctor, called with excitement over my interest. She told me that the committee wanted a tape of a worship service I'd led, in addition to my statement of theology and mission. I quickly sent these to her, feeling a mixture of trepidation and exhilaration. The thought of breaking new ground as the first woman pastor still pushed my prophetic button. Then I waited and waited. After several months had passed, I began to get anxious. If I waited too much longer, the position at Baylor might not be open anymore. I called the physician on the St. Charles Avenue search committee.

She said, "I'm so disgusted with this process! So far the committee's considered only male candidates, even though we all agreed to give equal treatment to women. When I asked what they thought about you, no one had even seen your materials except me. And I was quite impressed. I'd given your tape and papers to the chairman to pass around. Just yesterday he told me he'd misplaced them. All this time I've been thinking you were being considered along with the other candidates. He hadn't even bothered to tell me he lost your materials so I could've asked you to send them again."

"Do you think it'd be worth it if I did? How much longer do you think the process will take?" I asked.

"It may be a while. And I can't honestly say you have a chance. It's clearly gender discrimination, although nobody will admit it. I know the chair of the committee doesn't want a woman pastor, and I don't think many of the others on the committee want to recommend a woman. I thought the church was ready, but I guess I was wrong. I'm sorry. I didn't mean to lead you on." I thought she was about to cry.

"I don't blame you. You did all you could. It's bigger, bigger than you or I," and my voice began to crack too.

I had told my ordaining council that I felt called to pastor a Baptist church someday and then laughingly added, "It may not be before I'm eighty." Confronting the realities of resistance even in these so-called progressive Baptist churches left me weary and discouraged. I wondered if I'd live to be eighty if I had to go through many more such experiences.

No Retreat from Controversy

I went to Baylor wanting a retreat from controversy and causes. Learning a new hospital and chaplains' policies took time. And here I was again, spending hours on I-35 between Waco and Dallas. I often played a tape Chad had given me of

Willie Nelson singing "On the Road Again." We didn't move to Dallas until June of 1993, after Brett had graduated from high school.

One of the big advantages of the job in Dallas, I knew, would be that it brought me closer to Anne. She had been living in Dallas for many years and was now director of psychology at Texas Scottish Rite Hospital for Children, not far from Baylor. We got together for lunch, though not as frequently as we'd hoped, and we talked on the phone several times a week. Our bond grew deeper as we discovered more similarities in beliefs and thought processes. We could talk for hours, without realizing the time, on questions like whether the universe is basically benevolent or malevolent. We concluded that, at least, having a close sister relationship was a great good.

I had been at Baylor only a few months when I learned that I had inadvertently stirred up trouble in the pastoral care department. Maybe my friend Trish Holland was right when she told me after I'd become a chaplain at Hillcrest, "Every time you walk in a room, you're inviting change. You don't have to say a word. Your very presence as a woman minister challenges tradition." My colleagues in the department knew my work as a feminist minister. Perhaps it was my very presence in the department that stirred things up. Or maybe it was the hyphen. Also, some of the chaplains didn't appreciate the way I edited their prayers in our pastoral care tracts. I'd assumed, wrongly, that requests for my editing meant that they wanted any suggestions I might offer. Some became incensed when I changed "He" and "Lord" to "God." In addition, there were grumblings when I began meeting with the two other women chaplains, Nancy Ellett Allison and Mitzi Ellington. Even though they'd been getting together before I came, I was accused of dividing the department along gender lines. Mitzi quipped, "One woman's a token, two are okay, but three women are a threat!"

We had a department meeting to deal with the conflict. It felt more like a trial with me as the defendant. Mitzi sat on my right, impervious and proud, looking like the guard at the tomb of the unknown soldier. I could tell she was determined not to react to anything anyone said. Nancy, on my left, started tearing up as the first accusation came my way.

"How dare you change my prayers! I didn't ask for your opinion."

"I thought, that is, you asked me to read the tracts and make editorial recommendations," I began defensively.

"Well, we weren't asking you to come in here and be the feminist monitor."

"I'm sorry . . . but I thought you welcomed any suggestions I might have; I guess . . . I suppose I was wrong . . ." I felt my confidence melting down into the floor as I fought back tears and anger at my new colleagues and at myself for apologizing.

"What if I want to keep calling God 'He'? You can't make me change."

"No, I can't. But I'd like for you to consider . . . the strong sanction that these masculine references give to the dominance of men. I thought you knew my deep convictions on this," I said, trying to keep my voice and my body from shaking.

The accusations continued, like volleys coming faster than I could dodge:

"You've come here trying to force your feminist agenda on our whole department."

"Yes, nobody asked you to do that!"

"And you're dividing this department. You're leading Mitzi and Nancy to follow your agenda."

"Yeah, I feel left out when you women have your exclusive meetings."

Mitzi left her guard to angrily interject, "Nobody's leading me anywhere. I'm the one who asked Jann to start meeting with Nancy and me. I wouldn't have minded if ya'll had wanted to get together and read *Fire in the Belly*. You guys meet with each other all the time for coffee or lunch or whatever. What are you so afraid of? Do you think we're plotting a takeover?"

"Well, I just know things feel different around here since Jann came. And I don't like it."

Now I'd lost all power to control my tears and my breathing. I felt suffocated and ashamed that I'd lost control.

Nancy came to my rescue, "Jann's just trying to bring us a word of liberation. Like Martin Luther King, Jr., she's suffering because of her efforts. Bearers of a new truth have always been persecuted."

I winced with embarrassment over Nancy's exaggerated defense, yet felt grateful for her support, along with Mitzi's. I don't remember saying much else for the rest of the meeting. Finally, after two hours, it ended. I went to my office and sobbed. I wondered if I'd made a big mistake in taking this job. Was it too late to go back to Hillcrest? We hadn't moved from Waco yet. I called Anne, and she came to my defense with the anger I couldn't yet express, "How dare them! They knew your beliefs before you came, and now they have the nerve to blame you for their own insecurities. It's about power, not theology, Jann. They're intimidated by you." My colleagues' reactions still perplexed me.

A Less Threatening Role

Just the year before, I'd led the Baylor chaplains in a retreat seminar entitled "Feminist Theology and Pastoral Care." On a cold January afternoon I had driven about three hours from Waco to the retreat at Kaleo Lodge, nestled in the piney woods of East Texas near Tyler. The next morning in a cozy meeting room with a glowing fireplace in the center, I sat in jeans and blue denim shirt with the Baylor chaplains—ten men and two women—gathered in a circle around me. They looked eager and receptive. Their good will radiated as I began with Linda Ellerbee's definition of feminism: "Feminism does not mean turning the tables on men, but throwing out all tables except round tables." And I quoted theologian Leonard Swidler: "Feminism is personalism extended to women, and is a constitutive part of the gospel of Jesus." Energized by the rapt expressions and nodding heads of my audience, I moved on to invite them to explore with me new ways of thinking and speaking about God, new forms of worship, new spiritual discoveries, and new ways of doing pastoral care.

For the next two days and through six sessions, the Baylor chaplains continued to respond enthusiastically to my presentation. They had read *In Whose Image? God and Gender* before coming to the retreat. Before that, most of them had never even thought about calling God anything but "He." At the retreat they seemed more open than I thought they'd be as we considered such topics as Feminine Divine images in Scripture, the ambivalence toward the feminine in Christian history, feminist theology and women, feminist theology and men, and new images for healing.

On the second evening I led the group in a consciousness-raising experience—a reversed worship service with all women leaders and all feminine language. I explained that while I advocated a balance of male and female in worship, reversing traditional patterns could help emphasize the need for change. Mitzi Ellington, Nancy Ellett Allison, and I led the men in litanies and Scripture readings, changing all the traditional masculine language to feminine. We even changed the Apostles' Creed to begin, "I believe in God the Mother Almighty, Maker of heaven and earth, and in Jesus Christ her only Daughter." We sang "Rise up, O women (instead of men) of God," "Glory be to the Mother, and to the Daughter and to the Holy Ghost," and "Wherever She leads I'll go." I glanced over toward the back of the meeting hall at one of the lodge managers clearing our dinner tables. She stood gaping at us as though we'd landed there from another planet. I looked out at the ten men standing in front of me, some at first snickering and others with a sheepish is-this-really-okay look on their faces, singing softly and tentatively but then growing louder and surer. Their harmonious baritone and tenor voices lifted in praise of the Feminine Divine filled me with hope and confidence.

After the reversed service, I invited the chaplains to talk about their feelings.

Mitzi began, "Wow! That was powerful! I felt fully, totally affirmed as a woman—more than ever. It was great to call God

'Mother' and 'Daughter' and 'She.' And also wonderful to hear the men call God 'She.' When I heard those male voices singing, 'Rise up, O women of God,' I felt they were saying, 'Go for it! You can do it!' In addition to needing strong sister support, I feel the need of male advocates. I experienced both in this service. Thank you."

"I agree," Nancy chimed in. "For once I felt fully included in worship. I've had some painful experiences of being denied leadership opportunities simply because I'm a woman. Calling God 'She' feels a little strange, but makes me truly feel that I'm created in God's image."

The male chaplains also expressed positive feelings about the reversed service:

"It was quite an eye-opener for me! I never realized how much masculine language is in our traditional worship services."

"No wonder women feel excluded. I certainly felt excluded by all the feminine language."

"At first I felt a little anxious, like I might get struck by lightning or something. Then I looked around and saw the other men participating, so I joined in. I'll have to admit it felt weird, but nobody got struck down and the roof didn't cave in."

"Yeah, it seemed strange and kinda funny to me at first. But when I started seriously entering into the service, I felt a sense of comfort and grace. I guess because of my good relationship with my mother, I like the image of God as Mother."

In the cafeteria line after the last session, one of the chaplains leaned over to me and asked, "How'd you feel your seminar went?"

"Oh, everyone seemed so responsive and receptive. It excited me to hear all of you talk about creative ways you plan to use feminine images in pastoral care."

"Don't think they're really going to change," he whispered. "They're just going along to be nice."

Idealistically, I responded, "Oh, I don't think so. This was one of the most open groups I've ever had. I believe all of you were sincere when you talked about changing divine imagery for our ministry of healing and justice."

"Well, everyone enjoyed talking about new ideas, but I just don't believe anyone's going to change," he repeated.

I didn't see the foreshadowing in this pessimistic pronouncement. If I had, I might have thought harder about accepting the offer the next year to go to Baylor. It was only after that painful meeting about my dividing the department along gender lines that I realized I was more threatening as a colleague than as a guest speaker. My presence in the department made it harder to ignore my call for change.

New Job, New Book, New House

In spite of my ambivalence and that of my colleagues, I settled into my new job at Baylor as one of the chaplain coordinators for oncology. As I led support groups for cancer patients, however, I began to discover the purpose in my coming to Baylor. The painful experience of Daddy's cancer translated into understanding of cancer patients and families. I could see how my theological education, pastoral training, and personal experience merged in this new specialized ministry. Somehow I would fit the feminist piece into this new setting.

God, a Word for Girls and Boys, completed in Waco, came out in the spring of 1993. The more resistance I had met to changing worship language and imagery, the more convinced I had become of the need to start with children. If all they saw in their Sunday School rooms were pictures of a white male God, it would be difficult for them to replace these images when they grew older. My friend Sally Browder told me that the masculine language of the church had already taken root in her three-year-old daughter Annie. One day Sally referred to God as "She."

Annie promptly corrected her. "No, Mommy, God is a He."

Sally replied, "God can be a She and a He."

Annie insisted, "No, Mommy, that's not right. God is a He. God is a word for boys."

This story gave me the title for my children's book while strengthening my resolve to provide religious education resources that encouraged gender and racial inclusiveness. I gathered up many of the children's sermons I'd given at St. John's, designed activities to accompany these, wrote prayers, hired Pam Allen to create illustrations, wrote and collected songs. Sally Browder had written two of the songs for the Inclusive Worship Community. One, called "Miriam's Tambourine," corrects the picture most children receive of Moses alone leading the children of Israel out of bondage. Sally's song shows that the prophet Miriam, Moses' sister, also led in the Exodus. Miriam celebrated the victory by leading all the women in playing tambourines and dancing. Sally wrote a bouncy tune for her words: "Miriam and her brother crossed the desert sand, leading all the people to the Promised Land. Miriam, shake your tambourine; Miriam, shake your tambourine; Miriam, shake your tambourine, and dance for the love of God." Making tambourines out of paper plates and jingle bells, Sally and the children of the Inclusive Worship Community frolicked around the church.

I gave each of my colleagues at Baylor a signed copy of *God, A Word for Girls and Boys*. Together we had worked through some of our misunderstandings. My colleagues gave me respect as a pastor, whether or not they agreed with all my beliefs. And I walked a fine line between speaking my truth and alienating them. Some of them told me how much they enjoyed reading *God, A Word for Girls and Boys* with their children or grandchildren.

Also that spring David and I began looking for a house in Dallas. We wanted to "downscale," in current lingo, or to "simplify, simplify," in the clearer language of Thoreau. We found a small house that delighted us from the moment Sue Ringle, our unflagging realtor, pointed to it. Hot pink azaleas in the front yard and baskets of ferns hanging on the porch greeted us. Two of the rooms could double as offices for David and me and bedrooms for Brett and Chad when they came home. Across the street from a luscious greenbelt, the house felt like a sanctuary away from the stress of job and big city.

Aftermath of Re-Imagining

Several weeks earlier, while Sue drove David and me around on a Tuesday afternoon to look at houses, I got a call on her cell phone from an editor with United Church Press. I'd been waiting for a response to a manuscript I'd sent. Wanting to make sure the editor could reach me, I'd given her Sue's cell phone number in addition to my work and home numbers.

As Sue drove up to a house with a "for sale" sign in the yard, I heard the editor say, "We really like your work on Christ-Sophia and want to move forward to publish it. We have some suggested revisions that we hope you can make in the next few months."

"Of course, I'll be able to do that. I look forward to working with you," I said as we got out of the car. Elated by the good news from the editor, the house Sue was showing us looked marvelous to me. I had to settle down a bit to see that it was really lackluster.

About a year after the publication of *In Whose Image? God and Gender,* I had begun a manuscript that I hoped would answer questions people had asked me about feminine references to God. The most often raised objection in Christian groups had to do with the gender of the historical Jesus. One of the Baylor chaplains at the retreat said that his main problem with including the feminine in his naming of God was his belief that Jesus and God are one and that Jesus was male. After I'd done seminars for several Sunday School classes at Seventh and James Baptist in Waco, the issue of inclusive language came up for debate at a Wednesday evening business meeting. The discussion became heated as some accused others of tampering with the Word of God and destroying the beauty of familiar hymns. The other side argued that inclusiveness was imperative for the egalitarian church they wanted their daughters and sons to grow up in. One church member walked authoritatively to the pulpit. He spouted out every argument he could muster against including Feminine Divine images in worship. Leaning over the pulpit with eyes glaring and finger wagging, he delivered what he considered the crowning blow: "And Jesus was a man! None of you can dispute that." At the retreat I attempted to give a complicated theological explanation, and at the business meeting I chose to stay out of the fray. Not until giving a seminar months later did I come up with a simple answer. An earnest woman asked, "You do believe Jesus is male, don't you?" I replied, "I believe Jesus *was* male, but I don't believe Jesus *is* male because I believe in the resurrection."

I went home and started a manuscript, which I tentatively entitled, "In Search of the Resurrected Christ-Sophia." I researched the biblical parallel between Wisdom (*Sophia* in the Greek language of the New Testament) and Christ. I discovered that New Testament writers linked Jesus Christ to Wisdom, a feminine symbol of deity in the Hebrew Scriptures. My study of church history revealed that the earliest Christian communities connected Jesus with Sophia to establish the divinity of Jesus. I saw the irony in current efforts, including mine, to support the divinity of Sophia by linking her to Jesus. My manuscript included worship resources from our Waco Inclusive Worship Community, along with the biblical and historical discussions.

Wanting to avoid what author and friend Miriam Therese Winter told me that publishers referred to as "sleeping around," I first approached Crossroad Publishing Company with my Christ-Sophia manuscript. I'd liked working with Crossroad editors John Eagleson and Pamela Johnson on *In Whose Image* and had also approached them with the children's manuscript. I learned that Crossroad didn't publish children's books, so I found Glad River Publications, which Bill Thomason had recently started as a moderate alternative to conservative Baptist presses. Bill did an outstanding job on my children's book, but the demands of another full-time job kept him from taking on many books. So I sent the Christ-Sophia manuscript to Crossroad, naively believing that since they'd published one of my books, they'd be overjoyed to get another. I got only a conditional acceptance. The editorial committee said that I had tried to do too much in one book and wanted me to drop the worship resources while expanding the theoretical portion. I didn't want to comply with this condition. I had come to appreciate more fully than ever the importance of ritual experience to bring change. Perhaps in my grandiosity I had tried to do too much. But knowing I might have only one chance with the people in the pew I was trying to reach, I wanted my book to include strong appeals to both head and heart. So I cast about for another publisher. Upon receiving the manuscript, an editor from the publishing house of the United Church of Christ denomination expressed interest. A few months later I received the exciting acceptance call on Sue Ringle's cell phone.

I'm not so naive as to believe a phone call equals a contract. But the publishing of my other books began with phone calls of acceptance. That summer I rushed to make revisions on the Christ-Sophia manuscript while scaling down and packing up to move from Waco to Dallas. Brett and I loaded books and magazines in the car and took them to sell at used bookstores. I gave Brett the incentive of splitting the proceeds. We also took piles of clothes to Goodwill and Caritas. Mother came to Waco to help with a garage sale. I've never seen a more consummate salesperson than Mother. She actually got money for old dishes and clothes that I planned to throw away. As I feverishly cleared out the kitchen, she called to customers, "Here she comes, bringing out more treasures!"

Within a few months of the cell phone call, I sent the revised manuscript to the editor at United Church Press, according to my promise. I expected to receive a contract shortly thereafter. Months passed. Every day I checked the mailbox for the contract. Finally, I called.

The editor explained, "I'm sorry about the delay, but the New Testament scholar who's reading the manuscript has such a busy schedule this fall."

"What New Testament scholar? I thought you told me you'd already accepted the manuscript," I said, trying not to let too much surprise and disappointment into my voice.

"Well, yes, that's right, but the editorial committee just

wants to make sure there are no theological problems. Don't worry; I'm sure everything will go just fine. But it may take a little longer than we expected."

"I thought you wanted to bring the book out soon, so I rushed to make the revisions you suggested. But I guess a little delay won't hurt." I didn't want to sound accusatory.

That fall I continued to wait for the contract. In September I had heard about a Re-Imagining Conference to take place in Minneapolis in November. Carolyn Bullard-Zerweck brought conference brochures to our clergywomen's meeting and told us she planned to attend. I liked the name "Re-Imagining" and the purpose of the conference—to explore theology from women's experience. But I didn't think I had the time or the money to go. When news from this global ecumenical event started breaking, I wished I'd gone. More than 2,000 people from forty-nine states and twenty-seven countries, representing nearly forty Christian denominations, participated in rituals that included Feminine Divine images. The celebration of Sophia especially resonated with my recent study. I would have loved to experience the hymns and litanies to Sophia. The Sophia ritual sparked the most media attention and the greatest fury of conservative denominational leaders. People who hadn't even attended the conference misconstrued reports and used the inflammatory phrase "goddess worship" to discredit it. The Re-Imagining Conference achieved such notoriety that *Christian Century* listed it among the top religion stories of 1993. One top official in the Presbyterian denomination lost her job because of her role in the conference.

Not until a cold, late afternoon near the end of January did I receive word from United Church Press. Trembling with anticipation, I opened the letter in my office at Baylor. My tears blurred everything past the first few lines: "I'm sorry that I can't report a better outcome after these months. But the New Testament scholar found some problems with your manuscript, and we will not be able to proceed with publication." By the time I got to my car I was crying so hard I had trouble seeing as I drove home. Without turning on the lights, I lay down, shivering and sobbing, on the couch in our den. I think David thought somebody had died when he walked in and saw me. I showed David the letter. Even though David had expressed his fear about my writing a book on Christ-Sophia, now he came to my defense and helped turn my hurt into anger over the unfairness of this rejection.

"That's just not right," he sympathized. "They told you they would publish your book, and now they've reneged after keeping you dangling for so many months."

"I never got a contract, and I was beginning to get worried. But I trusted the editor's word."

"There's more to this than she says in this letter. She's not telling you everything. Something happened that made the company pull back from publishing your book." David's words brought sudden recognition. United Church Press may have been scared off by the controversy over Sophia that had been brewing in mainline Christian denominations since the Re-Imagining Conference.

The next day I called the editor and asked her for a more thorough explanation. She hemmed and hawed and repeated what she'd said in the letter about the problems cited by the New Testament scholar. But these criticisms, I told her, seemed minor, and I could easily make revisions. She said no and wouldn't give me any more substantial reasons for the rejection. I'll always believe that the controversy in the wake of the Re-Imagining Conference influenced United Church Press to reverse its decision concerning my manuscript, even though the editor denied any connection.

I recalled lines Grandmother Hickerson used to quote from an old Scottish ballad called "Johnny Armstrong": "I'll lay me down and bleed awhile, then rise to fight again." In my memory Grandmother does more rising than bleeding, even through the loss of her son and husband and through ten years of pain from shingles. Like her, I couldn't stand to be down for long. I had to keep moving.

Rising Again

About a week after the rejection letter, I picked up my wounded confidence and started looking for another publisher. No matter what the United Church Press editorial committee said, I reconvinced myself that the manuscript had merit. I read back through it, pausing over passages I especially liked. In the same folder with the manuscript were letters giving me copyright permission for some of the worship resources. As I was flipping through the pages, the word "Mystic" jumped out at me like a figure in a children's pop-up book. I stopped to look at the letter. Twenty-Third Publications in Mystic, Connecticut, had given me permission to use a prayer from a collection called *Women's Prayer Services*. I hurried to the Dallas Public Library to find more information about this publisher. When I learned it was Catholic, I hesitated. Although the leading feminist theologians were Catholic, I doubted that many Catholic presses would publish their books. Twenty-Third was probably a traditional Catholic publishing house that would be no more open to my feminist christology than a Baptist publisher. But still, I felt drawn to Twenty-Third Publications. So I sent the manuscript to Mystic.

Less than two weeks later, I was standing at the work desk in the middle of our Pastoral Care Department office on a busy morning with chaplains scurrying around. One of the secretaries called to me, "Jann, somebody who says he's from some publishing company wants to talk to you." In a daze, I answered the phone.

"Hello, is this Jann Aldredge-Clanton?" a resonant voice asked.

"Yes, this is she."

"This is Tom Artz, one of the editors at Twenty-Third Publications. We received your manuscript, 'In Search of the Resurrected Christ-Sophia,' and our editorial committee is quite impressed with it. We would like to work with you to publish it as soon as possible. I would like to discuss with you a few suggestions for revision." From the tone of his voice and the preciseness of his enunciation I would have thought it was Ted Koppel from *Nightline*.

"Thank you for calling so promptly, Mr. Artz," I said, trying to get some of the Southern out of my accent while kicking myself for not getting the number from the secretary so I could call him back from my office where I'd have some privacy. "I'd like to explore possibilities of working with you as a publishing partner," I continued, in my most professional tone, but softly to keep anyone from overhearing.

"The main revision the editorial committee would like to see involves the structure. Instead of interspersing the worship resources throughout the book, what about pulling them all together in a separate section or an appendix?"

"The rituals are an integral part of the book, so I definitely would not want them in an appendix. But perhaps a separate section would work." I stopped short. Why had I jumped into this discussion of revisions so quickly? Hadn't I been burned so recently by taking an enthusiastic phone call as a promise of publication? I swallowed my fear and risked, "Before we talk any further about revisions, I'd like to have a contract from Twenty-Third."

"Of course, of course. I should have made that clear. We're sending out the contract tomorrow. You should have it within a week." He sounded trustworthy, but I still felt cautious. I hung up the phone and tried to hide, even from myself, the elation and apprehension that churned inside me.

The contract came five days later. *In Search of the Christ-Sophia: An Inclusive Christology for Liberating Christians* came out in the fall of 1994, even sooner than my original goal for publication. "A Catholic press publishing feminist theology written by an ordained Baptist woman—now that's a miracle!" a friend remarked. I knew she was right. Fundamentalist Baptists often use belief in miracles as a test of faith. It might surprise them to know that I can pass this test. I do believe in miracles.

My experience with Twenty-Third had gone beyond my explanations and expectations. Tom turned out to be the best of editors for my book—thorough, flexible, and insightful. Over the phone and through the mail, we negotiated revisions that undoubtedly improved my manuscript. Tom remained accessible and encouraging throughout the process. I had thought that only a female editor would understand my purpose and only a liberal Protestant press would touch my book. But just as I had labored in the book to open people's minds, my own thinking expanded in the publishing process. I felt I had been guided to Twenty-Third. On my own, I wouldn't have picked Twenty-Third as my publisher or Tom Artz as my editor. My mystical experiences tend to come when I'm exhausted from my own efforts, but keep going anyway. So it was with my finding the Catholic press in Mystic, or its finding me.

Woman as Healer Conference at Baylor

As I made the revisions on *In Search of the Christ-Sophia,* I helped plan a regional conference called "Woman as Healer." I worked with my chaplain friend Nancy Ellett Allison and physician friends Margaret Christensen, Sandy Steinbach, and Renee Woods to set up this conference at Baylor. It delighted me that even with one of our stated program objectives being the identification of feminine images of God to empower women healers, we gained support from our Pastoral Care Department and from Baylor's administration. In fact, Nancy and Margaret persuaded the CEO to allot Baylor funds to the conference. He did raise questions so Nancy asked me, "Now what are some of those Bible verses with the feminine images? Refresh my memory." Nancy satisfied Baylor's CEO to the point that I had freedom to bring Mother God, Sophia, Ruah, and other Divine Feminine images out of the closet and into the large conference center at Baylor Medical Center.

Jeanne Achterberg, author of the book *Woman as Healer,* came all the way from California to be our keynote speaker. Some of Baylor's oncologists expressed reservations about Jeanne's coming to Baylor because of their skepticism about her book *Imagery in Healing* and her previous work in Dallas with Stephanie and Carl Simonton, who had stirred controversy over their use of visualization with cancer patients. Jeanne began the conference with an overview of the history of women healers, beginning with ancient cultures in which belief in the Great Goddess prevailed. She demonstrated that in those times when the deity had a feminine or androgynous nature, women were able to exercise the healing arts with freedom. Slides of ancient goddess statues accompanied her lecture. Moving around in her long, flowing purple silk dress and golden hair, Jeanne looked like a goddess. I sat there marveling as goddess pictures flashed large and bold on the slide screen in Baylor's Davis Auditorium. Jeanne went on to lament the holocaust of women healers condemned by patriarchal religion as "witches" during the sixteenth through the eighteenth centuries, and the subordination of women healers by the dualistic approach to medicine begun by the Scientific Revolution. Nobody had screamed out in protest yet, so I breathed a little more freely as I anticipated my presentation.

At the beginning and between speakers, Sandy Steinbach, petite and charming, flew around the room like Tinker Bell, spraying lavender and rose aromas. We wanted to create a different atmosphere from that of many of the dry, sterile medical conferences we'd attended. We had planned for this conference to stir the senses as well as the mind, drawing on the wide variety of women's healing gifts. The auditorium overflowed with rainbow arrangements of flowers. Also at intervals throughout the day, the live music of harp and violin filled the room.

Invigorated by Jeanne's words and the lovely setting, I rose to give my presentation entitled "Wholeness and Power for the Healer." I looked out and saw Anne beaming at me, and I knew I could deliver this message. Before the gathering I had practiced my presentation, making sure I could handle the mikes and the slide equipment. Out in the lobby Anne and Bev, one of her friends who is a biofeedback therapist, heard my voice projecting out from the auditorium. Bev gave Anne a shocked look and said, "That's your voice! But you're standing right here!" Anne too was startled that my voice sounded so much like hers. Our connection seemed to be growing closer in every way.

I began my presentation by telling a dream I'd had one night about leading a group of women of diverse races and ages, gathered in a circle in a meeting room at a large church. I felt deep satisfaction as we shared our joys, pains, and visions for wholeness. Down the hall were our children—babies, toddlers, and preschoolers. Several older adults were caring for them. Somewhere in the midst of our meeting, a three-year-old came gleefully bounding into the room—covered from head to foot in flour. Her mom and I jumped to our feet and carried her down the hall to the nursery. To our dismay, we found several older children distributing flour to the others who were happily pounding it on the floor, "making cakes," smearing it on one another, making "flour" designs on the walls and mirrors. Their caregivers were scurrying around, trying in vain to stop the children and clean up the mess. Since I was in charge of the meeting, I felt I had to take control, especially since there was to be a big conference of church leaders in several hours. I had to get the church back in order before they arrived. I set the nursery workers to cleaning up the children, while I seized a huge broom and began sweeping up the flour.

In my dream I swept and swept, uncovering half-eaten donuts and other trash beneath the flour. When the nursery was once again in order, I started back to the group of women, but found the hall also filled with flour and scraps of food. So I grabbed the broom again and resumed sweeping. I rounded the corner into the parlor—that room sacred to every church, the room where the important meeting was to take place in less than an hour. To my horror, the parlor also looked like an acid rain disaster. Flour all over chairs and tables, as well as on the new rose carpet. So I dusted and vacuumed, moving feverishly but getting nowhere in that leaden dream state.

When the church officials arrived for the conference, I was

still frantically sweeping. They began to berate me: "Weren't you in charge here? Why did you let those people make such a mess?" Behind this question I could feel their disapproval of the group of women I had gathered in the church. I tried to explain the significance of this gathering—the healing that was taking place among these women. But all they said was, "We hired you to keep order in the church. You are to see that things are kept clean and in order so that the important work of the church can go on." In vain I tried to get them to understand that my calling was to bring people together for spiritual healing and growth and that I never should have left the group to clean up after the children. I woke up wondering, "Why did I leave the group of women to clean up the church? What did I really believe to be my calling? What did I value most?"

The message for me in this dream, I told the conference participants, was that I had to learn to say "no" so that I could say "yes" to what I valued most. Women, I went on, especially have learned to take care of people, to keep everything running smoothly at home and at work, to be agreeable and sweet. We have paid a price for this inability to say "no." Too often we have sacrificed our creative spirits. If we say "yes" to other voices all the time, we never stop to listen to our own voices. Saying "yes" to our own deepest longings moves us toward wholeness.

In the second part of my presentation, I discussed Feminine Divine images that give power to women healers. Two projectors flashed side by side slides of feminine images with supporting biblical references. The first picture slide was an artist's depiction of *Ruah* accompanied by a Scripture slide of Genesis 1:1-2: "In the beginning God created the heavens and the earth. The earth was without form and void, and darkness was upon the face of the deep; and the Spirit (*Ruah*) of God was moving over the face of the waters." I pointed out that the Hebrew word translated "Spirit" was *Ruah,* a feminine noun, and that these verses, at the very beginning of the Bible, pictured God giving birth to the universe. When women discover

that the Creative Spirit is feminine, I said, we increase our belief that we are in the image of the Creator and feel greater
power to embrace our own creativity.

During the break after my presentation, Anne rushed up
and hugged me, exclaiming, "You were wonderful! Powerful
and persuasive! I'm so proud of you." Her friend Bev said,
"Yeah, and it took a lot of nerve to begin with your dream, especially with so many counselor types in the audience!"
Rosalie Beck, professor of Church History at Baylor University
and also a speaker at the conference, laughingly said, "You
sounded like the Mr. Rogers of feminist theology. As you
talked about Ruah and Sophia and the Divine Midwife, giving
Bible verses to back them up, you kept smiling and asking,
'Did you ever learn this in Sunday School?'"

My friend Sally Browder had come to the conference from
New Orleans, where she now taught psychology at Dillard
University. She and Margaret Christensen sat together on a
panel responding to Jeanne Achterberg's talk on the challenges
women healers face in the present. As Sally spoke eloquently
about the healing potential in women's mutual relationships, I
realized how much I missed the relationship we'd had in Waco
and her creative work in the Inclusive Worship Community.
Margaret discussed ways in which she focused on health, not
illness, in her ob/gyn medical practice. She talked about the
importance of health care professionals' taking care of ourselves so that we can model wellness to those who come to us
for healing.

The Woman as Healer Conference concluded with a service
of worship. Nancy and I wrote several litanies for the empow-
erment of healers. We also asked Dawn Darwin and Tracy
Dunn-Noland, idealistic young women who'd sought guidance
from Nancy and me as they moved toward ordination as Baptist
ministers, to write a litany. Tracy and Dawn created a moving
litany called "I Am," celebrating the voices of Mother, Sister,
and Daughter. Each of the three poems in the litany took the
form of an acrostic, spelling out "WOMAN AS HEALER." Dawn
and Tracy began each "S" line with "Sophia." In the poem

featuring the Mother's voice, the line read, "Sophia's gentle wisdom beckons me again"; the Sister's voice, "Sophia's gentle wisdom can be easy to forget"; and the Daughter's voice, "Sophia's gentle wisdom has torn down walls with our cheers." In one of our preconference planning meetings several women from Baylor's Continuing Education Department raised strong objections to Sophia in the service of worship. It saddened me that these women couldn't understand the importance of Sophia for themselves and that, again, it was okay to talk about Sophia but not to worship Her. The continued resistance to feminine language in worship showed me how devalued the feminine is, even by women. It became all too clear that if we kept Sophia in the worship service, She would cause as much or more of a stir at Baylor as She had at the Re-Imagining Conference. To keep from derailing the Woman as Healer Conference at Baylor, we had to ask Dawn and Tracy to amend their litany. They changed "Sophia" to "Spirit," cleverly keeping the acrostic intact. Tracy and Dawn gave me permission to publish the original "Sophia" version of their litany in the worship resource section of *In Search of the Christ-Sophia*.

Stirring Up Fears—and a Party

As the publication of *In Search of the Christ-Sophia* drew near, some of the people closest to me grew more anxious. I wondered if they'd have been as nervous if I'd written a pornographic novel.

David kept trying to get me to take "Sophia" out of the title: "People just aren't going to understand 'Sophia.' And if they do, they won't like it. Remember how inflammatory it was at that conference in Minneapolis. You're taking a big risk if you don't change that title. 'Sophia' will get you in trouble."

I tried to explain that the symbol of Christ-Sophia formed the foundation of the book and thus had to be in the title. "And besides," I said with a strained laugh, "it won't be the first time Sophia has gotten people in trouble. The prophets of

Wisdom have been killed down through the centuries." By the look on David's face, I could tell that my attempt at humor had not helped my case, but rather increased his fears. And the truth was that I wanted to avoid martyrdom in any form.

Some of my Baylor colleagues made ominous predictions:

"You'll lose your job over this book."

"If some Baptist pastor on Baylor's board of trustees sees your book, you're history. That's not Baptist theology."

"You'd better not put anywhere on the book that you're a chaplain at Baylor." I already had.

"Don't expect me to put my job on the line to come to your defense."

All these comments stirred surprisingly little fear and doubt in me. Nothing could shake my profound belief that I'd been divinely guided in the writing and the publication of this book and that it would thus reach a receptive audience.

When *In Search of the Christ-Sophia* came out in November of 1994, I didn't get fired. Rather, I got a book-signing party in the elegant home of Baylor physicians Sandy and Herb Steinbach. Other Baylor physicians and several Baylor chaplains attended. My chaplain colleague Nancy helped plan the event, and my mentor Martha Gilmore smiled her blessing as I began a brief explanation of Christ-Sophia as a sacred symbol of shared power. I led the gathering of about sixty people in a litany from the book that began, "O come, let us worship God, our Mother and Father. Let us worship Christ-Sophia, our Sister and Brother." At the center of the group my sister Anne nodded and beamed her pride. From the beginning, Anne had stretched my thinking and encouraged me to believe in my work. I also saw David, standing near the back of the room, joining in the litany: "Christ-Sophia, our Wisdom, come to us. Give us new visions. Set us free to be your new creation." David looked proud, and surprised to hear all these Baylor people saying "Christ-Sophia" without gulping. Driving home, he expressed relief that I still had my job.

Chapter Eight

Finding a Place

Finding a church in Dallas where "Christ-Sophia" was part of
the worship would have been even more impossible than finding an integrated church in Minden when I was growing up.
When we moved back to Dallas, David and I didn't rush into
joining a church. David had been heavily involved on committees at Seventh and James Baptist in Waco, and he welcomed
a break. I'd grown weary of advocating for change, trying to
translate worship language to feel included, and suppressing
anger over the exclusive theology. We didn't just quit going to
church, but we took our time visiting around. Sometimes we
stayed home and leisurely watched *CBS Sunday Morning,*
David's favorite show on TV. David jokingly called Charles
Kuralt his pastor, and grieved for him when he died.

At Baylor I soon got the message that I best not be too dila-
tory in joining a church, a Baptist one, because Baylor was
supported by the Baptist General Convention of Texas and all
the full-time chaplains must be Baptist. By this time I'd had
enough conversations with clergywomen friends in other denominations and enough experience giving presentations on
feminist theology in a variety of churches to know that I would

not be too comfortable in any traditional religious setting. And I continued to believe that my call had to be worked out, somehow, within my own Baptist heritage.

So we joined Royal Lane Baptist Church, one of the few Baptist churches in Dallas that ordained women. I could not with any integrity consider a church that still refused to ordain women as deacons and pastors. David agreed. Royal Lane also seemed appealing because my friend Nancy Ellett Allison had at one time been the associate pastor. Nancy had come back as a member of the church when she became a chaplain at Baylor after a tenure as a missionary in Liberia. The first few Sundays we visited Royal Lane, mostly men led the services and all the language was "Father," "Master," "King," "He," "He," "He." But Nancy assured me that the church was working toward more inclusiveness and that she had awakened some consciousness by teaching my book *In Whose Image? God and Gender* at a women's retreat. On the first Sunday we visited I did notice that someone had scratched through many of the "He's" in the hymnal and inked in "God."

Creating "New Wineskins"

Not more than a month after we joined Royal Lane, Jo Ferguson ran up to me exclaiming, "I'm so glad you're here! We really need you. I hope you'll start an inclusive worship group. At the women's retreat Nancy asked us, 'Now just what are you going to do about all this?' Right then I knew I had to do something to get out the message. I just love your books; they changed my life. And now you're here with us! Will you start a group?" I didn't know whether to crawl under the pew or to shout, "Yes!" Jo towered over me in her bright red dress and hat, waiting for my response.

"Well, you know . . . we just joined the church, and I'm not sure, not so sure yet how involved I want to get," I hesitated.

"Oh, I'll help you, but I want you to be the leader. Ever since the retreat and Nancy's challenge, I've felt this strong urge to do something here at Royal Lane, but I didn't know how. And now God's sent you to us; She knew we needed you." Jo was one of the first persons, besides myself, I'd heard call God "She" in a church without laughing. So I began to take her more seriously. But I still felt cautious.

"I'm reluctant to begin a group here because of experiences I had in Waco. At Seventh and James the inclusive language issue caused quite a conflict, and I got blamed for some of it. I really wanted to be low profile here. Maybe we could start a group that meets somewhere else."

"No, no. It needs to be here. I'm sure of that. This church is open and needs us here. Royal Lane's had a history of being out front on liberal causes." With her dark hair and bright clothes and persuasive power, Jo reminded me a little of Mother. She convinced me that the pastor would be fine with an inclusive worship group at the church as long as we didn't involve him because he hated controversy. And there would be little controversy, Jo assured me, because most of the people in the church were open-minded.

"I'll be part of the group," I told Jo. "But I won't be the leader. I feel strongly about shared leadership and mutual re-lationships."

On a Sunday morning in January of 1995 a group of six women, including myself, met in a small storage room at Royal Lane. Old furniture and books stacked high on one side of the room left space for a circle of only seven portable chairs. We could have taken this as a message of our marginalization from the beginning, but Herman, the minister of education, assured us that we would soon have a better meeting place. And our spirits soared so high that location seemed insignificant. We were creating new possibilities for ourselves and for the church. And in our grandiosity, we compared ourselves to other reformers who changed the world.

Jo Ferguson, Karen Ivy, Elizabeth Watson-Martin, Renee Woods, Mitzi Ellington, and I spoke our visions of creating new rituals, of true mutuality in a faith community. For over a month we brainstormed names for our group. Every Sunday morning Herman would catch me in the hall before our meeting and ask the name of our "Sunday School class." I'd say, "We don't have a name yet and we're not a Sunday School class. We're a worship community." In the church newsletter Herman listed me as the teacher of this nameless class. I told him that I wasn't the teacher. He asked, "Then who is the teacher?" I responded, "We all are." Again he asked for the name of the group, and I replied, "It's emerging." He stared at me as though I had green hair. Our group completely blew every religious education paradigm he had. Perhaps "It's Emerging" would have been the most appropriate name for our community.

We finally selected the name "New Wineskins." "Matchsticks" came in second. We decided people would hear our message better if we chose the more biblical, less inflammatory, name. Elizabeth Watson-Martin proposed "New Wineskins" from a metaphor in Matthew 9:17: "Neither is new wine put into old wineskins; otherwise, the skins burst, and the wine is spilled, and the skins are destroyed; but new wine is put into new wineskins, and so both are preserved." Later we came up with this mission statement:

> New Wineskins will explore new ways of seeing divinity and interpreting Scripture so that the spiritual gifts of everyone are equally valued and nurtured. The name "New Wineskins," coming from the metaphor in Matthew 9:17, describes our search for new language and symbols to proclaim liberation and shalom. We will include feminine and masculine divine names and images to symbolize shared power and responsibility. New Wineskins will welcome and invite people from various faith backgrounds. We will celebrate diversity and actively encourage the discovery and exercise of everyone's gifts. The mission of New Wineskins will be to expand experience of Divine Mystery and to contribute to healing, peace, and justice in our world.

A Room of Our Own

New Wineskins soon had a room of our own, a big-enough room right in the middle of the educational building of the church. New people kept coming, some just to quell their curiosity and others to stay. Barb Middleton unequivocally came to stay.

One day at Baylor I got a call: "Hello. My name is Barb Middleton. I've been trying to find you. I called Hillcrest Hospital in Waco, and they told me you were here. I was at Borders looking for books to help me with a paper I'm writing for the World Conference on Women that's meeting in Beijing this September. Your book just fell off the shelf into my hands! I'd like to meet with you."

As Barb talked, I kept trying to figure out why she'd called Waco for me. Then I remembered that the back cover of *In Whose Image? God and Gender* identified me as a chaplain at Hillcrest. "I'm glad whoever you talked with at Hillcrest didn't say, 'We never knew her,'" I quipped.

Barb met me at Baylor for lunch. Over veggie burgers and fries we talked excitedly about our passion for social justice causes, about her Russian Orthodox background and my Baptist background, about how we'd become feminists, about the diverse paths her social work career had taken. A woman with strong features and shoulder-length salt-and-pepper hair, Barb spoke with intensity about her visions for women and men sharing power, working together for peace. She sang my song, and it sounded stronger through her voice.

Barb became one of the most faithful and creative members of New Wineskins. She joined us in time for our first Easter celebration. That Christmas I'd begun writing new words to traditional carols because I'd gotten so tired of singing "O come, let us adore *him*." I wondered how different our world would've been if we'd adored *her* as well. To the tune of "O Come, All Ye Faithful," I wrote "O Come, Christ-Sophia." Then I wrote "Christ-Sophia Now We Praise" to the tune of "Hark, the Herald Angels Sing." New Wineskins sang these carols with such delight and eagerness that I kept writing new words to traditional hymn tunes. I didn't know it at the time, but I'd begun writing another book. For our Easter service I wrote "Christ-Sophia Lives Today" to the tune of "Christ the Lord is Risen Today." Jo made purple copies of the hymn, along with several litanies. She also brought each one of us a fan, like we'd used in the fifties at outdoor tabernacle revivals in Minden, on which she'd written "Tawanda." When Jo explained, I remembered the woman in the movie *Fried Green Tomatoes* who'd taken on the name "Tawanda" as a symbol of her consciousness-raised power. Ten of us gathered on that Easter Sunday morning to sing praises to Christ-Sophia, to speak of our newfound freedom and power through the resurrected "She" as well as "He," to loudly proclaim that we all had risen indeed. We ended with fans raised high over our heads and shouts of "Tawanda."

Losing Our Room But Not Our Mission

Not long after that Easter Sunday, New Wineskins lost our room. People in the Sunday School classes on either side of us complained that we were too loud. They also criticized our singing. Sunday School time was supposed to be for Bible study, not singing, they said. We could tell that what they mostly objected to was the content of our songs and litanies. Herman moved us to the parlor-library, far away from the other groups. We soon discovered that this wasn't really our room. We couldn't leave our candles and symbols we'd brought to represent our spiritual journeys. People would often interrupt us to get a cup of coffee or a book. And we had to make sure we were out by the time the choir began gathering there for the 11:00 A.M. worship service. But we met in the parlor-library for almost a year, continuing to draw new members. Perhaps because we dripped candle wax on the carpet in that sanctum or perhaps because we didn't always clear out before the choir came in or perhaps because our theology was beginning to catch people's attention, New Wineskins had to move again—this time to a dark catacomb-like room in the basement of the youth center. When the young people needed this room, we moved to a children's classroom. After several months we moved, again, to a cramped and windowless room near Fellowship Hall. In a little over two years at Royal Lane Baptist, New Wineskins had to move six times. We felt like the children of Israel, wandering in search of the Promised Land, carrying our Ark of sacred symbols.

A few men joined the New Wineskins journey. Several others who came only a time or two misinterpreted our purpose. One man accused us of "male-bashing." Blood rising to my face, I quickly countered, "Three of the people I love most in this world are males—my husband and two sons. This is not about male-bashing. We're advocating change that will liberate men as well as women. I'm passionate about our mission for the sake of my sons as well as for all the daughters of the world!" In a calmer moment I also would have quoted Carol Lee Flinders, who wrote in *At the Root of This Longing*:

> The analogy I'd struck between Gandhi's followers and the contemporary women's movement seemed to me well worth pursuing. Whenever I've brought this up with others, though, a very pointed question arises: Who, for women, are the British? Who is the *enemy*? Feminism's opponents are quick to leap in with what they suppose to be the answer: men. It's *men* women see as the enemy and the oppressor. Which, of course, is nonsense, but it's nonsense that persists. Gandhi didn't see the British as the enemy, and feminists don't see men as the enemy, either. The enemy, rather, is the theory and practice of male superiority. The role that racism played in the British *raj* is played by sexism in the lives of women and girls.

My sons and husband, along with other men, had also suffered under this system of male dominance. I had taught, preached, and written about the importance of change for the good of men as well as women. In New Wineskins we were seeking divine symbols to support shared power to counter the worship of a male God, who sanctioned the dominance of men. David, from a distance, supported my involvement in New Wineskins. Like many men, David could see the value of the group for women more than for men. Because they're the dominant group it's hard for men to feel themselves as also oppressed. Although at times I wished David would join our group, I respected his choices as he did mine. I believed that what we were about in New Wineskins benefited him, whether he attended our meetings or not. And I believed that my efforts to change the system of male superiority also gave Brett and Chad greater freedom of choice.

Liberating Sons

Brett gave me much cause to "bust my buttons"— Daddy's ultimate expression of pride. Brett chose to major in English, even though many of his friends majored in business so they'd be assured of making a good living. He resisted cultural pressures in his choice of career just as he'd resisted his sixth grade physical education teacher's efforts to bully him into playing football. Brett was tall for his age and well-built. The PE teacher tried to shame Brett and other large boys into playing football by calling them "sissy" if they refused. But Brett picked up a tennis racket, strummed a guitar, and followed his own music. At UT he joined service organizations instead of a fraternity. He became fluent in Spanish through a semester's study in Argentina. His love for literature rekindled mine as we talked about Shakespeare, Hemingway, Emily Dickinson, and other writers. It thrilled me to see Brett develop his writing skills with Professor John Trimble, who later became a mentor to me as well. Brett studied hard and made the Dean's List every semester.

Brett had many choices upon graduation. He entered the Mississippi Teacher Corps and took an assignment as a teacher of English and Spanish at Gentry High School in Indianola. In his first year he struggled daily with one of his students, who was every bit as recalcitrant as Fred in my first year of teaching but without the socioeconomic advantages of Fred. Brett filled journals with accounts of other teaching challenges, as well as with funny and poignant stories. I lasted only a year in high school teaching. Brett stayed twice as long. On our visit to Gentry High, I loved watching students flock around "Mr. Clanton" while he directed their creative energy into skits based on Willie Morris's *Good Ol' Boy* and Margaret Walker Alexander's *Micah*. Brett told me that he survived those two years with the help of a daily mantra: "I'm doing a good thing."

While teaching at Gentry, Brett also worked as a freelance journalist for the Indianola weekly newspaper, *The Enterprise-Tocsin*. A year later, when he'd become a writer for *New Orleans CityBusiness,* David and I proudly watched Brett receive a first-place award from the Mississippi Press Association for a feature story he'd written for the Indianola paper on the local black gospel singing tradition.

After graduating with honors from the University of Texas, Chad joined AmeriCorps, to work with San Antonio's Habitat for Humanity. With his degree in economics and government, he could have begun a more lucrative career. But he didn't succumb to our culture's pressure, especially on men, to equate significance with money. Chad flourished as a community organizer for Habitat, bringing people from various races and social classes together to build houses for people in need. Semesters in Mexico and Costa Rica, through UT's Study Abroad Program, equipped him to converse with San Antonio's Spanish-speaking community. He addressed churches and civic organizations all over town, passionately quoting Habitat's motto: "Every person deserves a decent place to live."

Chad tells me that one of the times when he's felt most alive was at a Habitat benefit concert he organized in San Antonio's Majestic Theater. He enlisted Texas musicians Tish Hinojosa, Jimmie Dale Gilmore, and Sara Hickman to give their talents to this fundraising event. David and I drove down, arriving in time to see Chad scurrying behind the scenes and people running up to him for directions. He introduced us to San Antonio business owners who'd made large contributions to the event. Chad and his cousin David got their talent for selling from Mother, who could've sold Bibles at a convention of atheists. On stage Chad dazzled more brightly than the florescent stars painted on the domed ceiling of the newly refurbished Majestic Theater. With poise and wit he welcomed the crowd, acknowledged the many contributors to the event, and introduced the performers. Even if I hadn't been his mother, I couldn't have resisted his boyish, disarming appeal for contributions to Habitat. At the conclusion of the program, Chad came back on stage and announced that the event raised $30,000, reaching the goal of collecting enough money in one night to build a Habitat house. David and I proudly rose with the crowd of over 2,400 to clap and cheer.

Brett and Chad both resisted traditional messages about male-female relationships. Chad broke off a relationship with a young woman in San Antonio "because she had babies in her eyes." Both sons were attracted to women who had intelligence and career goals, as well as looks. Although there was no way for them to escape all the cultural messages about proving their masculinity, they didn't indulge in sexist remarks or jokes, at least not around me. I didn't like their going to James Bond and Terminator movies and had trouble believing their assurances that they weren't affected by the violence and sexism, but I was glad that they acted on other peaceful models. Chad and Brett encouraged my work for mutual gender relationships, including my writing of new hymns. Brett worked out a guitar accompaniment to "O Come, Christ-Sophia" for a family Christmas gathering.

Mixed Reactions

Later I realized how naive I was to take "O Come, Christ-Sophia" to a family Christmas in San Angelo. I had persuaded

Mother that we could create our own service instead of going to the Christmas Eve service at First Baptist Church. I'd brought some new carols I'd written, and others could contribute readings or whatever they wanted. "That'll be great," Mother said, welcoming any opportunity for the family to worship together. So we all gathered for the service—Mother, my stepdad Taylor, Anne, her husband Mike, her son David and daugher DeAnne, our cousin Cindy, David, Chad, Brett, and I. After I distributed the words of my new carols, Brett gave his guitar introduction, and we began singing to the tune of "O Come, All Ye Faithful":

O Come, Christ-Sophia, full of grace and wisdom;
Come bless us, come challenge us to make life anew.
Come bring us power, beauty, hope, and harmony.
O come, thou Christ-Sophia,
O come, thou Christ-Sophia,
O come, thou Christ-Sophia, wisdom and peace.

As we sang this first stanza, I tried not to notice reactions to my new words. Taylor sat grim-faced, not singing a word. Mother sang as she looked anxiously at Taylor.

After we finished singing all three stanzas of "O Come, Christ-Sophia," Mother tried to make everybody happy by jumping up and saying, "Let's sing 'It Came Upon a Midnight Clear.'"

Anne responded, "Those are great words, Jann. I want to sing this other hymn you brought."

DeAnne chimed in, "Yeah, I just love these powerful words. Let's sing the other one Jann wrote."

Brett didn't have a guitar version of "Hark, the Herald Angels Sing," so we sang a cappella:

Christ-Sophia now we praise; joyful songs our voices raise;
For new life in us to birth, for deep healing of the earth.
Long her face we did not see; blind no more our eyes shall be.
Long we've needed her embrace, glory and power of her grace.
Christ-Sophia now we praise; joyful songs our voices raise.

Anne and DeAnne sang exuberantly. Cindy also sang out in her strong soprano voice. I could hear the softer, lower notes of Chad and Brett as they tried to support me. Taylor still sat close-mouthed. David, who never liked conflict, had quit singing and was giving me a look that said "you should have known this wouldn't go well here." My voice dwindled on the next two stanzas of the carol as tension filled the room.

The minute we finished, Mother tried again, "Now let's sing 'It Came Upon a Midnight Clear.'" But nobody seemed in the mood to sing anymore. So Mother prayed, and Cindy gave a reading about the "true meaning" of Christmas. Then Taylor prayed in a somber voice to "Our Father." Anne tried to keep some emotional distance behind her new movie camera.

My childlike wish for my family to receive my carols as joyfully as I'd written them ended in a dose of reality. In the fresh flush of creating the hymns, I'd believed that they'd catch on widely, contributing to freedom and peace around the world. Now my idealism shattered like ornaments dropped under the Christmas tree. I thought I could change the world, and now I wondered if I could even change my family. As always, I wanted Mother's approval. Now I also longed for her to see the value of Christ-Sophia for herself.

I should have remembered her remarks after she read *In Whose Image:* "You did a great job of demonstrating that the Bible has female images of God. And I've tried to pray to God as Mother and to call God 'She.' But when I do, I don't feel I'm giving God as much respect." This comment, I thought with sadness, also shows what Mother feels about herself. She'd grown up in a religion and culture that didn't respect women enough to even consider feminine references to deity. And now she was a faithful member of a church that still wouldn't ordain women as deacons or pastors even though Mother had been advocating it for years. At this time the gap was too great for Mother to leap—from a church that didn't even consider women fully human to a God who could be called "She" and "Christ-Sophia."

My hymns played better with Neil Kluepfel, publisher of

Twenty-Third. The hymns kept coming and with greater joy than I'd ever experienced in my writing. Along with them came a first in my writing experience—a contract before finishing a manuscript. Near the end of February 1996, I received a contract for *Praying with Christ-Sophia: Services for Healing and Renewal*. Months earlier Neil Kluepfel had responded enthusiastically to my hymns. In one telephone conversation he told me that he and others at Twenty-Third had been walking around the office singing them. Neil wrote me that although Tom Artz was leaving Twenty-Third, two other senior editors would work on my book. Mary Carol Kendzia worked most closely with me, proving to be an outstanding editor through her suggestions of creative changes to the rituals included in the book and her meticulous placement of the words of my hymns with the music. In March, Neil and his wife Pat came through Dallas on a business trip, and I met them for dinner at a Ramada Inn. A handsome couple, gray and wise, they spoke passionately about their commitment to publish religious books promoting social justice. I liked them immediately, and my trust in Twenty-Third Publications continued to soar.

In Search of Creativity

The previous summer, on our way to creative workshops in Maine, David and I had stopped in Mystic, Connecticut. I wanted to see if Mystic lived up to its name. It was a balmy Sunday afternoon in July. We parked on a hilly street downtown, close to "Mystic Pizza," where a movie of that name starring Julia Roberts had been made. We asked shopkeepers for directions to Twenty-Third Publications, and no one knew. Finally, we found a police officer on the street who pointed the way over a bridge and along a harbor where bright-colored sailboats danced in the breeze. We rounded a corner. There on the coast stood a three-story white frame building crowned with the sign "XXIII." To me it looked like a castle rising up from the sea. I recalled lines from a poem I'd memorized in junior high school, Edgar Allan Poe's "Annabel Lee":

> It was many and many a year ago,
> In a kingdom by the sea,
> That a maiden there lived whom you may know
> By the name of Annabel Lee.

How thrilled I was that my books lived in this white castle by the sea. David took pictures of me standing there in my black slacks and tank top, beaming as though I were queen of this castle.

Freshly inspired, I couldn't wait to begin the workshop on creative potential when we reached Rockport, Maine. In his workshop David photographed breathtaking coastal landscapes, while I joined eight other people in search of our creativity. Our instructors, David Lyman and Ann Marie Almeida, tried to persuade us that rock climbing would help. I stared at them with disbelief and up at the huge, sheer rock with terror. It didn't help that I had developed a bad case of acrophobia when Brett and Chad as little boys had tried to scare me by hanging over railings on towers at amusement parks. But if these gurus at the workshop said rock climbing would help my creativity, then I would give it a try. Hugging the rock, I slowly inched my way from one tiny foothold to another with only a thin rope keeping me from plunging to my death. On the way down, instead of leaning back in the harness as instructed, I slithered down the rock, scraping my hands and ankles. About the only thing rock climbing did for my creativity was to increase my drive toward sedentary activities, like writing.

One afternoon I stayed in my room and wrote a worship service on celebrating diversity to be included in *Praying with Christ-Sophia*. The service included a fictional story about a straight-haired cocker spaniel, drawing from the life of my own Flossie. Another afternoon I sat out on the rocky seashore and wrote the story of my ordination. My writing received affirmation from the creativity group, especially from Ann

Marie, whose Reiki treatment certainly did more for me than the rock climbing had. Ann Marie and a poet named Robyn Jacobson sang the loudest on a hymn I'd just finished: "We Sound a Call to Freedom" to the tune of "Mine Eyes Have Seen the Glory." The first stanza goes:

We sound a call to freedom that will heal our broken land;
As the call rings out more clearly, violent forces will disband.
Prison doors will open; bonds will loosen by the Spirit's hand;
The truth will set us free.

Celebration of *Praying with Christ-Sophia*

When *Praying with Christ-Sophia: Services for Healing and Renewal* came out in November of 1996, New Wineskins members and my chaplain friend Nancy threw a celebration in the fellowship hall of Royal Lane Baptist Church. The hall overflowed with people, and my heart surged with renewed hope. Maybe now would be the fulfillment of Taylor's prophecy at my ordination: "A new day has dawned." In that moment, I believed it. And I knew I was not alone as I looked around the room at friends from Baylor, Royal Lane, New Wineskins, and Dallas Clergywomen exuberantly singing my words to the tune "Hymn to Joy":

Celebrate a new day dawning, sunrise of a golden morn,
Christ-Sophia dwells among us, glorious visions now are born.
Equal partners 'round the table, we make dreams reality;
Calling out our gifts we nurture hope beyond all we can see.

How could anyone ever object to this message of partnership and peace? Again, I naively underestimated the power of resistance to change.

I stood before the group gathered there in fellowship hall on that rainy Saturday night in November and read from the Introduction my purpose in writing the worship service book:

My strong conviction of the power of communities to bring healing and blessing through sacred rituals has led me to create the services in this book. Developed from the belief that all are created in the divine image with abundant creative gifts, these services invite all to participate as equals.

Feeling my voice grow stronger with the passion I felt when I wrote these words, I continued:

All of the services in this collection are intended to break down hierarchies and to heal wounds inflicted by oppressive institutions and traditions. Because of my strong belief in the power of sacred symbols to shape our values and actions, the symbols of divinity in these services suggest partnership in restoring all creation to beauty and freedom.

I looked out and saw Anne smiling at me. The book, I told the group, is dedicated "to my sister Anne, who embodies the mutual love and power of the Divine Sister," and "to the New Wineskins Community, whose creative partnership and encouragement served as Divine Midwife to this book."

Karen Ivy led the group in singing several other hymns in my book; she included movements to "Praise Ruah, Spirit Who Gives Birth." Karen had us flapping our arms, bird-like, as we sang the refrain: "Praise the great creative Spirit! Come and praise her!" If this movement felt awkward, no one could complain that it was unbiblical. After all, Scripture included many winged images of the Spirit, including the dove. David escaped the bird motions by retreating behind his camera as he photographed the whole event. The clergywomen and New Wineskins flapped most freely. My new friends Meg Gloger and Pat Jablonski, who had driven up from Nacogdoches, also participated with gusto. I had met these delightful former nuns at an Episcopal Women's Caucus meeting in Fort Worth and learned about New Creation Ministry that Meg had started.

After the program New Wineskins members served punch, sandwiches, and cookies from a table which Jo Ferguson had elaborately decorated with doves and a flowing fountain. I signed books and received comments like, "This is the first time I've felt truly included in a worship service. I wish I could be in a service like this every week. I love the new hymns and wish we'd sing them in our church. It'll be hard to go back and sing the old words." I, of course, invited everyone to our Sunday morning New Wineskins services.

New Wineskins Bashers

The detractors of New Wineskins at Royal Lane Baptist Church gained numbers and power. Although I heard no direct criticism of the November celebration in fellowship hall, I knew it had stirred things up. For the good, I had hoped. In addition to the earlier accusation of "male-bashing," we heard comments against the candles we used in our New Wineskins community. One man walked by our door, saw our lighted candles on the small table in the center of the room, and muttered, "Since when did we become a bunch of Catholics?" His insensitivity angered me. I felt ashamed to be a Baptist. The candles and other visual symbols contributed by those in New Wineskins from the Catholic tradition—Margaret Christensen and Elizabeth Zedaran calling themselves "recovering Catholics"— had greatly enriched my spirituality.

The New Wineskins bashers' voices grew louder when Elizabeth brought in a three-foot-tall Mary statue she had transformed into Christ-Sophia. Elizabeth had found the statue, dingy and dusty and handless, stashed away in a corner of the basement room we'd had at Royal Lane. New Wineskins had been discussing Rebecca Wells's *Divine Secrets of the Ya-Ya Sisterhood* and relished the story of the girls' putting make-up and jewelry on a Madonna statue to the horror of one of their mothers.

Elizabeth took home the Mary statue and began by painting Mary's robe a rich purple dotted with shiny gold stars. Where one hand had been, Elizabeth glued a silver styrofoam moon and in the place of the other hand, a larger golden sun. Elizabeth saved the face for last. When she rubbed off the crusted paint, Elizabeth watched, in amazement, as Mary's face shone with dark and light tones in perfect balance. At once Elizabeth recognized Christ-Sophia, holding sun and moon, black and white in equal balance. Elizabeth also tells of a deeper discovery of herself as she recreated this sacred image. As she restored this wounded and rejected image, Elizabeth was at the same time reclaiming her own feminine power. Slowly working for months, in the midst of chaos and questions, she touched the divinity within herself. For the first time she saw herself as fully created in the divine image.

It became harder and harder for me to conceive of any Royal Lane members' objecting to such profound spiritual discovery, especially since Baptist tradition had always championed soul freedom and Royal Lane specifically prided itself on being "a community that values each person's faith and gifts." Many members of Royal Lane did wholeheartedly support New Wineskins. Others said they'd support us if we modified our practices. The harshest critics wanted us to leave. Some people in the middle wanted us to turn our attention to other less controversial social causes that they deemed more important. Royal Lane, from its inception, had been a moderate Baptist church with a social conscience that had supported such organizations as Habitat for Humanity.

Since moving to Dallas, my conscience at times stung because I'd left behind some of the activism of my Waco years. Now the inner tape began to run: "Maybe I'm putting too much energy into New Wineskins and writing feminist rituals when so many people in this community are starving and assaulted and homeless. I should volunteer with Habitat or Genesis Shelter or Wilkinson Center." Sue Monk Kidd in *The Dance of the Dissident Daughter* said she struggled with similar feelings:

One of the primary forms that resistance takes is trivialization. Surely I was making a big deal out of this, I began to tell myself. So maybe there is a feminine wound in me, in women, in the church, in the earth, but what about all those other major problems I should be concerned about—the environment, crime, war, homelessness? What is a little feminine wound by comparison?

But I soon recognized, as did Kidd, how deeply connected all these social ills are to the feminine wound. And I rededicated myself to our group's mission of healing and liberation.

"The Winepress"

Palm Sunday afternoon, 1997, deacon co-chairs brought New Wineskins members together with our critics and supporters for a mediation meeting in a classroom at Royal Lane. With a passion in my voice that surprised even me, I declared, "New Wineskins' mission is to bring the Good News of liberation through sacred symbolism that values women and men as equally created in the image of God."

"We've all suffered religious abuse from worshiping only a masculine God," Barb interjected.

"I never knew my spiritual worth and power until I started coming to New Wineskins," Elizabeth began her story. Margaret, Jo, Melanie, Brian, Barb, and I joined in telling our stories. The critics sat unmoved. One even slept through the meeting.

A portly deacon accused, "I heard ya'll engaged in male-bashing."

Brian Burton quickly countered, "That's absolutely false! Would I be in this group if it were about male-bashing?"

Brian later brought us comic relief through his satire of this meeting in "The Winepress," a newsletter he had created. I couldn't take myself quite so seriously after reading Brian's description of me:

Rumors spread that Dr. Jann Aldredge-Clanton, founding theologian of New Wineskins, would arrive at the church through a back entrance under heavy guard. Arriving at the church in a black stretch limo, reporters swarmed Aldredge-Clanton for comments. Wearing dark sunglasses, a veil, and an ante-bellum hoop skirt, Jann emerged from the limo with great difficulty. Once at the podium she began waving her arms like Eva Peron as she articulated the crusade for justice, inclusiveness, and kindness. Aldredge-Clanton announced that if the attacks on New Wineskins continued, she would declare a state of "Holy War" and bring the Feminine Divine power upon the church with full force.

The attacks did continue. The deacons appointed a special committee to determine what to do with New Wineskins. This committee met without any members of New Wineskins present. Finally, on June 15, Father's Day, the committee invited New Wineskins to a second mediation meeting. This meeting turned out to be less mediation and more pronouncement by the chair of the committee, a woman. To keep the church from splitting, the committee had decided that New Wineskins could continue meeting only under these conditions: (1) drop litanies and hymns to Christ-Sophia; (2) remove all candles and other visual symbols; (3) drop use of feminine references to God. I found it fitting that the church tried to reestablish the rule of the Father on Father's Day. Also I understood, more fully than ever, the power of naming the Divine Feminine in worship—power to split the church, according to some members of Royal Lane. In reliving this meeting as I look back over the written responses of New Wineskins members, anger and tears well up. Also, I'm laughing out loud, thanks to Brian's account in another issue of "The Winepress":

During the mediation meeting, New Wineskins members learned that many distortions and untruths have circulated during the last two years about our group. "Dismayed, disappointed, and disgusted," was how one member reacted to news of the gossip. One detractor spread the news that New Wineskins talked a lot about "Mother Hen" and "Mother

Eagle." Apparently the church member concluded that we were teaching a "bird theology," and needed to be "de-beaked." Responding to this charge, Jann Aldredge-Clanton confirmed that members were mining scripture and discovered feminine images of God complete with feathers. In response, New Wineskins members surprised church officials the following Sunday by dressing up as birds. Jann came as a mother hen, saying that if she had to, she would hover and protect her chicks if she sensed any approaching danger. Sprightly Melanie fluttered in as a Carolina chickadee, a bird known for its acrobatic dance and antics. Barb winged into the room as a pelican, a symbol used in Christian art representing a Mother Christ. Jo donned her pheasant feathered hat, and Elizabeth dressed as a wood duck, the most colorful waterfowl in the world. Jeannine came as a peafowl with stunning tail plumage and memorable call. Karen blew in as a roadrunner, darting from place to place in case New Wineskins needed to make a quick getaway. Anna Lou came as a quail, making low-level chortling sounds. Margaret had a bad night at the hospital and waddled in as a penguin, hoping some deacons might mistake her as a man in a tuxedo with hemorrhoids. Reminding his sisters that dynamite comes in small packages, Brian flitted in as a hummingbird.

Splitting New Wineskins

We could not, of course, succumb to the conditions set by the committee. As Brian said in his more serious response, "In the name of heading off a church split, New Wineskins is being asked to split off from who we are and who we feel called to be. To ask us to refrain from our present course is akin to asking the Royal Welcome class to stop welcoming people." We began to experience the reality of external pressure causing internal conflict within a group. Those members who'd been part of Royal Lane Baptist Church the longest wanted to adapt New Wineskins, somehow, to pacify the critics. Jeannine Owens and others who weren't members of Royal Lane felt it impossible to stay under the restricted conditions. Jeannine had come to New Wineskins after painful experiences in churches of several denominations and a long period of separation from any religious community. She had taught our group a chorus that repeated over and over the words "love and respect to you." I felt guilty to be a member of a church that couldn't fully respect her beliefs. Jeannine wrote in a letter to the church, "Your rejection of the celebration held in New Wineskins has ended my participation. I am grateful it was allowed to survive long enough for me to find this special group. Inclusive language is soothing, comforting, and inspirational for many others and me. I am saddened and disappointed by the patriarchal system that continues to control religion." Barb and Elizabeth wrote, "Since both the visual and vocal aspects of our celebration have been suppressed, we will take these to another sacred space."

So, in order to keep the church from splitting, New Wineskins split. Some stayed at Royal Lane and became a book-study group. Others began meeting in a meditation room over a restaurant called "Cosmic Cup." I went back and forth between the two groups. I wanted to maintain relationship with everyone. And I felt torn between my longing for feminist ritual and my call to bring change within my Baptist tradition. But the question Rex Lewis had asked in my College of Chaplains interview came nagging back, "So why are you still Baptist?" And then his interpretation, "You're just like an abused woman who won't get out of a marriage."

Karen Ivy, who'd decided to remain with the New Wineskins group at Royal Lane, accused the church of abuse. In her response to the Father's Day meeting she wrote, "I feel that I and my New Wineskins sisters and brothers have been bound, betrayed and assaulted. Royal Lane Baptist Church, through New Wineskins, had delivered a message of love and acceptance to some people who had rejected their traditional church experience. Our group was helping them look through the window of Christianity without the curtain of patriarchy. Now they have been battered by patriarchy once again."

Patriarchy was everywhere, I told myself, not just among Baptists. I could leave the Baptist church, but I couldn't escape patriarchy. I remembered stories of my Methodist clergywomen friends who juggled two or three small churches while their younger, less competent male counterparts received appointments to large churches. I knew of no worship services of any faith where I could experience an equal balance of feminine and masculine images of divinity. All religion worshiped a masculine God. Our whole society worshiped the masculine. There was no escape. I might as well work for change within my own Baptist tradition, I thought. So my inner dialogue went.

Soon I began to feel that I created more stress for myself than change within any institution. Whether sitting cross-legged in the upper room of the Cosmic Cup, or cramped in the classroom at Royal Lane or numbed in the sanctuary worship service, I rarely felt at home. At the Cosmic Cup surrounded by pictures of Buddha on the walls, I felt blown, like Dorothy in *The Wizard of Oz,* to a foreign land. And it saddened me to be with the New Wineskins at Royal Lane, because we didn't sing or dance anymore. Our detractors had succeeded in clipping our wings. For more than a year I'd dash back and forth between Royal Lane and the Cosmic Cup. Often I'd stay for the 11:00 A.M. worship service at Royal Lane to be with David. Sometimes Brian Burton sat with us, and we'd laugh and change the masculine language in the hymns. But mostly, I quit singing. It took too much energy to fight against the words that pelted my spirit like stones. I tried to block them with fantasies of worship that included the Feminine Divine. Or I flipped through *The Baptist Hymnal* and started writing new words to some of the hymn tunes.

Vision Restored

On a day when my heart weighed heavy with discouragement, I found in my Baylor mailbox a letter Bill Holub had forwarded. I appreciated Bill, the author liaison for Twenty-Third

Publications, as an encouraging friend and diligent promoter of my Christ-Sophia books. He promptly sent me any reviews or comments he found about my books. This letter had come to Bill all the way from Australia. Eileen Ray wrote to ask permission to use services from *Praying with Christ-Sophia*. She explained:

> I am an unemployed Baptist minister (there aren't a lot of openings for women here), and am in the process of responding to requests from several women to establish a women's worship time. This has grown out of courses I have run on an introduction to feminine images of God, including the biblical/cultural/historical background to Sophia and Christ-Sophia. I used material based on Jann's other book for this course. The growth of interest in Christ-Sophia is very exciting—it is amazing how women grow and change when they discover for themselves the feminine side of God.

The words of this Baptist minister reenergized me more than my favorite Whole Foods Power Smoothie. And my vision suddenly came back into clear focus. This woman halfway around the world had reminded me of the purpose of my work.

One day Harriet Boorhem called with an idea for a new meeting place for New Wineskins. Harriet and Barb had co-hosted a book-signing party for me and later a croning ritual for my fiftieth birthday in the offices of their Gaia Institute for Feminist Therapy. And I'd given a lecture on feminine sacred imagery in Harriet's psychology class at the University of North Texas.

"Jann, I have the perfect meeting place for us," Harriet said.

"For whom?" I didn't at first follow Harriet because she had attended only a few New Wineskins' meetings.

"For New Wineskins."

"Really?"

"Remember, when you came to my class at North Texas I told you I'd gotten involved again with my Methodist church. And I wanted you to come and do your feminine images lecture in my Sunday School class."

"Oh, yeah," I said cautiously.

"I've been talking with our pastor, and he thinks it's a great idea to have New Wineskins at our church. Would you be willing to meet with us to get things started?" The phone vibrated with Harriet's excitement.

Trying not to get my hopes up, I drove on a crisp autumn Sunday afternoon to Kessler Park United Methodist Church in the Oak Cliff area of Dallas. In the parlor Harriet introduced me to the pastor and to the minister of education. For over an hour the four of us talked about possibilities for New Wineskins at Kessler Park. Harriet had already given them copies of my Christ-Sophia books, so they knew my theology. And to my surprise, they celebrated it. They told me that they knew people in the church who longed for this inclusive theology and others in the community who would be attracted to it. Still, I felt wary. I knew I had to be honest with them about the history of New Wineskins at Royal Lane so they'd know what they might be getting into. Not everyone in the church might be as enthusiastic about Christ-Sophia as they were, I told them. But they felt certain they could deal with any conflict that arose. They would take the proposal to the Council on Ministries for a vote.

Harriet called several weeks later to tell me that we had received full approval for New Wineskins to meet at Kessler Park. We decided to begin with the new year. To everyone who'd ever been connected with New Wineskins or expressed any interest, we sent flyers with this message in large magenta letters: "NEW WINESKINS GIVES BIRTH TO A NEW COMMUNITY. JOIN THE CELEBRATION AT KESSLER PARK UNITED METHODIST CHURCH, BEGINNING JANUARY 10, 1999."

Anne with New Wineskins

The September before, Anne had left Mike after nineteen years of marriage. This is Anne's story to tell, not mine. So I'll say only that for a while Anne had known the marriage wasn't good for her, but she'd tried to hang on to keep from going through another divorce. Mike tried to get Anne back until the divorce was final the following June. But Anne continued to gain strength to follow her own voice and to find her separate identity.

New Wineskins, she said, helped her regain power to stand up for herself. She'd wanted to come to New Wineskins meetings before, but Mike didn't want to come and discouraged her from going anywhere without him. Now Anne gave birth to her new self as New Wineskins gave birth to a new community. She joyfully came to our beginning celebration on January 10 and every Sunday thereafter. We often led rituals together.

I remembered playing church with Anne when we were children. Because she was older, she always got to be the preacher, and I directed the music or played the piano. Maybe I'd entered my ministerial vocation so that I could at last be the preacher, I laughingly told Anne. But in New Wineskins we stood side by side as proclaimers of truth.

Harriet led our singing with her vibrant soprano voice that had gotten her into the Dallas Women's Chorus. Sometimes when we sang "Celebrate a New Day Dawning" or "We Sound a Call to Freedom," I looked over and saw Anne's eyes glistening with tears.

On June 6, 1999, two days after Anne's divorce settlement, New Wineskins gathered in our spacious, sunny room at Kessler Park. We sat in a circle around an altar on which lavender candles surrounded Elizabeth's Christ-Sophia statue, her purple star-bedecked robe gleaming more brightly than ever. Floating over the altar was a butterfly-shaped balloon, in rich shades of gold and purple and emerald. Light streamed in through the large windows, setting the butterfly aglow. During the ritual, participants told of new experiences in their lives and of their hopes for newness in the future. After each one spoke, together we proclaimed the vision in Revelation 21:5: "Behold, I make all things new!" The ritual concluded with our singing "We Sound a Call to Freedom" to the tune of "Mine Eyes have Seen the Glory," growing louder and stronger as we came to the refrain:

Free at last, O Hallelujah!
Free at last, O Hallelujah!
Christ-Sophia, you have freed us!
Your truth has set us free.

We swayed to the music and pointed to the butterfly, our symbol of metamorphosis and freedom.

After the service we gave the butterfly to Anne to symbolize the new adventure she had entered after completing her divorce. Elizabeth, Anne, and I walked out together. Anne held the butterfly balloon by a thin ribbon—but not for long. The butterfly broke loose and took off on her own, slowly drifting skyward.

"Oh no, we've lost her," I said.

"Look! She's free!" Elizabeth said. We laughed and stood staring as she soared more rapidly now. The three of us watched as the sun sparkled through her, lighting up her golds and purples to even more brilliant hues.

Anne said, "I wonder where she'll land."

"Wherever she needs to," I replied.

Elizabeth countered, "Wherever she *wants* to!"

The balloon butterfly was all of us, breaking free. She soared upward through pearly clouds in the ocean-blue sky, until she was only a speck of deep purple in the distance.

Dislocated Again

A few weeks later a new pastor came to Kessler Park United Methodist Church. This pastor didn't support New Wineskins, reminding me of the biblical story of the king over Egypt who "knew not Joseph." The former Pharaoh had welcomed the children of Israel, but the new Pharaoh began enslaving them. The new pastor of Kessler Park didn't approve of our free, inclusive community. Harriet grieved the departure of Jim, the former pastor, and warned us that this new pastor would seek to stifle us.

One Sunday morning Harriet told our group that she could no longer come to the church for anything, not even for New Wineskins, because she felt estranged from Kessler Park and from institutional religion in general. Especially upsetting, she said, was the United Methodist Church's discrimination against homosexuals.

Enthusiasm and attendance at New Wineskins meetings waned. One Sunday morning when only Anne, Elizabeth, and I were there, we began talking about possibilities of other meeting places. Elizabeth told of disapproving stares she'd gotten from some members of Kessler Park when they saw her carrying the Christ-Sophia statue into the church. Anne said she thought the church simply tolerated us and that we should look around for a more welcoming place. I'd grown weary of moving.

Several months later, Harriet called to tell me she'd heard indirectly that the new pastor felt that New Wineskins shouldn't be at Kessler Park because our theology didn't fit that of the congregation. He'd visited our group one Sunday morning when Meg Gloger led a ritual including a variety of feminine sacred images. He didn't say anything to Meg or to any of us that Sunday. Instead he told the minister of education, who called Harriet. Now we knew we had to move, again.

"I have the perfect place for us," Elizabeth said one Sunday.

"I've heard that before," I thought.

"Grace United Methodist Church," Elizabeth continued. "I met the pastor and several members of the church at a party the other night. We got to talking, and I brought up New Wineskins. They said they'd love to have us at Grace, that we'd fit right in."

"Grace . . . well, that may be a possibility. I know one of the lay leaders there, Kathy LaTour. She's a breast cancer survivor who's written this wonderful book I recommend to patients, and she gave one of our big lectures on cancer survivorship at Baylor. Kathy's been telling me for a while that Grace would be the perfect place for New Wineskins," I said.

"Kathy's one of the people I met the other night!" Elizabeth's voice rang with excitement. "That's more than coincidence! It's meant to be, that's clear. Sophia's been preparing the way."

Welcomed by Grace

In December Elizabeth and I met with Pastor Charles Cox and Kathy LaTour at Cafe Brazil to talk about moving New Wineskins to Grace United Methodist Church. Just as in the meeting with church officials before we moved to Kessler Park, I expressed caution. Again, I recited the history of New Wineskins—the conflicts at Royal Lane and our various locations. I told Charles and Kathy about the objections the new pastor of Kessler Park had to New Wineskins. They assured me that Grace would celebrate our presence, and had already voted unanimously to welcome us. And if conflicts arose, Grace had a history of dealing with controversy. The church had already survived becoming a Reconciling Congregation, a United Methodist local church that makes a public statement welcoming all persons, regardless of sexual orientation, to participate fully in their congregational life. Soon after Grace voted to be a Reconciling Congregation, the national General Assembly of the United Methodist Church voted that churches couldn't be "Reconciling." It struck me as deeply ironic that any religious group would vote not to be "Reconciling." In spite of the General Assembly's edict, Grace continued as a Reconciling Congregation. As I listened to Charles and Kathy talk about Grace, new hope beat in my heart.

Wanting the invitations to our first meeting at Grace to be different from the invitations the year before to Kessler Park, I struggled with the wording. I didn't want to say "New Wineskins Community moves again." Several of us laughingly thought about "You're invited to the first meeting of the new new New Wineskins." Finally, I wrote: "New Wineskins on pilgrim journey gives birth to a new community. Join the celebration at Grace United Methodist Church, beginning January 16, 2000."

That Sunday morning dawned bright and unseasonably warm. Though the middle of January, it felt like spring. Arriving early, I walked up the stairs to our third floor meeting room. Kathy, Charles, and a sunny room with two big windows greeted me. In the center of the room was a small table with fifteen chairs arranged neatly around it. I draped a purple silk cloth over the table. On this altar I placed five votive candles, a black ceramic Madonna, and a porcelain Madonna. The room soon filled with people and pulsated with expectancy. Elizabeth entered, placing on the altar the purple-robed Christ-Sophia figure and a gloxinia plant with purple velvety blooms.

Our ritual began with a litany in celebration of beginnings. Then we stood and sang: "Celebrate a new day dawning, sunrise of a golden morn; Christ-Sophia dwells among us; glorious visions now are born." These words sounded more joyful, more hopeful than ever before. Maybe this time, I prayed. Maybe now, at last, a new day has dawned for New Wineskins. A new century, a new millennium had dawned. Maybe, just maybe, things will be different now.

We went around the circle telling our visions for New Wineskins. Anne expressed her hope that the community would always be open to new ideas and would continue to grow more inclusive. Margaret spoke of the power of circles to bring change. We agreed that we'd come to Grace not to change that church, but to change the world. And in that holy moment we believed we could.

Mother with New Wineskins

A year later Mother visited New Wineskins for the first time. On previous weekend visits, she'd rush back to teach her Sunday School class, or I'd take her to a more traditional worship service. I felt apprehensive about what she'd think of

New Wineskins' feminist rituals. I appreciated her efforts to call God "Mother" or "She" to support me, but her tongue tripped on the words. They were just too foreign to what she'd always heard and spoken. So I worried about how Mother would participate in our liturgies with references to "Christ-Sophia," "Mother and Father," "She and He."

On Mother's first Sunday with New Wineskins, I led a blessing ritual. All her life Mother has been a faithful minister, but she's never received an official blessing because she's been in Baptist churches that refuse to ordain women. At my ordination I longed for Mother to receive this powerful affirmation of her ministry. Now her chance had come. I could hear Mother's strong voice on the unison invocation to the "Spirit from whom all blessings flow." As a solo reader in one of the litanies, Mother came to the line "for all of you are one in Christ-Sophia." She began loudly and trailed off on the "Sophia." She became reenergized, however, as we took turns ordaining one another, passing around a multicolored Guatemalan ministerial stole Chad had given me. Anne wept when Mother gently laid her hands on her shoulders and blessed her ministry of healing. And Mother gave a whole-hearted affirmation of my ministry, though it had taken a different direction from what Mother expected. Then Mother proudly draped the stole around her shoulders and proclaimed her call as a minister of Jesus Christ. Her face glowed, and her eyes filled with tears as we ordained her. I wanted to stay in this holy moment.

But my mind flashed back to the reason for Mother's visit to Dallas. For three weeks Mother had been struggling with what her San Angelo physician had diagnosed as pneumonia. The antibiotics he prescribed weren't helping. San Angelo's only pulmonologist had died several months before, so we scheduled an appointment for Mother with a Dallas specialist.

The Friday before the New Wineskins blessing ritual, Mother and Anne and I sat in Dr. Berdine's office. Clad in silver shin-high boots and flowing red cape, Mother began filling out the seven-page intake form as she talked to us. She read the checklist out loud: "diabetes, high blood pressure, cancer, heart palpitations, ulcers, glaucoma, venereal disease. Thank God, I can check 'no' to all these." Then she came to "unusual thoughts." We all cracked up. Anne said, "For heavens' sake, Mother, don't check that!"

A nurse came to lead us from the outer to the inner sanctum of Dr. Berdine's office. She pointed Mother to the examining table and Anne and me to the chairs beneath. Mother's silver-booted legs dangled from the table. Dr. Berdine entered, wearing a turquoise and neon gold tie. "Oh, what a lovely tie!" Mother remarked, launching Dr. Berdine into a long explanation of how his wife picked out all his clothes because he had no sense of color.

When Dr. Berdine asked Mother her age, she replied, "I don't tell that. You should never ask a woman her age." When Dr. Berdine insisted that he needed to know because he was her doctor, Mother relented, "Well, then, I was born in 1918—you can figure it out for yourself!"

Anne, squirming in her chair, asked Dr. Berdine about Mother's chest x-rays that Dr. Schultze sent from San Angelo. I gave Anne a grateful look because I also wanted to conserve our limited time with the doctor. We'd come to discuss weightier matters than neckties and age. Dr. Berdine expressed his concern over a questionable spot on Mother's right lung that hadn't improved with antibiotics. He would put her on another round of antibiotics to give it a little more time to respond. Mother cut through the tension in the room, telling Dr. Berdine, "I didn't check 'unusual thoughts' on your form, but I want you to know that I don't have any usual thoughts. All my thoughts are unusual, creative, big thoughts. Who wants to have usual thoughts?" I laughed along with Dr. Berdine and Anne, while I prayed that she had a "usual" pneumonia that could be treated with "usual" antibiotics.

Downstairs in the Baylor Plaza Frullati Cafe, Anne and Mother and I ate tuna sandwiches and drank strawberry banana smoothies fortified with green spirulina and soy powder. If anything serious even threatened Mother's lung, we would stave it off with all the weapons in our nutrition arsenal. Our conversation ran in stream-of-consciousness, from Dr. Berdine's comments about the spot on Mother's lung to his prescription of antibiotics to the merits of vitamin and herbal supplements to ways of reversing the aging process to living to the age of at least 150. Anyone listening would have checked "unusual thoughts" for all of us.

That afternoon Mother had two more doctor appointments. Anne and I went with Mother to each one, and she told the doctors we were her "honor guard." First, we went to orthopedic specialist Dr. Rathjen because of Mother's persistent pain in her hip. On his intake checklist, Mother found "hair problem." In a voice loud enough for all the people in the large waiting room to hear, she said, "Hair problem! Of course I have a hair problem, at least once a week. That's why I go to the beauty shop." The woman sitting across from us looked up from her *Time* magazine and smiled. Chest pains had put Mother in the San Angelo hospital the week before. When her friend Joan tried to help her into the wheelchair in the emergency room, Mother protested, "There's nothing wrong with my legs! It's just my heart."

In the office of Dr. Donsky, a cardiologist at Baylor, Mother continued to entertain Anne and me, along with other people who'd been reading or staring silently at the aquarium. I'd never been more grateful for Mother's gift of bringing humor to stressful situations. Thank God, Dr. Rathjen recommended more water therapy, which Mother loved, instead of hip replacement surgery. And Dr. Donsky, with the help of a thallium scan, found nothing wrong with Mother's heart.

When Mother went back to see Dr. Berdine the next Friday, the spot on her lung hadn't decreased. He led us into the hall and pointed to a white blob on Mother's x-rays hanging on the light board: "In fact, it may have gotten larger. I'm concerned that your lung hasn't responded to all the antibiotics you've taken. We need to do a bronchoscopy and a biopsy." The word "biopsy" sent chills through my body.

The following Monday morning at 7:30 Mother checked into

Baylor's outpatient surgery unit. As Mother, Anne, and I walked to Room 249, I thought of all the early mornings I'd spent on this floor making pastoral calls to patients before surgery. But now Mother was the patient, and I was the family member. I called chaplain friends Ella, Lee Ann, and Travis to come see Mother. Dark hair softly curled and mouth glowing with red Revlon lipstick, she looked elegant even in the hospital gown.

Ella commented on how good she looked, and Mother responded, "You look great too! And so young. You must be in your twenties."

"Thank you, but, no, I'm Jann's age," Ella responded.

"No, not really!" Mother exclaimed.

Then realizing what she'd said, she tried to assure me that I looked young also, much younger than my age. My heart felt 100 years old, weighed down with fear of what Dr. Berdine might find. I couldn't hold back the tears when we joined hands as Ella prayed, in a voice as commanding as Barbara Jordan's, asking Mother God to heal our mother. I looked at Anne and saw tears streaming down her cheeks also.

Outside the radiology testing room, Dr. Berdine spoke the terrible word: "cancer." He was sending the tissue for more extensive pathology tests, but he felt sure it was lung cancer. Anne burst into tears, while I started questioning Dr. Berdine. "How do you know? You said it might be some form of TB or rare fungus. Mother can't have lung cancer! She's never smoked or anything. Couldn't it just be a resistant form of pneumonia? How can you know before you get the pathology reports?" He admitted that there was a small chance that it was something else, but it looked like cancer. The pathology report would reveal what kind of cancer, and then an oncologist would know how to treat it.

I held my composure until we got to my office, which fortunately was just around the corner. Then Anne and I sobbed together. Part of me still refused to believe Dr. Berdine. I could not speak the dreaded word.

That night Mother stayed with Anne. I was glad to have time alone to write in my journal.

I sit here on this cold night in my warm red socks with white polka dots. Mother gave me these socks. My feet feel warm and cozy, but my heart aches. I remember how Mother always tried to keep my feet warm when I was little. She'd heat a soft pink flannel blanket over our floor furnace and then wrap it around my feet under the icy covers. Now I long to keep her warm and safe. If I just keep writing, I can keep Mother alive and safe. I'm obsessing over whether or not I picked the right doctor. I can't even write the words Dr. Berdine spoke today after Mother's bronchoscopy. It's too absurd and scary to think something serious might be wrong with Mother. She's invincible, a force of nature. If I just keep writing and praying, she will survive. Please Mother God, help Mother to be all right. Yesterday at CityChurch, I touched Mother's arm during the prayer time and saw deep purple surrounding and flowing through her lung. Purple replaced the white spot on Mother's x-ray. Strong, healthy, deep purple.

The next Wednesday Dr. Berdine told us that Mother's pathology reports came back negative. But he interrupted our shouts of joy and relief, telling us not to get too excited because he didn't have the answer to the spot on Mother's lung. He still thought it might be malignant. So he scheduled a CAT scan for the next Sunday. That Monday he told us that the scan showed "suspicious" fluid on Mother's lung. Dr. Berdine sent Mother immediately to the second-floor outpatient surgery unit. When he drained the fluid, to his surprise it looked clear. But he'd have to send it to pathology, he said. He prescribed another round of antibiotics and scheduled Mother to come back in two weeks to see if the lung spot had diminished. My nephew David Herring picked Mother up from the hospital and rushed her to the airport to catch a flight that very evening. She had to get back to San Angelo the next day for a beauty shop appointment and a church speaking engagement.

Two weeks later, Mother, Anne, and I gathered with New Wineskins for a healing ritual in the upper room of Grace

United Methodist Church. We sat around the purple-draped altar adorned with gold and purple votive candles and chrysanthemums. We joined in litanies of lament for the abuse women and men have suffered from patriarchal cultures and religions. Then we took turns sitting in a chair in front of the altar, expressing our specific needs for healing, and receiving healing touch and prayers from the others. Mother prayed fervently for each of us, invoking Christ-Sophia and Mother God in a voice as bold as her red cape. Now she didn't shrink from these Feminine Divine names. They sounded like a burst of energy from a place deep in her soul, a place that had long been covered over by layers of dogma against women. At last Mother had found a place where she could be deeply affirmed as a woman and as a minister. New Wineskins had ordained Mother. And now New Wineskins reached out to heal her. As Mother sat in the purple glow, we prayed for the healing of her lung, but also for healing from all the sexism and ageism she had suffered.

The next day I knew. I knew even before Dr. Berdine clipped the x-rays up on his light board and said, "Well, the spot responded to antibiotics. That means it was pneumonia or some kind of infection." The cancer cloud had finally lifted. This time he didn't stop our hugs and shouts. Mother exclaimed, "Praise God! Praise Christ-Sophia! And I'm going to tell all my friends about the powerful healing service with New Wineskins."

Mother, Anne, and I had found a place where we could come together for our healing.

Chapter Nine

Still Preaching Freedom

♦

At a meeting of the Baptist Studies Advisory Board at Brite Divinity School, I proudly introduced myself as a "Baptist feminist." Everyone laughed.

"Though some people think this phrase is an oxymoron," I went on, "I see 'Baptist' and 'feminist' as highly compatible, even inseparable."

"Amen," cheered Leon McBeth, the author of *Women in Baptist Life* who'd taught church history at Southwestern Baptist Theological Seminary for years and and who now also taught Baptist history at Brite.

Although there wasn't time on this occasion, I had come to relish opportunities to launch into discourses on the connection between feminist values and the Baptist heritage of religious freedom.

I'd speak of Baptist forefather John Leland, who led the effort to get religious freedom into the First Amendment of our U.S. Constitution, and of Roger Williams, who founded Rhode Island on the principle of religious liberty. I'd speak of Baptist foremothers Eunice Marshall, Martha Marshall, Margaret Clay, and Hannah Lee, who freely preached in eighteenth-century America. I'd speak of seventeenth-century British

Baptists who were ridiculed for having "she-preachers." Thus, I would declare, Baptists should now be the strongest advocates of women's liberation, ordination of women, equality of women and men as pastors, complete freedom for women to use our gifts in church leadership. A true Baptist would surely champion the full personhood and liberty of women, and would therefore be a feminist.

Accused of Heresy

Surely my colleagues in the Pastoral Care Department of Baylor knew my theological convictions. From the time I'd done the retreat on feminist theology, through my joining the department complete with hyphenated name, through my suggesting inclusive language for pastoral care tracts, through my leading discussions with chaplain residents on expanding divine images, through my publishing two books on Christ-Sophia, I'd made my beliefs clear. At the Woman as Healer Conference at Baylor, I'd openly presented my theology outside our department as well. A Baylor physician whom I'd worked with on the Institutional Ethics Committee had even introduced me to his rabbi as "a feminist theologian in the guise of a Baptist chaplain." So I sat stunned, listening to members of our department's education committee say they felt betrayed by my Feminine Divine references in my manuscript *Counseling People with Cancer*.

About six months before, they had invited me to deliver our department's endowed James Lecture. Pastors, pastoral counselors, and chaplains from all over the Dallas area attend this annual event. At first I expressed caution about accepting the invitation. "We've never had anyone in our department do the lecture. How will others feel about this? And besides, some of the more conservative pastors who attend might have problems with my theology."

"We'll all be proud to have one of our own give the lecture. You're the one who's written a book. And since the lecture will be from your pastoral care book, not the ones on feminist theology, no one should have a problem with it," one of the committee members said.

"Well, in some ways it's the most conservative book I've written. But still, my theology on images of God comes through because it's foundational to my ministry. Also, my doing the lecture may call attention to my other books."

The committee assured me that there'd be no problem, and continued to encourage me to deliver the lecture. I accepted, still feeling some trepidation. In the next few months I began preparation for the lecture. I gave Baylor's Continuing Education Department the required objectives, outline, and biographical information. On a cold Wednesday morning in early February 1998, the education committee asked me to attend a meeting concerning the lecture. Members of the committee had now read my manuscript.

I walked into the stuffy office of one of the committee members, sat down in the only empty chair, and looked around at the seven men holding pages of my manuscript. Several greeted me, but no one smiled. Then they started.

"I have serious reservations about your manuscript. Now, don't get me wrong. I appreciate you, and I know you do fine ministry."

"We have questions about your doing the James Lecture."

"All this discussion about sacred images—and you refer to 'Mother God.' That could really get us in trouble if you say this in the lecture."

"I feel betrayed! I thought this book would be different—that you'd just focus on pastoral care, not get into feminine images."

I tried to defend myself by reminding them that I'd told them that the book integrated my theology on divine images into my pastoral care ministry—that it was all part of who I was. And I'd been open with them about my beliefs. But my voice began to crack and my body to tremble. I got mad at myself because I couldn't hold back the tears. The accusations continued.

"You've got to take responsibility for putting us into this position. You should have known that what you wrote could cause problems. And I don't think you could leave out the feminine images in your lecture."

"This isn't Baptist theology."

"Yeah, some Baptist pastor could really cause us trouble over it."

"Frankly, I don't mind saying that I'm scared. I don't want you or any of us to lose our jobs. I don't think you should do the lecture. You're a good chaplain, and I'd like to see you stay around here."

"I'm offended that you give so many good traits to Mother images of God. I'm a father, and I think I'm also nurturing and gentle."

"This is heresy!"

Now I was feeling the walls coming closer and the air becoming thinner until I could hardly catch my breath. I kept trying to tell myself that this one lecture couldn't possibly matter so much. But I felt that much more was at stake: my whole ministry and theology seemed to be on trial. And I'd received the verdict—heretic. I didn't want to indulge any martyr complex, but I remembered Jeanne Achterberg's statement at the Woman as Healer Conference that even modern women may be stifled by horrible Inquisition memories in our collective unconscious. In that moment I felt the truth of her words.

Later I realized that my panic came also from my deep fear of failure. I had blown up the retraction of the invitation to do the lecture into a rejection of my work and even of myself. A few days later, I wrote in my journal that "part of the deep pain I felt Wednesday was from lack of appreciation of my labor." My raw feelings continued to flow into my journal:

Write, just keep writing. Keep writing and keep breathing, and I will survive. Both are necessary to my survival. I counsel people with cancer to write their feelings. So today I'll write mine. It's not my fault! I'll take responsibility for my work, but I won't take responsibility for what's not my fault.

I didn't ask to do the lecture. I tried to tell them my honest reservations. I've never hidden my theology from them. How could they think that I would cut off my deepest beliefs from my pastoral care? And their mixed messages stung: "We love you, but hate your belief system. It's heresy." Am I masochistic to stay at Baylor? Am I selling out? I can't stifle my spirit. Then I have nothing. I don't feel I have a home— at Baylor, with Baptists.

David came adamantly to my defense: "How can they do this? They offered you the lecture with full knowledge of who you are and what you believe. They can't just pull back now after all the work you've done. And I'll go tell them so, if you want me to." It helped for David to lament with me the unfairness. He also made me feel better by reminding me that my work as a chaplain and as a writer didn't depend on that lecture. Remember, he said, your book will still come out and will reach receptive people.

I looked out the window into our front yard and noticed the peach-pink blossoms on our tulip tree, a promise of spring.

My Cancer Book as Gift

Counseling People with Cancer came out, without fanfare, that April of 1998. And only a few weeks later, David's prophecy came true. One of the marrow transplant physicians I worked with told me how much he appreciated the book. Usually reserved, he said with more emotion than I'd ever heard in his voice, "It's an awesome book, just what I've been looking for . . . Amazing! It helps me understand some of the things my patients are going through and how I can help them." Now I knew I hadn't labored in vain.

In the middle of writing *Counseling Pople with Cancer*, I dreamed one night that I'd had a bone marrow transplant to treat leukemia. For a little while after I woke up, I felt too exhausted to move. The book had drained more energy from me than any other book I'd written. But how could I have expected anything else from a book about cancer? I remembered the reluctance I'd expressed to Andy Lester when he asked me to write the book: "I'm not sure I want to come home and write about what I've been doing all day with people struggling with cancer. I want my writing to give me a creative break." I'd met Andy at a Brite Baptist Studies Advisory Board meeting. After Southern Baptist Theological Seminary fell under fundamentalist control, he had moved on to chair the Pastoral Theology Department at Brite. A gentle but determined man, Andy persuaded me to write the book for a pastoral counseling series he was editing.

As I worked feverishly on the book, using weekends and vacation days to write about cancer, I thought I must have been crazy to have agreed to it. Or maybe just egotistical. I'd received a contract before finishing *Praying with Christ-Sophia,* but now I was being offered a contract before I wrote a page of the manuscript. And I'll have to admit that I felt flattered that someone as prominent in pastoral theology as Andy Lester had sought me out.

There were other gifts along the way. My colleagues at Baylor generously gave me extra weeks off to finish the book. Now I understood that their fear, not lack of respect for my work, had led them to retract the invitation to give the pastoral care lecture.

My colleague Travis Maxwell spent his own time reading the manuscript and offering valuable insights from his twenty-five years of experience as an oncology chaplain. Travis and I had co-authored an article on survivor guilt in cancer patients for the *Journal of Pastoral Care.* The research Travis had been gathering for many years contributed to this article and to my book. Other colleagues and pastor friends gave perceptive critiques. And David always listened when I felt overwhelmed by the emotions of the people I wrote about. One woman with breast cancer gave me excerpts from her journal to include in the book. Later, at her funeral, I quoted her vivid personification of hope.

In the end I discovered the purpose of my writing the book. It had been my way of giving back—to my pastoral colleagues, to all the people with cancer who'd opened their lives to me, and most of all, to Daddy. One day as I struggled with the Introduction, in a flash I knew I had to begin with the cancer story closest to my heart. I told about Daddy's agonizing disease, and then I wrote:

> I realize that I have written this book as a gift to my father and to all the other people who have profoundly influenced my life by the way they met the challenge of cancer. These courageous people have given to me from the depths and heights of their experience as I have been in relationship with them, first as daughter with my father and then as friend with several people and then as minister with people in a local parish, in a counseling center, and in several medical centers. My gift to them is this effort to represent and interpret the cancer experience in ways that will deepen the understanding and improve the art of those who minister with people going through cancer.

Brenda's Legacy

Standing in the pulpit of the chapel of First Baptist Church of Dallas, I understood more clearly my calling to people with cancer, and my purpose as a Baptist minister. I was conducting the funeral of a young woman who had died of colon cancer. I'd first met Brenda Brame in a support group I facilitated. Later, she'd come to my office with poems she'd written about dying and about all the things on earth she'd miss and about what she hoped heaven would be like. Brenda had grown up in First Baptist Church, but rarely attended any church as an adult. She'd expanded her beliefs beyond those she grew up with and had come to me to continue her spiritual exploration. Brenda seemed to take some comfort in my being a Baptist minister, but not like any she'd ever known. For one thing, she'd never seen a Baptist woman pastor. And, she said, "It's about time!"

We laughed and connected out of our similar background. When things got too heavy, Brenda started singing choruses from her Baptist camp days. Of course, I knew them. Together we sang:

> *Give me oil in my lamp, keep me burning;*
> *Give me oil in my lamp, I pray.*
> *Give me oil in my lamp, keep me burning;*
> *Keep me burning to the break of day.*

We sang these lines over and over. Perhaps we could keep Brenda "burning" against the cancer if we could just keep singing.

At her funeral service I told about our singing camp songs, and I read some of her poems and the Scripture passage she'd chosen from Ecclesiastes: "For everything there is a season, and a time for every matter under heaven: a time to be born, and a time to die." I didn't say that I couldn't believe it was time for Brenda to die. She was only thirty-two and wanted desperately to live. I knew I wouldn't have been able to do her service if I hadn't been Baptist. Her parents, staunch members of First Baptist, wouldn't have considered having a pastor other than Baptist and certainly wouldn't have asked a woman if Brenda hadn't insisted. It was probably the first time a woman had ever been in the pulpit at First Baptist, where famous fundamentalist leader W.A. Criswell had been pastor more than forty years. And I could see Brenda smiling down and saying, "It's about time!" At that moment I felt deep gratitude for Brenda's gifts to me. Also, I was glad to be Baptist so I could give this memorial service to her.

At the graveside we released white helium balloons into the sunny August sky and sang a song Brenda had written. I went home and opened my journal to write my feelings that I'd kept at bay so I could get through the service. I came across an entry dated May 4. On this evening I had joined

Brenda and some of her friends to celebrate her TV debut. CNN had interviewed her concerning her feelings about a "miracle" cancer drug that would be approved in about a year. It would probably be too late for her, she said in the interview. She also said that while most people her age were planning weddings, she was planning her funeral. Many times Brenda had expressed concern about leaving a legacy. She lamented that she'd not had enough time to do much that people would remember. I'd reminded her of the vital contributions she'd made as a volunteer toward the founding of the Dallas chapter of Gilda's Club, a support center for people with cancer. But the CNN interview convinced her that she'd have a legacy.

That balmy evening in May, after the interview, we gathered for dinner—Brenda, Diane, Deb, Martha, Kathy, Mary Jo, and I—knowing that Brenda didn't have much time left. But she looked radiant and said she felt fine, except when she tried to eat. She did, however, drink wine with us as we toasted and prayed around a table in Deb's back yard—lush green and blooming like Eden. In my journal I had jotted down these lines:

> Surrounded by flowers and music,
> seven women joined hands
> in a circle for grace,
> more felt than said.
> We drank in the moment, holy, with the wine,
> laughing and longing
> for the feast to go on past the night.

A month after Brenda's funeral, Diane and Deb looked out the window of their plane headed for Washington D.C. and saw an angel cloud flying along beside. Trembling, they said together, "That's Brenda. She is coming." And she went with us through her picture on T-shirts we wore in D.C. that September at "The March: Coming Together to Conquer Cancer." Brenda had made big plans to go. Diane had said she'd take her in a wheelchair, if she had to. Instead, we took her in memory and spirit.

Mother Preaches Freedom

Daddy also went with us on The March in September of 1998. I could hear his deep baritone voice cheering us on. It didn't seem possible that it had been thirty-two years since Daddy died of lymphoma. Mother jumped at the chance to rally for a cancer cure and flew with me to Washington. Chad, who worked there as a communications director for Senator Mary Landrieu of Louisiana, took off to join us for The March. The three of us wore placards with Daddy's picture and the caption in bold black letters: "Conquer Cancer! In Celebration of the Life of Truman Aldredge." On the Friday night before The March, we stood with thousands of people in front of the Lincoln Memorial to shout with Jesse Jackson, "Pain to power! Pain to power!" Prostate cancer survivor General Norman Schwarzkopf, the leader of The March, challenged us to work together to fight cancer with the zeal that we've used against other common enemies.

The next day, on the National Mall, Chad, Mother, Diane, Deb, and I walked past forty-three patchwork quilts with little faces stitched in the squares. Beneath the pictures of the children were their ages and the kind of cancer they were fighting. Some had died, the quilts said. An oncology nurse stood near us, looking at the quilts, and told us that she couldn't work with children anymore. It was too heartbreaking to see children suffer, she said.

We moved down the Mall to hear Vice President Al Gore promise more money for cancer research and news commentator Cokie Roberts tell about her sister who died of breast cancer. We were pressed in a crowd of thousands of people—standing, in wheelchairs, or huddled on the ground. A group of ten women elbowed their way closer to the platform, wearing identical T-shirts with the words "Fight Ovarian Cancer, the Silent Killer." The parents of David, a thirty-two-year-old with lymphoma, showed us his wedding pictures of a year before his cancer diagnosis. I heard their anger as they told us that David couldn't have children because of all the chemotherapy he'd taken.

Mother stood sweating and taking copious notes in the 100-plus-degree heat. She went home and wrote an article that was printed in the *San Angelo Standard Times* and the *Minden Press-Herald*. Her article ended with these words:

Imagine a cancer-free America. Imagine waking up in a world where no child knows the word, "chemo," where every child is given immune shots for cancer. It will come to pass. Hope, triumph, and grief were all part of The March experience for me. We will win the war against cancer. "NO MORE CAN-CER" is the battle cry!

As I read her words, I realized that Mother could be just as powerful a preacher of freedom as Daddy. It upset me that her Baptist church in San Angelo still refused to ordain women.

Mother continued to stand strong for full rights for women, even through her grief over the loss of another husband to cancer. About five months after the Washington March, my stepfather Taylor was diagnosed with multiple myeloma. The pain became so excruciating that he could barely walk, but for almost a year he continued to lead mission groups to Russia, refusing even a wheelchair at airports. And Mother hated people's comments that he was "going downhill" or "getting bad," preferring to say he had "experienced changes." The night the doctors told her he had only a few hours or days, she called and told us he'd undergone "dramatic changes." Denial, some said. But Mother's attitude through Taylor's dying, as it had been through Daddy's, felt life-affirming to me.

After Taylor's death, several men offered to take over Missions Our Mission, the organization she and Taylor had founded. She said she could lead it herself. I told Mother that I thought the acronym for Missions Our Mission, "MOM," signified that she should indeed lead it and that Mother God would bless her work with MOM. She seemed pleased, but said she'd probably not share that insight with the men. One man told her he'd be glad to take care of her, but she said, "Thank you very much, but I can take care of myself and Missions Our Mission." She refused to be patronized because of her gender or age, and told me she would prove that a woman could be a strong leader.

Mother stood firm in her resolve to release something at Taylor's funeral. First, she wanted butterflies. She'd gotten this idea at my nephew David Herring's wedding in October. When she discovered she couldn't get butterflies in January, she turned to doves. Anne and I dissuaded her by saying, "The doves might decide to perch on a low limb instead of fly heavenwards, and then what would become of the symbolism?" So Mother turned her focus to balloons. Her friend Joan had told her about balloons released at a graveside service in Austin. Mother asked if I'd ever seen anything like this, and I described Brenda's service. Also, Anne and I told Mother about the butterfly-shaped balloon we'd released after the freedom ritual at New Wineskins. That did it. She could have her butterflies and balloons all in one.

"I don't think my dad would want the balloons," Taylor's son John said.

"He'll love them now from his higher perspective," Mother countered.

"You've got to talk your mother out of the balloons," David told me. "You know how dignified Taylor was. Balloons just wouldn't be appropriate."

Anne and I began to wonder. We asked Mother if balloons had ever been released at a funeral in San Angelo.

"I don't think so, but this will be the first. Won't that be great?" she answered.

Mother could not be deterred from the balloons. We found only one butterfly-shaped balloon in all of San Angelo—at a Super Wal-Mart. At midnight Mother, Anne, and I stood outside Wal-Mart, exhausted, with the butterfly balloon tightly in hand. We had a local florist deliver to the graveside this balloon along with fifty other helium-filled, transparent balloons in colors picking up those on the butterfly—purple, gold, rose, emerald, blue. At the close of the memorial service in First Baptist Church, Anne and I gave a reading celebrating resurrection, interweaving a vivid description of a butterfly emerging from a cocoon with a passage in I Corinthians: "This mortal will put on immortality. Death has been swallowed up in victory."

At the conclusion of the graveside service, Mother popped out from under the funeral canopy, holding the butterfly balloon. In a loud voice she cried, "I release you to new life," and let go of the balloon. As the butterfly balloon floated up into the cloudless sky, Taylor's grandchildren distributed the other balloons. Lyndel Vaught began slowly singing that old gospel hymn "When the Roll is Called Up Yonder." When he got to the phrase "and the morning breaks, eternal, bright, and fair," somehow we all knew it was time to let go. Fifty shimmering balloons rose upward, straight into the sun. We stared transfixed as the balloons ascended, filling the sky with their radiant colors. Mother had preached another powerful sermon of freedom.

A little over two months later, Anne and I sat on the second pew of Cockrell Hill Baptist Church in Dallas, listening to Mother preach on her mission activity in the Ukraine. Anne whispered, "This feels like a time warp," and I nodded agreement. Images of Anne and me as little girls on the second pew of First Baptist in Minden flashed through my mind. Only then, we looked up at our daddy, not our mother, in the pulpit. And the Minden church was always packed on Sunday mornings, downstairs and balcony, with adults of all ages and children and teenagers. Cockrell Hill Baptist on this Sunday morning in April of 2000 felt like a morgue in comparison. Only about seventy, mostly elderly, people rattled around in a sanctuary that seated over 600. But like our Minden church in the 1950s, Cockrell Hill's ushers and ministers were all men. Mother, no doubt, was the first woman to preach in that church.

In the restroom before the service, women in their seventies and eighties—with teased and plastered white hair, portly bodies, drab print dresses, and clodhopper shoes—stood at the sinks alongside Mother, in her trim red skirt and blouse with vest of many colors, red high-heeled shoes, and hair softly styled and colored her natural dark brown. Although Mother was probably as old or older than these women, she looked at least twenty years younger.

As the choir laboriously filed into the loft at the beginning of the service, Mother sat on the front pew blowing up a red balloon. As when we were little and came across "my spirit pants for thee" in the hymnal, Anne and I had to choke back our laughs. Several people in the choir grinned, but most stared blankly. If angels descended through the ceiling, their expressions wouldn't change, I thought.

At the appointed time, Mother sprang up to the pulpit, launching into a story of a young woman transformed through the work of Missions Our Mission in the Ukraine. Mother appealed for money to purchase a building for a church in Odessa, Ukraine. By preaching in churches all over Texas she had already raised more than $80,000 toward the $150,000 building, and she was determined to raise the rest. She talked about saving people in the Ukraine, but I could think only of her saving herself from grief through her all-consuming mission work, and of the possibility that her bubbly red presence might bring some life to this church. My heart ached with love and pride as I watched her. Yes, at one point in her sermon, Mother burst the red balloon—to illustrate, she said, that no matter how bright and shiny a person's exterior, if he or she didn't have Jesus on the inside, everything would shatter. Not even the balloon exploding into the microphone stirred that church. No wonder the service ended with a lugubrious hymn pleading for salvation from despair and "infinite sin."

After the service Mother stood near the front pews, where she'd lined up Kinko-copied color pictures of the mission in the Ukraine, stacks of brochures, and offering envelopes. Only a few people came by to look at the pictures and take envelopes. But I'd like to believe that the image of Mother blowing up a red balloon and preaching in her red outfit made some lasting impression on Cockrell Hill Baptist Church. I longed for the women of the church to see that they could preach from the pulpit, not just sit in the pews. And I dreamed that the whole congregation would quit singing of "infinite sin" and start welcoming red balloons in church.

"Why are you still Baptist?"

"So why are you still Baptist?" There was that pesky question again. But this time it came from someone trying to understand rather than challenge me.

Dana Durham, a pastoral intern who'd worked with me in Waco, and I sat in a small coffee shop in Albuquerque, having breakfast with Miriam Therese Winter. I had asked Miriam Therese why she remained Catholic, so it was only fair that she ask me why I stayed Baptist. When I had learned that Miriam Therese was one of the leaders of the Women-Church Conference, I not only rushed to get my plane ticket to Albuquerque but also boldly called her to see if she could squeeze me into her schedule while she was there. She graciously consented to meet with me. For many years I'd admired Miriam Therese's prophetic voice and had celebrated rituals in her books *WomanPrayer, WomanSong; WomanWord;* and *WomanWisdom.*

As we ate breakfast, Rosemary Radford Ruether, another of my heroines in feminist theology, spotted Miriam Therese and asked if she could join us. Dana stared in amazement. It took me a little while to collect my voice to tell Rosemary how profoundly influenced I'd been by her books, especially *Sexism and God-Talk* and *Women-Church.* Our discussion turned to our ambivalent relationship with our religious traditions. Listening to Miriam Therese and Rosemary talk about reasons for their continued connection to the Catholic church, I realized more clearly my reasons for staying Baptist. Much of what Miriam Therese said that morning she later stated in an interview published in a journal called *Sojourners:*

First of all, I don't stay within. That's not the terminology I would use. I am the church. We are the church. And then, where would one go? I try to live faithful to the Spirit in the tradition in which my roots are planted. But I don't just follow the path. You make the path as you go toward the destination, and in some ways remake the maps. I find the challenge of that exciting. Blessings come with new insights that fit within the tradition, even though the tradition doesn't yet understand it. . . . I think the preference by the hierarchy would be that women would just leave and leave everything alone. For we're staying with our new understanding that church is not just an institution—we are the church. And it is our dream that we will transform the structures of power so that the church becomes a community of energy and commitment from which we can go out to transform society.

"Maybe I stay Baptist also," I told them, "because I've always loved a challenge."

"And where could a feminist find a bigger challenge than in the Baptist church?" Dana chimed in.

"Or the Catholic church?" Miriam Therese added, and we all laughed.

Later I would read the following passage in a book by Carol Lee Flinders, *At the Root of this Longing:*

Organized religion has been no great friend to women, but that must not discourage women from reaching out to reclaim the connection with the sacred that has so long been denied us. And if we restructure entire denominations in the process, well and good. Feminism *catches fire* when it draws upon its inherent spirituality.

I was just stubborn and idealistic enough to believe I could take part in restructuring the Baptist denomination, drawing from its roots in religious liberty and soul freedom. There might be many Baptist leaders who wished I would leave, but they'd have to keep on wishing.

So what, if people saw me on the margins of the Baptist church? I would be in the company of many people I admired, like Phyllis Trible, Will Campbell, James Dunn, and Peter Gomes.

Feminist scholar Phyllis Trible had contributed significantly to my theology, especially through her book *God and the Rhetoric of Sexuality*. I especially loved her translation of divine "mercy" as "womb-love" and had drawn from her exposition when I wrote *In Whose Image? God and Gender*. Trible had graciously written an endorsement, commending my "irenic spirit, clear writing, and passionate conviction" that made my book "accessible and instructive for all who have eyes to see and ears to hear." In a lecture at Southwestern University in Georgetown, Texas, I heard Trible refer to Girls' Auxiliary (GA's). Of course, I recognized GA's as Baptist, so after the lecture I asked her about her denomination. She said, yes, she'd grown up Baptist, but was now a "peripheral" Baptist.

Will Campbell called himself a "renegade" or "bootleg" Baptist preacher. He'd been among my heroes since I'd read of his activism in the civil rights movement. And then I heard him speak at a T.B. Maston Ethics Banquet shortly after the Southern Baptist boycott of Disney because of the company's policy of nondiscrimination for gays and lesbians. Campbell said he'd gone out and bought all his grandchildren stock in Disney because of this courageous stand. My admiration of Will Campbell continued to rise when Chad and Brett told me of his tribute at the funeral of Willie Morris in Yazoo City, Mississippi. Campbell and Morris had fought together against racism in the South. Never one to stick with tradition, Campbell concluded his eulogy with these words: "Willie Morris gave us a speech of sixty-four years. A good speech deserves a good round of applause." The congregation responded with an unforgettable standing ovation.

James Dunn, executive director of the Baptist Joint Committee on Public Affairs (BJCPA) in Washington D.C., and I together made a Baptist fundamentalist "hit" list. The

October 1998 issue of a right-wing newsletter called *Plumbline* denounced James Dunn and the BJCPA for their "leadership role in the production of a far-left political training manual entitled *How to Win: A Practical Guide for Defeating the Radical Right in Your Community.*" Fundamentalists condemned this manual especially because the contributing organizations included the National Gay and Lesbian Task Force, National Abortion Federation, and Planned Parenthood. The *Plumbline* article also insinuated that Dunn's activity as trustee of Americans United for Separation of Church and State was reprehensible. Reading this slam on Dunn made me proud to be Baptist and proud that he was Chad's godfather. James Dunn had been a good friend since he and David had worked together at the Baptist General Convention of Texas. Chad was born on Dunn's birthday, and they quickly developed a close relationship that continued when Chad went to work on Capitol Hill. I'd long admired Dunn's work for freedom of conscience. So I felt honored to be listed with Dunn as a threat to the religious right. The *Plumbline* article referred to me as "a feminist theologian calling for the worship of Christ-Sophia." I celebrated this one accurate statement. The rest of the paragraph misquotes and distorts my writing on Christ-Sophia.

Virginia Ramey Mollenkott, another of my mothers in the feminist faith, reminded me that Peter Gomes is Baptist. An African-American out-of-the-closet homosexual minister of Harvard University's Memorial Church, Gomes challenges racism, sexism, and homophobia through his prophetic interpretations of the Bible. I met Virginia Mollenkott when she preached at the Cathedral of Hope in Dallas. I told her how profoundly she'd influenced my theology by her book *The Divine Feminine,* the first I'd read on female images of God in Scripture. I was elated when she replied, "Oh, you're Jann Aldredge-Clanton. I didn't know you lived in Dallas. Your Christ-Sophia books are wonderful; I've referred to them in my lectures. And you're Baptist, like Peter Gomes. He's Baptist and what a prophet, astounding!" And then she threw her hands into the air and shouted, "Hallelujah, the Spirit moves in many ways!" I joined her: "Hallelujah, She certainly does!"

Choosing When to Speak

More and more, I realized I needed to free myself if I were going to preach freedom for others. I'd turned down several interviews with the *Dallas Morning News*. My colleagues had voiced anxiety that my feminist theology would cause trouble, and I didn't want to hurt them. But I had to admit that I shied away from controversy too. Sometimes I felt like a coward. Crying, I called Anne.

"I'm just chicken. I don't have the guts to speak out. It's like I'm trying to hide what I've poured so much of my soul into and spent so much time writing."

"Did you really feel you should do the interviews?"

"Yes and no. That's my problem. I'm so wishy-washy. That's why people don't take me seriously."

"Oh, they take you seriously, all right. That's why they're so afraid."

"If I keep stifling my spirit, it might die," I moaned.

"Oh, no, your spirit can't die. Look at it this way. When you're silent, you're not stifling your spirit. You're just choosing when to share your spirit. You knew on some level that the interviews weren't worth risking your job."

I had no doubt about what I should do when Brian called and asked to have a prayer meeting in my office before the vote over ousting University Baptist Church (UBC) from the Baptist General Convention of Texas. UBC's ordination of two openly gay men as deacons had fomented controversy among Texas Baptists. The Executive Board of the Convention was meeting at Baylor to decide the fate of UBC. I told Brian I'd be honored to have the prayer meeting. So they squeezed into my office—the pastor of UBC, the two deacons in question, and some members of Honesty, the support organization for gay and lesbian Baptists. We joined hands and called earnestly upon the God of justice. The deacons' gentle prayers for understanding brought tears to my eyes. Nancy saw us walking out of my office and said, "Jann, if you don't get fired for one thing, it'll be another!" University Baptist, not I, got booted that day. It grieved me to watch Baptist leaders ignore the fervent call for justice for homosexual persons, as well as the pleas for the basic Baptist doctrines of freedom of conscience and autonomy of the local church.

Healing Environment

Chad told his friend Cary Pierce, "My mom's doing the Patch Adams thing at Baylor Hospital." Cary had been with the nationally acclaimed group "Jackopierce" and now had launched out as a solo performer. He generously volunteered to come play at Baylor as part of our Healing Environment Program. Like a troubadour, Cary went room to room with his guitar and mellow voice, delighting patients and their families. After a concert he'd given in the family room of the marrow transplant unit, one of the young nurses said to me, "Cary Pierce is awesome and so good-looking! I couldn't believe it when I heard you'd gotten him here." I knew my stock had risen. She'd probably thought I was some stodgy chaplain, and now her opinion had changed, thanks to Chad and Cary.

The Healing Environment Program had begun with a small group of oncology professionals meeting in a basement room in the cancer center. For almost two years we ran the program with volunteer clowns and musicians and meditation tapes contributed by the Pastoral Care Department. Our mission was to empower patients with treatments that complemented the physical treatment they received. Social worker Greg Powers was chair. Later, when Greg was in Slovakia with the Peace Corps, another social worker, Kathy Thomas-Welch, and I became co-chairs. Two women with hyphenated names were bound to stir things up.

Customer demand spurred all medical centers to take a

more serious look at complementary treatments. Baylor formed a Complementary Care Team. The chair of that team invited me to speak on the Healing Environment Program. In my red and black power suit I stood before the group to proclaim the healing power of meditation and music and art and humor. I quoted Florence Nightingale on the power of beautiful objects to effect outcomes in illness, William Congreve on music's "charms to sooth the savage breast," and the book of Proverbs on a cheerful heart as good medicine. And since my audience consisted mostly of physicians, I also quoted extensively from empirical research studies listed in the bibliography I'd attached to my handout. I had that exhilarating feeling I got when I knew I was on. After I finished, everyone applauded. Then one of Baylor's medical directors said he'd love to see the Healing Environment Program all over the medical center, not just in oncology. "If anyone here doesn't agree," he said, "just go see the movie *Patch Adams*." Not long after that, he helped us get the money for Baylor TV's meditation channel with peaceful music, nature photography, and instruction in relaxation—one of my big dreams from the beginning of Healing Environment. Then contributions from Baylor's auxiliary and several foundations made possible our placement of splendid backlighted nature scenes and aquariums throughout the medical center.

I also dreamed of a labyrinth in an Interfaith Garden of Healing at Baylor. Margaret Christensen had loaned me a book on this ancient circular prayer path. At Chartres Cathedral in France, on our thirtieth wedding anniversary trip, David and I had stood with awe in the center of the oldest known labyrinth. The guide told us that it probably originated in pre-Christian days. I'd also experienced the healing power of the labyrinth in Dallas at the Episcopal Church of the Transfiguration. At a meeting of the Interfaith Task Force, Margaret proposed this prayer path as a symbol accessible to all faiths. Everyone agreed. I relished chairing this task force which brought together physicians and other health care professionals from six faith traditions.

In response to a physician who expressed dismay when one of her Jewish patients couldn't get matzah at Baylor during Passover, the Interfaith Task Force worked with dietary services to provide options for various religious traditions. We also sponsored a cultural diversity conference to educate Baylor employees. From the beginning we planned a sacred place where people of all religions would feel comfortable coming for prayer. Our mission was to advance the goal of Baptist pastor and founder George Truett that Baylor be "a great humanitarian institution where people of all faiths and those of none can come with equal confidence." I could preach this vision of freedom. And I did, every chance I got to promote the Interfaith Task Force. George Truett made me proud of my Baptist heritage.

Look, She is Here!

The voices of my radical Baptist foremothers and forefathers came swelling through my voice at the International Peacemakers Conference on September 9, 1999. After my blessing during the Women of the Cloth ceremony, Barb hugged me and exclaimed, "You were so powerful! You didn't sound like the gracious Southern lady up there."

For over a year Barb Middleton had led in planning this four-day conference which she called "Rights of Passage: Healing Through Chaos into the Millennium." Ten years earlier she'd participated in the first Peacemakers Conference held on August 8, 1988 (8-8-88). She wanted to follow up with an even bigger celebration on the eve of the millennium, on 9-9-99. I accepted Barb's invitation to lead a workshop on "Expanding Our Images of the Divine" and to take part in the Women of the Cloth ceremony at the close of the conference.

Meg Gloger and Kathryn Marshall coordinated the Women of the Cloth ceremony. While Kathryn recruited women clergy of many religious traditions, Meg poured her liturgical talent into creating the ritual. Meg had moved from Nacogdoches to

Dallas to go through Baylor's Clinical Pastoral Education Program, and now she worked as a chaplain with a Dallas hospice organization. Early on the Sunday before the conference began, Meg called and told me that during her morning meditation Sophia revealed to her that I was to wear red for the Women of the Cloth ritual. What I wore was the last thing I had time to worry about. The week before, Meg had talked about asking each woman to wear the worship-leader attire appropriate to her tradition. I told Meg I'd probably wear my black robe with one of my stoles.

When she told me that her revelation was of me in red, I said, "Red is the dominant color in the Guatemalan stole Chad gave me, so I guess I'm supposed to wear that."

"No, no. In my vision, you're wearing a long, flowing red dress. You know, red is the color of power."

"I don't have a long red dress."

"Then you owe it to yourself to go out and buy one," Meg said in a voice with more authority than I'd ever heard from her.

I needed to spend the little time I had in writing my blessing for the ritual, not in shopping. And besides, I hated to shop. I would have dismissed Meg's words, but she said that Sophia had spoken to her. Meg sounded so convincing that I had to listen. That Sunday afternoon I spent three hours in North Park Mall looking for a flowing red dress. It was a season of black and gray. I found few red outfits, and they were tailored suits or frilly evening gowns. The next morning at the conference I told Meg that she must have heard Sophia incorrectly and that I would just wear my black robe and the hand-woven Guatemalan stole.

Baylor paid my way and gave me four days off so that I could attend the entire conference. Also, I felt grateful to Baylor for making a contribution to support the conference, partly because Margaret Christensen and I took part in the program. On Monday morning, September 6, I gave my presentation on expanding divine images to ten women and one man, who kept popping up and taking pictures, he said, for his wife, who had attended another workshop. Excitement filled the room as everyone participated in a ritual for healing, ending with singing "We Sound a Call to Freedom."

Tuesday morning I did the same workshop for another group. It thrilled me to see our two newest Baylor chaplains, Lee Ann Rathbun and Ella McCarroll, in this group. They drank in every word. When we came to "We Sound a Call to Freedom," I could hear their voices above the other women—including two from Germany and one from South Africa. Another woman gave us a beat with her hand against the back of a folding metal chair. We all joined hands and danced around in a circle when we sang the final refrain:

Free at last, O Hallelujah!
Free at last, O Hallelujah!
Christ-Sophia, you have freed us!
Your truth has set us free.

I hadn't realized how sorely I needed recharging, and what this conference could give me. It invigorated me more than my kitchen cabinet full of vitamins or a week of workouts on the Stairmaster. In the sanctuary of the magnificent Cathedral Guadalupe in downtown Dallas, Barb welcomed the gathering of more than 700 people from all over the world. In her long black dress and purple shawl draped over one shoulder, Barb looked like an Egyptian queen as she declared the purpose of the conference: "Rights of Passage to peace will explore both rights and rites necessary to move through the chaos surrounding us and to live in peace, love and harmony in the next millennium." How proud I was to have Barb as friend and New Wineskins sister. That first night I got to hear Don Campbell, whose book *The Mozart Effect* I quoted in my Healing Environment promotions. Don had that large crowd swaying and clapping paper plates to Mozart's "Rondo-Allegro" from *Eine Kleine Nacht Musik*. I felt joyous and free like I did as a child in church rhythm band. Then on Tuesday morning I had the treat of China Galland's plenary address. China's book *The Bond Between Women: A Journey to Fierce Compassion* had recently aroused me more fully to the power of the Divine Feminine to bring liberation and healing around the world. On Wednesday morning Jeanne Achterberg challenged me with her reminder that healers are "in service to the Divine." Also, I had a restoring experience of walking the sacred path of the labyrinth with Mary Ann Reed, a labyrinth expert whom I'd first met at the Women-Church Conference in Albuquerque.

Tuesday afternoon at the Peacemakers Conference Meg, Marylou Ghyst, and I went to the arts and crafts display. Marylou and I had performed Meg's "unorthodox" ordination at the Unity church Marylou pastored. Because Catholics still don't ordain women priests, Meg couldn't be ordained in her own tradition. Not wanting to join any other denomination, she had chosen instead for us to ordain her as a "nondenominational" minister. Marylou had seen some handmade dresses in the display room. She and Meg convinced me to try on a dress—a red one. When I stood in front of the mirror, others gathered round, including Elizabeth from New Wineskins. The sleeveless dress hung loose in several layers from my shoulders to my ankles. The brushed cotton felt soft on my skin. The designer showed me how to pull up one layer like a shawl around my shoulders. Another option was to drape the cloth over one shoulder, like a Venus statue.

Marylou exclaimed, "You've got to have this dress. You look like a goddess!" Meg, Elizabeth, and of course the designer agreed.

Meg said, "Here it is—the long, flowing red dress. This is what you're to wear for the Women of the Cloth ceremony."

Maybe this was the fulfillment of Meg's revelation—a vivid red dress, long and flowing. But my cautious voice warned, "Don't do it. It's too bold. It's not me. This is something Mother would wear, but not me." And the thrifty Scot in me joined in, "Don't spend money on something I'll wear only for this occasion. I can never wear it again—to work or anywhere I can think of." But Elizabeth, Meg, Marylou, and other women who kept gathering told me I just had to have it. Perhaps it was Sophia who finally convinced me to buy the red dress.

The next morning I felt more playful as Brian Burton and I rehearsed our antiphonal blessing for the plenary session. He laughed as I kept waving my arms and saying "Let's *flow, flow* with the poetry." And we did. In strong, lilting voices we gave our blessing:

TOGETHER:	Celebrate the Divine Feminine and the Divine Masculine in all of us and in all creation.
BRIAN:	Let us celebrate the sacredness of every living being.
JANN:	Let us claim our holy power.
BRIAN:	Let us dare to dream big dreams of bringing peace to our community and our world.
JANN:	Let us dare to believe that we contribute to healing our global community by gathering here to share our visions.
TOGETHER:	Come to us, Spirit from whom all blessings flow; Wake us to see more than we know; Help us claim all our gifts and pow'r; Fill us with grace that we may flow'r.
JANN:	Sister Spirit moves around us;
BRIAN:	Brother Spirit joins in love;
TOGETHER:	She and He together dancing, Crowned with holy Heav'nly Dove. May we join this dance of freedom, Making heav'n and earth anew. All our gifts will blossom fully As our dreams come into view.
JANN:	Sister Spirit gives us power;
BRIAN:	Brother Spirit ends all strife.
TOGETHER:	She and He together lead us To a spring of flowing life. May we drink this gift of healing From a Giver wise and true. Now our voices join in shouting, "Come and see all things made new."

The chanter who was then supposed to lead us in a procession to another meeting room hadn't arrived, so Barb called out to Brian and me to go back on stage. I whispered to Brian that we could sing the last part of the blessing, which I'd originally written to the tune of the hymn "Servant Song." I announced to the group that singing wasn't my gift, but then proceeded to lead out in a loud voice, "Sister Spirit moves around us; Brother Spirit joins in love." Brian, thankfully, joined me in leading the singing. Later I marveled that I, whose greatest nightmare was being unprepared, felt confident enough to ad-lib before that large congregation—especially with singing. At this conference I was growing bolder by the day.

Wednesday over lunch, Meg announced that she'd had another revelation about my part in the Women of the Cloth ritual the next day. She passed me a sheet of paper upon which she'd written, "I am the breath of life. I am Sophia. She Who Is. She Who Dwells Within."

She said, "You're the one to give the final blessing. So you are to be Sophia. You are to speak her words."

"That feels a little awesome," I said, laughing.

Meg, dead serious, replied, "Think about it. This is the revelation I received in my morning meditation."

Again, Meg sounded convincing. So Wednesday night I sat down at my computer to rewrite my blessing. I stared at the words Meg had jotted down. It still felt too arrogant to begin with, "I am Sophia." Maybe I could speak for Sophia without presuming to be her. Some of the biblical writers showed me the way. They would begin with "Thus says the Lord," and then speak for the Almighty. So I began writing, "Hear the voice of She Who Dwells Within Us All." Now I could speak for the One far larger than I, the One within all those gathered at the conference.

Thursday morning we met at 8:30 to rehearse the Women of the Cloth ceremony. It became quickly apparent that the designer of the goddess dresses had done good business. I stood in my long flowing scarlet dress with women wearing the same dress in different colors—white, light blue, emerald, and royal blue. Meg arranged us in a semicircle on the platform of the cathedral, in front of a high altar over which hung an eighteen-foot tapestry of Our Lady of Guadalupe. Up until the last minute, Kathryn continued to invite women to join the ritual. Our group included a Jewish rabbi, a Christian Scientist practitioner, a Buddhist spiritual leader, an Islamic holy woman with scarf draped over her head, a former nun now ordained a nondenominational minister, a still-practicing nun, a Unity pastor, an Episcopal priest, a Methodist minister, and me, a Baptist minister. Meg, tall and regal in her white goddess dress and purple stole, began with a proclamation of the destruction caused by worship of a one-dimensional deity and the healing that comes through including the Divine Feminine. Marylou led the whole congregation, male and female, in marriage vows to the Divine Feminine. A religious leader from Kosovo gave a heart-rending, tearful plea for support for her sister, imprisoned in Serbia for her human rights activities. The women continued, one by one, praying and blessing until I felt a dam break in my soul.

It came time for my benediction. I stepped up to the mike and began: "Hear the voice of She Who Dwells Within Us All, 'I am the breath of life. I am the healing power. I am Wisdom and Love. I am a Fountain of blessings flowing freely through all creation.'" With arms stretching out and palms up I made sweeping gestures to include all those on stage and in the congregation. I could feel the red dress flowing with my arms. I'd decided to wear the Guatemalan stole with the dress because the colors went so beautifully together, and because the stole made me feel more ministerial.

From some deep well my voice rose, bold and clear, as I continued, "Come to me! Come to me! There is life in my words and healing in my touch." My voice came from a place without fear and timidity. Maybe it was the radiant dress, or perhaps the energy of that incredible gathering and all the marvelous blessings spoken by the Women of the Cloth. Or perhaps Meg had been right when she told me I was to be Sophia's voice. All I know is that I felt free and powerful and totally unafraid as I invited the congregation to "listen to Her voice and feel Her touch."

My voice continued to swell as I quoted lines from one of my hymns: "Long we've needed Her embrace, glory and power of Her grace." My bright and flowing arms stretched wider in a circular gesture toward all the women around me on stage as I continued, "Now we gather up Her blessings as we celebrate Her many names: Ruah, Creative Spirit, Sophia, Hokmah, Wisdom, Sister, Shekinah, Mother Eagle, Friend, Black Madonna, Divine Midwife, Mother Hen, Birth-Giver, Comforting Mother, Divine Healer, Holy Mother, and so many more." Then with even larger arms I reached up toward the eighteen-foot Lady of Guadalupe and then out toward the Women of the Cloth and all the people in the congregation as I exclaimed: "Look, look, for She is here! Her wisdom words have long been near. Now, now, behold Her grace, divinity in Her image." I continued with a supplication to the "Great Creator of the universe, She and He, all in all" to pour out blessings of hope and healing for the new millennium. And with arms lifted high above my head I called out in a loud voice: "Come, Spirit who makes all things new. Show us your wider, fuller view. Teach us our wholeness now to see. Stir us to be all we can be."

Everyone rose and shouted, "Amen!" Then I heard Elizabeth shout "A-she," our New Wineskins' prayer closing, a word from the mouth of a child. Harriet's six-year-old daughter Leslie asked why we say "Amen" instead of "A-she." Harriet, thrilled to see Leslie's consciousness already raised, didn't explain that "Amen" didn't have anything to do with "men." She just replied, "That's a good point. We'll say A-she." Upon hearing this story New Wineskins adopted "A-she." I joined Elizabeth's "A-she," and a chorus of "A-she's" followed.

Then the congregation stood and sang my words to Beethoven's "Hymn to Joy":

Celebrate a new day dawning, sunrise of a golden morn;
Christ-Sophia dwells among us, glorious visions now are born.

Equal partners 'round the table, we make dreams reality;
Calling out our gifts we nurture hope beyond all we can see.

Christ-Sophia lights the pathway to a world of harmony;
Sister-Brother Love surrounds us, nourishing our synergy.
Earth joins in our rich communion, grateful for our healing care;
Leaping deer and soaring eagles, all Earth's fullness now can share.

Sing a song of jubilation, dance with joyous revelry;
Clapping trees and laughing rivers join our call to liberty.
Free at last to blossom fully, flow'ring forth in beauty bright,
We become a new creation, bursting open into light.

We'd sung this hymn many times in small gatherings of New Wineskins and in workshops and even at the celebration when *Praying with Christ-Sophia* first came out. But I'd never before heard it sung so triumphantly in so lofty a sanctuary by so large a congregation. By this time I felt close to an out-of-body experience and at the same time more fully embodied than ever.

The next day at Baylor, Lucy Aguirre-Kelly, an occupational therapist on the Healing Environment Team, said, "You blew me away yesterday! Your blessing in the cathedral was amazing. I saw a different side of you." Jo Wharton called and said, "When I saw you standing up there with your arms held out under Our Lady of Guadalupe, I started bawling. You were so powerful. Your words, your voice, your gestures, the red dress—astounding. I felt Her presence. Thank you for such a gift." I thanked Jo for her kind words and for her dedicated leadership of feminist ritual circles. Other friends told me that they'd never experienced me so bold and compelling.

I too experienced myself in a new way as I gave that blessing at the Women of the Cloth ceremony. It was as though the threads of my life had come together to reveal a design as clear as that on the tapestry in the Cathedral Guadalupe. My interfaith thread shone through as I stood at the altar of a Catholic cathedral, surrounded by spiritual leaders from multiple faith traditions. My Baptist roots came forth in my proclamation of freedom. Granted, I preached a different kind of freedom than my daddy could have imagined, a freedom that my mother was only beginning to experience. But, nonetheless, I felt linked to those Baptist founders who preached religious liberty into our constitution. My Baptist heritage had also given me the model of dynamic preaching. Some of my clergywomen friends, from quieter traditions, seemed surprised to hear my loud Baptist preacher voice. And my feminism released my voice to its greatest freedom. Not until I'd experienced the Divine Feminine could I claim my full power as one created in the divine image. The collective voices of radical, freedom-preaching Baptists and suffragists like Susan B. Anthony and Elizabeth Cady Stanton and modern feminist theologians and people from many cultures gathered that day in the Cathedral Guadalupe. All joined together in my voice as it rose to fill that vast cathedral. And I felt the ecstasy.

Preaching at the Alliance of Baptists Convocation

Friday night, April 20, 2001, I stood before a large congregation gathered in Oakhurst Baptist Church in Atlanta, Georgia, for the Alliance of Baptists Annual Convocation. After going to the bathroom five times and getting twice that many drinks of water and sucking orange echinacea cough drops, I rose clear-voiced to the occasion.

Before the worship service, Andy Lester and I stood in the foyer of the church, waiting to march in with the choir. We were giving the "Covenant Addresses" at the convocation. Hands shaking and face flushed, Andy cleared his voice over and over. We both had been fighting upper respiratory problems all week. I told him I'd pray for his voice if he'd pray for mine. Also, the reason we were so nervous, I said, was that we were breaking taboos in the church: he was calling anger good, and I was calling God "She."

Andy jumped into the pulpit after the choir anthem, and in the first few minutes had everyone laughing about "compassionate anger." If he can get laughs out of this subject, surely they'll laugh at my story of the hyphen in my name, I thought. I couldn't help comparing my address to his as he spoke. Will mine be as witty? As profound? As erudite? Feelings of inadequacy always plagued me, but they soon gave way to admiration for Andy and appreciation of his humor. My laughter relaxed me. Also, I remembered that Mother was praying that my voice would be clear and that Christ-Sophia would give me power. I smiled as I thought of all the "Christ-Sophia's" in Mother's e-mails. If she could accept Christ-Sophia, maybe this congregation would be receptive.

In my sleek black dress and new crimson jacket, I rose to the pulpit. I looked out, unafraid, at that huge congregation. And I began, "The Sunday before this past Christmas I sat beside my mother in her moderate Baptist church's morning worship service. As the organ began playing, twenty men filed in . . . " Before I could finish this second sentence, the crowd burst out laughing in recognition. I knew I had connected. I remembered Chad's advice in his call to me that afternoon: "Speak slowly and clearly and connect with your audience." My story continued to draw the congregation in. My voice miraculously cleared—for the first time in five days. Now I could enjoy delivering my address. I could preach even the confrontational parts with love and passion. My voice came forth as strongly as when I gave the benediction for the Peacemakers Conference in the Cathedral Guadalupe. Christ-Sophia spoke through me again, and this time in a Baptist church.

After the service, Isabel Docampo, seminary professor and friend from New Wineskins, hugged me and said, "You held them in the palm of your hand." Steve Boyd, author of a book on men's spirituality, said, "You inspired me to continue working for change in the institutional church. I'd about given up on it." One young woman exclaimed, "You were marvelous! You gave me so much hope." Stan Hastey, executive director of the Alliance, told me I'd done a superb job and that the Alliance needed to hear my message. Deb Schoenfeld and Paul Richardson, active in The Hymn Society, praised my hymns

"Sister Spirit, Brother Spirit" and "O Spirit of Power," sung in the worship service.

That Friday night, back in my room at the Holiday Inn, I couldn't sleep. My address, almost memorized from repetitive practice, kept playing over and over in my head, like a CD stuck on "repeat." The adrenaline of hope shot grandiose images through my mind: images of my memoir influencing change, images of huge congregations singing my hymns, images of churches including the Divine Feminine in worship, images of people making *big* changes for peace and justice.

A few hours' sleep and the morning light scaled these images down to realistic size. But I still felt a deep-down assurance that my work would make a difference. Everybody and everything at the convocation confirmed this feeling. I had found a place where my voice was heard and valued. I felt an affinity with this group of Baptists.

At the convocation I saw some of the "radical" Baptists whom I'd long admired.

Stan Hastey has been an advocate for religious liberty and social justice for three decades. Before becoming executive director of the Alliance of Baptists in 1989, he served on the staff of the Baptist Joint Committee on Public Affairs. He led the Alliance to move from reaction to the fundamentalist capture of the Southern Baptist Convention to celebration of new opportunities as freedom-loving Baptists. With Stan's visionary leadership the Alliance has developed partnerships not only with other Baptist groups around the world but also with other faith groups.

Raye Nell Dyer beamed up at me from the second row of the church as I gave my Covenant Address. Afterwards, she ran up and hugged me, raving, "You were fabulous, sister! I knew you'd make us proud! Thank you, thank you!" Raye Nell, president of Baptist Women in Ministry, had been the one to call with the invitation to give the Covenant Address. My first response, as usual, was hesitancy. I told her I thought she should be the one to give the address. But she convinced me that the Alliance needed my message of the importance of changing worship to include the Divine Feminine. And I knew how much she had suffered from the exclusion. She'd lost her job at a Baptist institution because she took a stand for her divine call to ordination. Raye Nell has been a model of prophetic courage for me and many others.

At the convocation I also saw Ken Sehested, executive director of the Baptist Peace Fellowship of North America. For almost twenty years his vision for world peace has led the Fellowship to address conflict issues around the globe and to teach congregations and individuals to make peace. Ken has also been a prophet of justice for the gay community. The Baptist Peace Fellowship and the Alliance of Baptists are the only two Baptist groups, and among the few denominational groups of any kind, who are welcoming and affirming of homosexual people.

I left Atlanta, truly believing that the Alliance of Baptists Convocation and my sermon and hymns might make a difference, at least to some people and churches. Not until I got off the plane in Dallas, tired, did the fear creep back in that nothing would change. But hope continued to sing a soft tune in my heart for months afterwards. An e-mail from my friend Jeanie Miley helped. She had been elected moderator of the Texas Cooperative Baptist Fellowship. She wrote of her delight in the gender equality she saw in the Fellowship. I first met Jeanie in San Angelo, where she and Mother had become friends. Jeanie wrote witty columns on parenting and books on contemplative spirituality. Like Mother, Jeanie was a nonconventional Baptist preacher's wife. She was not invited back to speak at a Christian retreat because one of the leaders labeled her a "radical feminist."

A Journey Home

On a crisp October Sunday morning I sat alone where the steps to the sanctuary of First Baptist Church in Minden used to stand. I could still see those steps that rose up toward the four sturdy white columns—steps as steep and tall as Jacob's ladder, in my child memory. Almost fifty years before, I'd first lined up there to march in for Vacation Bible School. When Daddy came to pastor First Baptist Church, I was four. My sister Anne was seven, Mother was thirty-two, and Daddy was thirty-eight. Now before me stood a Family Life Center, part of the sprawling two-square-block church that replaced the church I grew up in. Gone were the tall steps and the sanctuary that faced Main Street and the Methodist church. But I could still hear Daddy's booming voice from the pulpit and see Mother in her wide-brimmed hat sitting about midway down in the center section, keeping a watchful eye over Anne and me on the second row.

First Baptist still has no women deacons. The pastor is a man. Only men preach and lead worship. I looked at my watch—8:40 A.M. Soon people would begin gathering for Sunday School. I'd leave. But they probably wouldn't see me anyway. That day, as the day before, I moved around Minden like Emily in *Our Town*. I walked invisible, just as much a ghost as Daddy. The young man at the Subway sandwich shop, the young woman at the Taco Bell, and the research assistant at the Webster Parish Library hadn't even been born when I lived in Minden. Daddy would have liked to come back on this solitary pilgrimage with me—to be sitting there with me remembering. He'd get a kick out of my fantasy of running into the morning worship service in my red dress and Guatemalan stole and proclaiming as I did at the Peacemakers Conference: "Look, look for She is here!" He would be smiling and saying, "I'm busting my buttons." And maybe he is, I thought.

The day before, I'd walked through the red-brick house on College Street, where we lived for sixteen years. The house now belonged to the Church of Christ next door. Workers were renovating our old house to use for Sunday School classes and social gatherings. A friendly woman named Sue greeted me and welcomed my visitation of the house. Sue, her son, and grandson were there on this Saturday afternoon setting up a jungle gym in the back yard.

As I walked through our house, images raced through my mind, as fast as the microfilm reader flashed pictures from the *Waco Tribune-Herald* several months before when I did research in the McLennan County Library. In the dining room, now bare, I stood on the freshly restored hardwood floor and remembered the wall-to-wall carpeting Mother had so proudly put there. I could see the mahogany dining room table set with white linen tablecloth, bright flowers, china, silver—twelve or more people crammed around the table for eight because Mother kept thinking of people to invite. In the living room I could see myself playing the upright piano in the corner beside a lighted Christmas tree that reached up to the ceiling, and across the room stockings hanging from the mantel, Anne and I posing in front of it, reluctantly, in our Christmas dresses. Against the wall in the middle of the room I saw the sofa where we sat for many family pictures, and hanging from the ceiling, the chandelier Mother broke when she flung her shoe in relief after a deacons' party. In the music room, I could see Daddy lying on the couch listening to classical music on the new stereo he so carefully guarded. There as a teenager I necked with boyfriends to the love songs of Johnny Mathis and Andy Williams, while Mother and Daddy slept (I hoped) in the back bedroom.

Going up the stairs, I opened the storage closet that looked exactly the same as it did when I was six and scrunched in there with a flashlight and a friend eating Ritz crackers and peanut butter. In the bathroom upstairs, also the same, I looked in the mirror and saw myself putting on a black dress and hat for Daddy's funeral. I saw my friends on pallets all over Anne's upstairs room and remembered how I thanked her for letting me use it for slumber parties. I opened the doors to attics we'd used for storage and could see myself hauling out loads and loads of magazines when we moved.

The gigantic, two-story house of my memory had shrunk. Now I could see that the house was really only one and a half stories, the rooms were small, and the garage looked like a child's playhouse. In the back yard the huge oak tree I loved to climb had vanished. The whole town looked smaller as I walked around, covering most of my old ground in about an hour—from our house to the high school on down to Eve Baskerville's house and back around to the Wests' and the Kitchens' and the Marshalls' and then to the church and then downtown. I remembered trick-or-treating about this time of year, walking all over town with Anne, dressed up as ghosts or gypsies or witches, without grownups or any fears of being poisoned. I felt again, even in October, the dense humidity that made my hair curl and my dress stick to my skin. Perhaps we sound so slow-talking down here because it takes so long for the words to travel through the thick air.

Although Daddy's body was out in the Garden of Memories and mine was walking around, eating bananas and ice cream that he also loved, I felt we moved through Minden together. He's guiding my steps, I thought, and whispering in my ear to look here once more, to linger, to feel the permanence and the impermanence of this place. McDonald's and Wendy's had sprung up on Homer Road in place of the Dixie Cream, where I used to hang out with Waynette and Mary Margaret and Eve. But the sweet-smelling magnolia trees on College Street on my way to the high school, the cracks in the sidewalks, the Southern accents, and the victory bell our student council had spent so much time discussing hadn't changed.

Minden High School looked the same as when I graduated in 1964, with one hopeful exception. An African-American greeted me. Stepfret Williams, Sr., now assistant principal, had come to Minden High with the consolidation. "They tried, unsuccessfully, to integrate in 1969," he told me, "so in 1974 the courts ordered the merger of Minden High and Webster High." To accommodate all of the students, the merged high school took in the building where I'd gone to junior high along with the newer high school building. The assistant principal and I, both fifty-three now, stood talking in the hall outside his office in the building that had seemed antiquated when I went through seventh and eighth grades there. It didn't look much different now. Mr. Williams told me he'd been in education for thirty-one years. Also, he served as director of probation for Webster Parish. I learned that Cynthia Robinson, my Baylor colleague, had been one of his students at Webster High, and that Cynthia's niece Cassandra Martin, a senior at Minden High, does office work for him. He told me that Minden High is now about 55 percent black and 45 percent white, a much better mix than most schools in the South.

There we stood together, a black man and a white woman—something that would have been impossible back when I went to school in that old building. Mr. Williams talked, without a trace of bitterness, of the long road toward integration in Minden. But mostly we talked about how proud we are of our sons. He had covered the high wall behind his desk with pictures of Stepfret Williams, Jr., who'd played football for the University of Louisiana at Monroe and then for the Dallas Cowboys and the Cincinnati Bengals. I thanked Mr. Williams for generously giving me so much of his time on that Saturday afternoon.

I walked down to the Minden Crimson Tide football field and tried to unlock the gate so I could sit in the stands. The gate wouldn't budge, but I could still see the field where I'd marched, often out of line, and the stands where I'd sat with the other majorettes, eager to twirl our fire batons at halftime. I thought about how much I'd missed by not having Stepfret Williams as a high school buddy. We could have run each other's student council campaigns and worked together in the Future Teachers' Association. It felt right that on my two-day pilgrimage back to Minden, Stepfret was the only live person I had a conversation with.

I drove out Lewisville Road to the cemetery and placed a big pot of yellow chrysanthemums on Daddy's marble gravestone. I wanted to feel closer to him. He wasn't there, never had been. But maybe I could feel his spirit also in this place. I began to talk to him, telling him that I missed him and that I knew he celebrated my ordination because I felt his presence at the service. And I believed he'd champion my feminist causes, or at least enjoy discussing them. He'd understand my passion to expand understanding of God. After all, I told Daddy, "You're there and know firsthand that God's not a white man." Surely he could understand why we so desperately need female divine images—black ones too—for the sake of justice. "You took hard stands for justice," I told Daddy.

The words from John 8:32 etched on his gravestone leaped out at me: "And ye shall know the truth, and the truth shall make you free." Daddy was reminding me again what this journey's about—finding freedom. Freedom to hear the voice of the Spirit within. Freedom to love. Freedom to speak our truth. Freedom to grow. Freedom to live joyfully. Freedom to become all we're created to be. The writer of the book of Hebrews was right: "he being dead yet speaks." Daddy is still preaching freedom, I thought. And so am I.

> We sound a call to freedom that will heal our broken land;
> As the call rings out more clearly violent forces will disband.
> Prison doors will open, bonds will loosen by the Spirit's hand;
> The truth will set us free.

Quote Citations

page x: Jeanne Achterberg, *Woman as Healer* (Boston: Shambhala, 1991), p. 200.

page xi: China Galland, *The Bond Between Women* (New York: Riverhead Books, 1998), p. xiv.

page 68: Kate Millett, *Sexual Politics* (New York: Doubleday, 1970), quoted in *And Then She Said . . . Quotations by Women for Every Occasion,* compiled by J.D. Zahniser (St. Paul, Minnesota: Caillech Press, 1989), p. 10.

page 79: Major DePingre, *A History of The First Baptist Church Minden, La., Part Two: 1970-1994* (Kilgore, Texas: Ford Printing Company, 1994), pp. 3-4.

page 87: Christiane Northrup, *Women's Bodies, Women's Wisdom* (New York: Bantam Books, 1994), p. 4.

page 143: Elinor Lenz and Barbara Myerhoff, *The Feminization of America* (Los Angeles: Jeremy P. Tarcher, Inc., 1985), p. 139.

page 173: Sue Monk Kidd, *The Dance of the Dissident Daughter* (HarperSanFrancisco, 1996), p. 72.

page 176: Bobby McFerrin, *The 23rd Psalm* (Prob Noblem Music, 1990).

page 183: Rosemary Radford Ruether, *Women-Church: Theology & Practice* (San Fancisco: Harper & Row, 1986), p. 62.

page 184: Rosemary Radford Ruether, "Feminism and Jewish-Christian Dialogue," in *The Myth of Christian Uniqueness,* ed. John Hick and Paul F. Knitter (Maryknoll, New York: Orbis, 1987), pp. 146-147.

page 185: Rosemary Radford Ruether, *Women-Church: Theology & Practice* (San Francisco: Harper & Row, 1986), p. 75.

page 220: Carol Lee Flinders, *At the Root of This Longing* (HarperSanFrancisco, 1998), p. 94.

pages 231-232: Sue Monk Kidd, *The Dance of the Dissident Daughter* (HarperSanFrancisco, 1996), p. 33.

page 265: Julie Polter and Anne Wayne, "From the Inside Out: Conversation with Miriam Therese Winter on Imagination, Women in the Church, and Finding God between the Lines," *Sojourners Magazine* 26, no. 4 (July-August 1997): 17-19.

page 265: Carol Lee Flinders, *At the Root of This Longing* (HarperSanFrancisco, 1998), p. 325.